SONGS OF THE
VIETNAM CONFLICT

SONGS OF THE VIETNAM CONFLICT

——————— JAMES PERONE ———————

Music Reference Collection, Number 83

GREENWOOD PRESS
Westport, Connecticut • London

Library of Congress Cataloging-in-Publication Data

Perone, James E.
    Songs of the Vietnam conflict / James Perone.
        p. cm.—(Music reference collection, ISSN 0736–7740 ; no. 83)
    Includes bibliographical references (p.), discography (p.), and indexes.
    ISBN 0–313–31528–0 (alk. paper)
    1. Popular music—United States—1961–1970—History and criticism. 2. Popular
music—United States—1971–1980—History and criticism. 3. Vietnamese Conflict,
1961–1975—Music and the conflict. 4. Music and society. I. Title. II. Series.

ML3477.P45 2001
782.42′1599—dc21   2001023868

British Library Cataloguing in Publication Data is available.

Library of Congress Catalog Card Number: 2001023868
ISBN: 0–313–31528–0
ISSN: 0736–7740

First published in 2001

Greenwood Press, 88 Post Road West, Westport, CT 06881
An imprint of Greenwood Publishing Group, Inc.
www.greenwood.com

Printed in the United States of America

The paper used in this book complies with the
Permanent Paper Standard issued by the National
Information Standards Organization (Z39.48–1984).

10 9 8 7 6 5 4 3 2 1

CONTENTS

PREFACE

At an Abilene, Texas, concert just after his return from performing for servicemen in Vietnam, well-known country/pop/folk performer Johnny Cash was quoted as saying that "the only good thing that ever came out of a war was a song." According to John Grissim, writing in his *Country Music: White Man's Blues*, when Cash made the statement "both hawks and doves [could] confidently construe that Johnny is behind them all the way" (Grissim 1970, 84). Such is the complexity of emotions reflected in and stirred up by the songs of the Vietnam Conflict.

The present book presents background information, musical and textual descriptions, analysis, and criticism of the songs that refer to, were affected by, and responded to the events of one of the most controversial eras in the history of the United States of America. Although I have not detailed every Vietnam-related song of the era—the databases of performing rights organizations BMI and ASCAP indicate at least a half-dozen songs with the title "Vietnam Blues" alone—I have tried to detail the songs that seemed to have affected, or at least were probably heard by, the greatest numbers of Americans throughout the period 1960-74; I have also included several post-war songs to show how American musicians dealt with the aftermath of the Vietnam Conflict.

Throughout the discussion of the specific songs of the era, I have consciously avoided providing direct musical and textual quotations for two reasons: (1) obtaining permissions was an insurmountable obstacle (there is at least one well-known composer of the era for whom permissions literally are never granted) and, much more importantly, (2) I strongly believe that it is essential to hear, to experience the music of this or any other era in order to more fully grasp its significance; to *very* roughly paraphrase a quotation that I have seen variously attributed to John Lennon and to Elvis Costello, reading about music (without experiencing it) is like dancing about architecture.

In an effort to present the reader with some basic background on the Vietnam Conflict and theories about the relationship between music and society, to generally categorize the songs with which we will be dealing, to make sources of information and sources for sound recordings accessible, and to make this book as easy to navigate as possible, I have organized it into the following chapters: (1) Background; (2) Anti-War Songs; (3) Pro-Government and Plight-of-the-Soldier Songs; (4) Selected Discography; (5) Song Title Index; and (6) Index.

The Background chapter provides basic information on the history of U.S. involvement in Vietnam, with a focus on some of the key battles, the progression and the regression of the size of the U.S. military presence in Southeast Asia between the late 1950s and the mid-1970s, and the evolving changes in public opinion that relate to the progress of the war effort as well as to the music of the era. The chapter also includes basic background on some of the theories of the relationships between music and society, a topic that will be more fully explored in the following chapters of the book.

Anti-War Songs and Pro-Government and Plight-of-the-Soldier Songs include general discussions of the nature of the material contained therein followed by specific discussions of individual songs and relationships between songs. Many of the songs of the era contained clearly articulated, unambiguous political messages in their lyrics. Some, though, were either written to serve multiple purposes or could be (and were) understood on several (sometimes conflicting) levels; therefore, some of the songs are difficult to categorize. The reader will also note that I have made reference to songs across chapter boundaries in comparing the ways in which differing political views were communicated and because the battles between the various factions on differing sides of the political issue of American involvement in Vietnam were sometimes played out musically: some songs (particularly of the pro-government type) are direct comments on or obvious reactions to some of the anti-war songs. Given the cross-chapter discussions and the fact that some songs were interpreted as somehow supporting competing sides in the controversies surrounding the war, the reader should be aware that I have broken up discussion of the songs of the war into these chapters for the sake of convenience. Lumping all of these discussions together in one mammoth chapter would have created more logistical problems than it would have corrected.

Generally, I have included first release and reissue information in the Selected Discography. In the case of songs that were known in several different recorded versions, I have included listings for each. Some of the songs of the Vietnam Conflict were reissued quite extensively on greatest hits albums, compact discs, and various other compilations; these I have included to the extent that space was available. While I found it necessary to limit this chapter to some extent, I have made every attempt to include information about recordings that are currently in print so that the reader might be able to get access to the songs. The internet-savvy reader may know that some of these recordings can be found on the web in MP3 format. I have not included any information about web-based sources of recordings, as they seem to appear and disappear so frequently as not to be of much use in a book such as this one.

The Bibliography includes references to books, journal articles, and articles in compilations all arranged in author-date format. Again, due to the transitory nature of the Internet, and the uneven quality of some of the information available on the World Wide Web related to the Vietnam Conflict, I have not included references to web-based sources of information on the war; however, I have cited a number of *All Music Guide*'s very thoughtful on-line reviews. I would like to cite one example of how very wrong some of the electronic "information" out there is. There is one Internet site devoted to the music of Bob Dylan, which shall remain nameless, in which the author of the site, in a supreme show of egotism, manages to "prove" that nearly all of Dylan's songs refer to him, the maintainer of the site! The reader is also cautioned about some of the print sources available, particularly some of those presenting interpretations of song texts. In at least one article I read in preparation of this book, Weberman 1968 to be precise, the author of the article claimed that the Lennon/McCartney composition "Fool on the Hill" and the Jim Morrison composition "Love Street" both refer to the Vietnam Conflict. For one thing, the author misattributed "Fool on the Hill" to John Lennon—the song was completely composed and sung by Paul McCartney—and McCartney himself claims that the fool in the song text was "someone like Maharishi" Mahesh Yogi (Miles 1997, 365), not an easy person to mistake for Lyndon Johnson! Incidentally, I find nothing in the literature on Jim Morrison and The Doors to suggest that he or any other member of that band intended "Love Street" to contain references to the war.

I have included a Song Title Index due to the fact that references to a particular song may be made in several locations in the text, and due to the fact that listing the titles exclusively under the headings for the songwriter(s) in the Index might make for some unnecessary hunting: the names of the composers of some of these songs are not necessarily well known. Note that I have included war-related song titles in the Song Title Index; I have mentioned other songs from time to time but I have not listed them in this chapter because they are often of only periphery interest.

The Index includes proper names of songwriters, performers, political figures, and military and civilian organizations and corporations.

My aim in this project has been to create a guide to the songs of the Vietnam Conflict, one that can be understood and appreciated by scholars and the general public alike. Although I have included discussion of the musical materials of many songs, I have tried to use as little musical jargon as possible. It is my hope that the reader finds this book to be a way into the music of one of the most sociologically interesting eras in American musical history, suggesting some of the reasons for the music, the relationships between the war and particular songs, and some of the relationships between the songs themselves.

ACKNOWLEDGMENTS

This book could not have been written without the valuable assistance of a number of individuals and institutions. I wish to thank Dr. Saundra J. Tracy, Dean of the College and Vice President for Academic Affairs at Mount Union College; the College's Faculty Personnel Committee and Faculty Development Committee; and those faculty and administrators who select the recipients of the College's Sponsored Travel and Research Grants. Without their help in navigating the tenure, promotion, sabbatical leave, and grant-writing process, this project never would have gotten off the ground.

I also wish to thank the Department of Popular Culture, Dr. Marilyn Motz, Chair, and the Center for Popular Culture Studies at Bowling Green State University for selecting me for a Research Fellowship during my fall 2000 sabbatical leave from Mount Union. The fellowship gave me access to probably the finest popular music recording archives in the world. Many thanks to William L. Schurk, Sound Recordings Archivist of the Music Library and Sound Recordings Archives at Bowling Green State University; on more than a few occasions, Mr. Schurk suggested songs and albums that I had never heard and that did not even seem to have been mentioned before in article or book-length studies dealing in whole or in part with the music of the Vietnam era. I also wish to thank Bonna Boettcher, Head of the Music Library and Sound Recordings Archives, and the rest of the library's professional staff for all of their valuable assistance.

Over the course of writing several books, the entire staff at Greenwood Press has been most helpful and cooperative. I wish to extend special thanks to Bobbie Goettler, copy and production editor of this book for helping me in the fine tuning of this book.

I wish to extend special thanks to my wife, Karen, for putting up with my long absences from home to do research in Bowling Green and for being a great sounding board, critic, and supporter.

1

BACKGROUND

HISTORICAL PERSPECTIVE OF THE CONFLICT

The history of Vietnam has been one of great struggle. The country had been under the rule of China over two millennia ago, had gained independence by the tenth century, only to fall under French dominance in the mid-nineteenth century. After World War II, nationalist and Communist factions sought to repel the French, and did so in the Indochina War, which ended in 1954. The Geneva Accord of 1954 split the country into two halves, the Communist North Vietnam, ruled by Ho Chi Minh, and South Vietnam, first ruled by Premier Ngo Ninh Diem. From the time of the arrival of the first U.S. military advisors to assist South Vietnam in May 1959, through the present, the Vietnam Conflict has been considered one of the most controversial wars in U.S. history. It has been suggested that the domestic situation in South Vietnam in the early 1960s virtually guaranteed defeat: the country had a revolving door of governments, none of which successfully united the various constituencies of the country; land reforms were slow in coming; recognition and tolerance of various religious groups was even slower in coming; and the various South Vietnamese ethnic groups were constantly at odds with each other. A possibly more significant problem may have been that Ho Chi Minh had once been supported by the United States, as he helped to lead Vietnam against the Japanese during World War II; Ho was also highly regarded by some citizens of South Vietnam due to his leadership during the Indochina War, which successfully took the Vietnamese peninsula out of the hands of the French. In fact, President Dwight Eisenhower has been quoted as suggesting that Ho could have been supported by up to 80 percent of the citizens of the Vietnamese peninsula, had unified elections taken place (Silber 1967c, 22), a figure that was reported to him by Undersecretary of State Walter Bedell Smith at the end of the Indochina War (Arnold 1991, 285). In retrospect, then, Vietnam might be seen as just another twentieth-century example of how artificial national borders, whether negotiated or imposed, tend to break down; other more recent examples would be the peaceful reunification of Germany, the peaceful splitting of Czechoslovakia, and the ongoing problems and bloodshed in the Balkans.

While it is outside the scope of the present study to detail the history of the conflict, a brief chronology must be established in order to better understand the changes that took place in musical response to the conflict between approximately 1960 and 1974. While there were many key battles, many changes in public opinion, and numerous facets to this war, I will focus on those events most directly relating to the music of the period.

In November 1961, U.S. President John F. Kennedy decided to increase military aid to South Vietnam, and by February 1962 approximately 4,000 American military advisors were stationed in the country (*The Vietnam War* 1988, 12). Apparently, at some point during the Eisenhower or Kennedy administrations, a decision was made to focus anti-Communism efforts in the divided Vietnam; however, Arnold 1991 suggests that Eisenhower and Kennedy discussed the situation in Southeast Asia on the day before the Kennedy inauguration, with Eisenhower stressing the strategic importance of Laos (apparently over Vietnam) (Arnold 1991, 391). (Eisenhower's feelings about direct intervention in Vietnam have been a source of contention for historians and biographers.) U.S. military advisors had been sent to train South Vietnamese troops so that they might better defend themselves against incursions from the North Vietnamese. The decision was based on the so-called domino theory, the belief that one nation falling to Communism would lead to a second falling, and so on. This theory, widely espoused by the government, found its way into virtually every song supporting the war effort. In hindsight, Vietnam might not have provided a true test of the theory, if the war was as stacked against the South Vietnamese, as even some of President Kennedy's advisors suggested, years before U.S. ground troops were committed to the war.

While 15,000 U.S. American advisors found themselves in South Vietnam in November 1963, U.S. Secretary of Defense Robert McNamara announced that 1,000 would be returning home: McNamara was convinced that the South Vietnamese military would be self-sustaining by 1965. On August 2, 1964, however, the destroyer USS *Maddox* was attacked by a North Vietnamese torpedo boat in the Gulf of Tonkin. A similar attack on the USS *C. Turner Joy* and the *Maddox* allegedly followed on August 4, 1964. I write "allegedly," as some U.S. intelligence officers suggested in the *Pentagon Papers* that the August 4 attack never took place, and that sailors aboard the Maddox had misinterpreted radar blips.

In response to the two alleged attacks, U.S. President Lyndon Johnson decided to bomb North Vietnam, but stated publicly that he did not seek a wider war. Johnson's statement, and the fact that it seemed to be contradicted by the reality of the growing U.S. military presence in Vietnam, was the subject of a number of songs, including, perhaps most obviously, the Phil Ochs work "We Seek No Wider War." The Gulf of Tonkin Resolution was signed on August 11, 1964, giving the President the authority to use whatever measures would be deemed necessary to repel attacks on U.S. forces and to prevent future aggression. By mid-November 1964, "Gallup polls revealed that the U.S. public now put Vietnam near the top of the list of problems it wanted solved" (Hammond 1988, 80). By December 1964, 23,000 Americans were stationed in Vietnam.

After attacks on American air bases in early 1965, U.S. aerial bombardment of North Vietnam was stepped up in early March. The use of jellied gasoline, or napalm, in these bombings, which even early on resulted in substantial numbers of civilian deaths and severe burn-related injuries, prompted a number of protest songs, including Malvina Reynolds's biting "Napalm." It was at this time that the first U.S. ground troops, in the form of a Marine infantry battalion, arrived at Da Nang, South Vietnam. Even at this stage, military experts in the United States thought it essential to Vietnamize the war. In other words, in order to defeat the North Vietnamese, it would be essential that the South Vietnamese military become self-sustainable: the South Vietnamese would have to win the war, not the United States. Experts also stressed the importance of pacification, the concept that the South Vietnamese government would have to win the hearts of the people in order to defeat the North. While historians likely will argue for years about the reasons for the eventual defeat of South Vietnam, many trace the defeat to the poor relationship between the South Vietnamese government and the people: pacification of the type envisioned by American military experts in the early 1960s simply never took place (Hunt 1988).

With the bombing raids and the introduction of U.S. ground troops in spring 1965 came the first organized anti-war demonstrations, including Vietnam teach-ins at Temple University, Swarthmore College, and the University of Pennsylvania on April 8, 1965. According to the *Skolnick Report to the National Commission on the Causes and Prevention of Violence*, the number of Americans taking part in anti-war demonstrations gradually rose from approximately 20,000 at the first organized demonstrations in spring 1965 to approximately 150,000 by spring 1967 (Skolnick 1969, 32, 94). Perhaps not surprisingly, the year 1965 was marked by an increase in the number of overtly anti-war songs being released as 45 rpm single records, as well as the first records both about the plight of the soldier and in support of official U.S. government policy in Southeast Asia.

Throughout his tenure, President Lyndon Johnson acted cautiously, generally committing fewer troops than requested by General Maxwell Taylor, U.S. Ambassador to South Vietnam, 1964-65, and General William Westmoreland, Commander, U.S. Military Assistance Command, Vietnam, 1964-68. During the last two years of the Johnson administration, Westmoreland estimated that, if he were given the troops he requested, the war should be over, with all U.S. troops returning in approximately five years. Westmoreland had in fact also predicted that withdrawals would begin by 1969. Although the course of the conflict did not necessarily always go according to plan, and although President Johnson made troop commitments conservatively, Westmoreland's predictions proved to be generally accurate. By the time all American troops had returned from Vietnam, some Americans may have remembered back to predictions made by the General and others and come to the conclusion that perhaps the war had played itself out in pretty much the way it would have, even if public opinion had not turned so drastically against the conflict. As we shall see later, this conclusion contributed to the eventual disillusionment a number of staunchly anti-war musicians felt with the protest movement.

By October 1967, U.S. Secretary of Defense Robert McNamara had become convinced that the American public would not allow the United States to remain in Vietnam for enough time to defeat the North Vietnamese, and that perhaps the administration should admit that the war was not winnable and pull out. Despite the Secretary of Defense's concerns, in late 1967 General William Westmoreland and President Johnson continued to assure the American public that the war was going well, according to plan. At the same time, however, the North Vietnamese army was preparing for a major offensive, an all-out effort possibly to induce a general uprising by the South Vietnamese people. This effort, the Tet Offensive, was to coincide with the traditional Vietnamese New Year celebrations, and began on January 31, 1968.

Although the Tet Offensive failed to rally South Vietnamese citizens to the Communist National Liberation Front, resulted in approximately 45,000 North Vietnamese Army and Viet Cong killed, and resulted in a general weakening of the North Vietnamese military, it was widely reported by the American press as a defeat for the South Vietnamese (MacDonald 1988). American reporters documented disastrous events in Saigon, and a famous photograph of Saigon Police Chief Nguyen Ngoc Loan executing a Viet Cong officer with his revolver "shocked world opinion" (MacDonald 1988, 155). When President Johnson decided to promote General Westmoreland to the position of U.S. Army Chief of Staff, the press widely speculated that the general had been "kicked upstairs" because of the President's dissatisfaction with Westmoreland's handling of the Tet Offensive. While there is evidence that many Americans were dissatisfied with President Johnson's hesitancy in committing more troops, the press speculated that most of the dissatisfaction was that the country was involved in the war in the first place.

Gallup Polls suggested that the number of Americans who answered "yes" to the question "In view of the developments since we entered the fighting in Vietnam, do you think the U.S. made a mistake sending troops to fight in Vietnam?" rose from 37 percent to 49 percent between May 1967 and March 1968, and that the percentage of Americans describing themselves as "doves" rose from 26 percent in February 1968 to 42 percent one month later (Skolnick 1969, 44). Between spring 1967 and spring 1968, the number of Americans taking part in anti-war demonstrations nearly doubled, from approximately 150,000 to nearly 300,000 (Skolnick 1969, 32).

The year 1968 saw the continuation of the gradual buildup in American forces until more than 500,000 U.S. troops finally found themselves in Vietnam. The size of the U.S. force, the controversies surrounding the handling of the Tet Offensive, the growing negative reporting on the war in the American press, and a growing visibility of youth anti-war protests all may have contributed to President Johnson's decision not to seek reelection, although his weakening health and the desires of the President's family have been given as the official reasons behind the decision. Following Johnson's decision, there was renewed hope among the anti-war factions that one of the other Democratic candidates, especially Senator Robert Kennedy, might be able finally to end the war. With Kennedy's subsequent death at the hands of an assassin, and the disastrous and violent breaking up of anti-war demonstrations at the 1968 Democratic National Convention by Chicago police, many in the anti-war movement grew disillusioned. The anti-war movement became more radicalized throughout 1968 and 1969, as some thought that the nonviolent rallies of earlier times had been ineffective.

As Richard Nixon took office as President in 1969, a gradual pullout from Vietnam began. However this may have swayed public opinion, the change was temporary, as two incidents brought into question the manner in which the conflict was being played out: the "Hamburger Hill" assault in May 1969 and, more importantly, the revelations of the My Lai massacre.

After the Tet Offensive of early 1968, the North Vietnamese troops and the Viet Cong largely had abandoned mass battles, focusing on more numerous, small-scale raids. For the press, and by extension the public, this meant that there were fewer large-scale battles won: the small-scale successes were not given the same kind of media attention as had the major battles of the past. When American troops had successfully taken Ap Bia Mountain (a.k.a. "Hamburger Hill") after a six-day-long, intensive battle in May 1969, one of the few battles of the year to receive much press coverage, only to abandon what was basically a militarily worthless hill just several days later, press and public alike saw the battle as another example of the pointlessness of the war.

In April 1969 Ronald L. Ridenhour, a Vietnam veteran, wrote a series of open letters to President Nixon and to other government officials telling of a March 1968 massacre in the hamlet of My Lai. After public disclosure of the incident, the Army appointed a review panel to study Ridenhour's allegations. The panel, which met between November 1969 and March 1970, recommended that charges be filed against fifteen U.S. officers: the American public was stunned, believing that such war crimes were always carried out by the enemy. Provoking even more outrage among the American public was the Army's eventual decision to dismiss outright charges against the higher ranking officers, focusing the blame on younger officers, like Lieutenant William L. Calley, Jr., who was charged with the murder of 102 South Vietnamese citizens and sentenced in March 1971 to life imprisonment (later reduced to 20 years). The My Lai massacre and the subsequent conviction of Calley provided much fuel for songwriters, and made for one of the fastest selling, and most controversial, single records in the history of the recording industry, "The Battle Hymn of Lt. Calley." The early work of the panel investigating the My Lai massacre coincided with the massive "Moratorium" anti-war demonstrations that swept America on November 15, 1969: anti-war rallies continued to become increasingly prone to violence.

It was not just ardent members of the anti-war movement and increasing numbers of the American public at large who were taking firmer stands against the war in the later 1960s. Members of the military, including some high-ranking officers, were increasingly speaking out. One of the strongest such statements came from Brigadier General Robert L. Hughes, who is quoted as saying, "We are prosecuting an immoral war in support of a government that is a dictatorship by design. In this new era of political unrest, we cannot police the world, we cannot impose our social system on other nations. We are losing the flower of American youth in a war that could stretch into perpetuity. After three years of fighting, we cannot be sure of the security of villages three miles from Saigon" (Dane and Silber 1969, 22).

By 1970 Viet Cong and North Vietnamese forces were massing strength in the officially neutral nation of Cambodia. Diplomatic and minor military campaigns by the U.S. and South Vietnamese troops in the eastern part of Cambodia had failed to weaken the Communist positions, and it had become clear that the Cambodian military would be no match for the Viet Cong. In April 1970 South Vietnamese troops undertook an invasion of Cambodia. A further assault launched on May 1, 1970, found U.S. ground troops also involved. This expansion of the theatre of operations, even as the U.S. troop withdrawal continued, provoked violent demonstrations in the United States, culminating with the Ohio National Guard killing four students and injuring ten others at an anti-war rally at Kent State University on May 4, 1970. The Kent State University incident brought a new wave of nationwide protests, commencing on May 9, 1970. Some writers, David Szatmary among them, postulate that the May 4, 1970, events at Kent State University "destroyed any remaining feeling of militant power that existed among sixties youth after Altamont" (Szatmary 1996, 212), the infamous December 1969 Rolling Stones concert at which members of the Hell's Angels motorcycle gang, hired to handle security, stabbed one concertgoer to death (three other audience members also died at the concert).

Troop withdrawals continued throughout 1970 and 1971, but the continued expansion of the theatre of operations into Cambodia and Laos, and heavy bombing raids by U.S. pilots kept the anti-war movement alive. In fact, according to Jacob Neufeld, a historian with the Office of Air Force History, "the peace movement, which had suffered from splits between outright pacifists and those who opposed only the Vietnam War—and from internal divisions in either camp—attained a new unity in the spring of 1971" (Neufeld 1988, 211-12). The rallies of April and May were not the one-day events of the past, but lasted for days on end. Attendance at these events not only included a broader spectrum of the population, but saw larger overall numbers of protesters involved: the April 1971 anti-war rallies in Washington, D.C., for example, drew 500,000 people. Another important part of the widening of the circle of anti-war protesters was the growing inclusion of Vietnam veterans. John Kerry, a former naval officer and Vietnam veteran and later a prominent U.S. senator from Massachusetts, emerged as a particularly strong spokesman in the anti-war movement. The growing disenchantment with the war among military personnel was also seen in the ever-increasing use of "hard" drugs, including heroin, among those serving in Indochina (Neufeld 1988, 212), as well as in increasing numbers of acts of insubordination and outright sabotage.

Jerry Lembcke, Vietnam veteran and sociologist, contends that the increasingly close relationships between returning, now anti-war veterans, World War II-era veterans opposed to the conflict in Southeast Asia, and the youth counterculture posed a major public relations problem for the Nixon administration by 1970 and 1971 (Lembcke 1998). He argues that the government was responsible for developing the myth of the "spat-upon" returning Vietnam veteran in an effort to drive a wedge between the various groups of anti-war allies. We shall see later that the relationship between the anti-war movement and soldiers was explored in a number of the songs of the 1969-71 era.

The June 13, 1971, release of the first installment of the *Pentagon Papers* by the *New York Times* provided more fuel for the anti-war movement. The top-secret study, undertaken in 1967 and 1968 and running to some 3,000 pages of text, detailed the diplomatic and military failures of the U.S. policy in Indochina between 1945 and 1968. The report, which had been leaked to the *New York Times* by Daniel Ellsberg, one of the writers of the study, made it clear that the government had "disregarded its obligation to South Vietnam" and "had not dealt honestly with the American people: it had not told them what was being done in their name in Indochina, and it had not truthfully reported to them the way the war was progressing" (Neufeld 1988, 214).

By March 1973 all U.S. troops had been withdrawn from South Vietnam. The Saigon government finally fell in April 1975 and Vietnam was reunified in 1976. Controversy still surrounds the war, its causes, its justification, the rebellion it caused at home, and its impact on the future of the United States of America. At the time of this writing, a quarter-century after the end of the war, the United States of America and Vietnam are in the process of exploring the possibilities for closer diplomatic and economic relationships.

THE RELATIONSHIP OF MUSIC AND SOCIETY

From at least the time of Plato and Aristotle, the question of whether popular music reflects or shapes culture has been debated. R. Serge Denisoff, one of the most prolific writers of the early 1970s on the subject of the music of protest, collected a number of essays expounding both views in the first section of *Sounds of Social Change* (1972a). Denisoff concludes that both viewpoints are (or at least were in 1972) at least partially correct, depending upon the specific song or specific social movement in question. Still today, the complex relationships between music and society are subject to debate. If one accepts the conclusion that music can be both reflective of society at large and influential upon society as I do, then one must attend closely to the details of particular musical works in terms of their either reactive or their promptive nature.

Although the focus of the present study is on music that received the greatest amount of exposure, primarily through record sales and radio airplay, but also through performance at political gatherings and popular music concerts, even music with a more limited audience changed as a result of the Vietnam Conflict. There was a radical paradigm shift in the response of composers of serious concert music to war. According to Ben Arnold, "the Vietnam conflict was a new age war, a war with a culture of protest.

Composers no longer wrote compositions to support war as had Aaron Copland, Samuel Barber, Roy Harris, Gail Kubick, and dozens of others during World War II; they openly protested the war and expressed anti-government sentiments directly and to a degree unprecedented in history" (Arnold 1993, 317). In his reference guide *Music and War: A Research and Information Guide*, Arnold presents information on approximately sixty concert compositions that either deal directly with the war or were heavily influenced by it. The author notes, however, that "while a large educated public reads novels about the Vietnam conflict, few (if any) of the art compositions dealing with Vietnam are known even in the music/academic world that produced so many of them" (Arnold 1993, 324). Indeed, perusal of concert programs of choral ensembles, symphony orchestras, concert bands, and even ensembles that predominantly perform music written in the past fifty years reveals that these works simply have not made it into the repertoire.

Why the change in the relationship between music, war, and patriotism during the 1960s and early 1970s? It has been widely suggested that the answer lies in the role of the media during the Vietnam era. Many commentators, including media expert Marshall McLuhan (McLuhan and Fiore 1968), have regarded the Vietnam Conflict as the first true media war: a war that was covered almost in real time on television sets across the country every day on the evening news. McLuhan referred to the importance of television in the development of public opinion when he wrote that "a new form of 'politics' is emerging, and in ways we haven't yet noticed. The living room has become a voting booth. Participation via television in Freedom Marches, in war, revolution, pollution, and other events is changing *everything*" (McLuhan and Fiore 1967, 22, emphasis in original). Within a quarter-century of McLuhan issuing his statements on the importance of electronic media in the shaping of public opinion, live news television, the fax machine, and computer networks have played crucial roles in the fall of the Soviet Union and the Iron Curtain, the conduct of the Persian Gulf War, the O. J. Simpson case, and many other situations.

How important a role was played by the songs of the Vietnam Conflict, the truly popular or well-known works influenced by the war? Study of the literature surrounding the way in which the war was conducted, the anti-war movement, and right-wing reaction to the music of the era yields varying results.

Right-wing writer David A. Noebel's *Rhythm, Riots, and Revolution* places the blame for the early anti-war movement and its attendant "subversive" and "atheistic" trends in American society squarely on what he calls "pro-Communist" musicians like Pete Seeger, Bob Dylan, Joan Baez, Phil Ochs, and others (Noebel 1966). While Noebel's views might easily be labeled extreme, it should be noted that at least one other writer, looking at protest songs through less-right-wing eyes, has credited Noebel with being perceptive as to the power of music. Jerome Rodnitzky wrote, that "Although Noebel's specific charges lean toward the ridiculous, as a frightened professional patriot, he is one of the few individuals besides folk performers themselves who seem to grasp the persuasive power of the musical idiom" (Rodnitzky 1971b).

In terms of the amount of importance placed on music in the shaping of public opinion during the time of the Vietnam Conflict, Charles DeBenedetti's scholarly study *An American Ordeal: The Antiwar Movement of the Vietnam Era* (DeBenedetti with Chatfield 1990) is at the opposite end of the spectrum from Noebel's 1966 opus. DeBenedetti's massive study, with its focus on organizations and individual leaders of the anti-war movement, includes only a handful of references to musicians, and only then when either they appeared at anti-war rallies, or when their compositions were sung at rallies: the power of the album or 45 rpm single record are not discussed. Along the same lines, some historians have duly noted that compared with the large number of total songs making the charts during the course of the war, there were really relatively few that even vaguely mention the war, let alone make a clear political statement about it. Bindas and Houston 1989, detailing strictly with anti-war material, found that only approximately 1.5 percent of the songs to make the pop charts during the ten years of the Vietnam Conflict have anything at all directly to do with the war. Since Bindas and Houston's study deals with the type of material it does, the reader will find further discussion of their findings and conclusions in the chapter "Anti-War Songs."

My look at the literature and my casual conversations with those who were either of high school or college age during the war suggests that a middle-ground assessment probably reflects the reality of music's role during the Vietnam Conflict. As Rodnitzky points out, the societal revivalism of the 1960s resembles to a certain extent the religious revivalism of nineteenth-century America (Rodnitzky 1971b). As had been the case in the nineteenth century, music was simply always there: one could not escape the presence of songs at patriotic rallies in support of the troops or at anti-war demonstrations. And the sales figures and power of radio simply don't lie: many more Americans heard anti-war songs, pro-war songs, and songs dealing with the plight of servicemen and women via purchased records or via the medium of radio than those who heard music or sang along at political rallies. That being said, however, it also seems not to have been the case that even the most politically charged songs of the era alone could be blamed for or credited with the wholesale shaping of beliefs or values. Indeed, there is evidence that the songs of the Vietnam era served more to reinforce already held beliefs and to reflect what was happening in American society at large than anything else.

Two examples, one general in nature and the other related to a specific event, serve to illustrate the reactive nature of music of the era, the way in which some scholars have suggested that the popular consumption of music changed with the changes in the course of the war and the development of the anti-war movement, and also suggest the difficulties found in trying to tie these together in any sort of scientific way. In his 1996 book *A Time to Rock: A Social History of Rock 'N' Roll*, David Szatmary attributes the rise in popularity of harder-edged, blues-oriented guitar-based rock in 1968 and 1969 to the increasing radicalization of college students in the anti-war movement (Szatmary 1996, 195-99). While it is true that the radicalization of the campus anti-war movement and the increased popularity of a harder, electric guitar-based rock style both occurred in 1968 and 1969, it should be noted that many musical ensembles, political and otherwise, reacted to the psychedelic music of 1967 by returning to the roots of rock, the electric blues, in 1968 and 1969. The sheer volume of this type of material (no pun intended) practically guaranteed that it would be heard over the airwaves more frequently and would enjoy greater record sales. The question must then arise, did a correlation really exist between the course of the anti-war movement and the popularity of a particular style of rock music, or was it simply a matter of coincidence? Could, in fact, the tables have been turned: could the popularity of hard rock have been responsible for the radicalization of the anti-war movement? At our present point in history, we may be able only to note that several possibly related things were happening at about the same time and speculate as to the relationships: studies at the time seem not to have proven definitively a cause-and-effect relationship.

A second, more clear-cut example of the relationship between music and the events of the Vietnam Conflict can be seen in "The Battle Hymn of Lt. Calley," a single that sold more than a quarter-million copies within a few weeks. The song was an obvious reaction to the legal proceedings against Lieutenant William Calley, Jr., the junior officer accused of the murder of civilians in the My Lai massacre. In this case one particular event can be seen as prompting the work of art. Not only was the massacre and the government's passing over of higher ranking officers in the legal proceedings controversial, the single, as the reader will see later, played on the emotional extremes of the general public, inciting fist fights and shouting matches.

Writing in the *South Atlantic Quarterly*, Rodnitzky places particular emphasis on the period 1960-63 in American popular music, a time period in which lyrics became more important (Rodnitzky 1971b). Generally, post 1960, 45 rpm single records feature easier-to-understand vocals: both advances in recording technology and a growing liberality with respect to allowing possibly suggestive or controversial lyrics to be understood probably played a role in this textural change. Just as important in the development of the battle of words played out on radio and on records was a basic paradigm shift in corporate control over musical product in the record industry: a change that coincided with the increased emphasis on lyrics described by Rodnitzky.

In his 1972 book *It's Too Late to Stop Now*, well-known rock critic Jon Landau wrote:

Rock, the music of the Sixties, was a music of spontaneity. It was a folk music—it was listened to and made by the same group of people. It did not come out of a New York office building where people sit and write what they think other people want to hear. It came from the life experiences of the artists and their interaction with an audience that was roughly the same age. As that spontaneity and creativity have become more stylized and analyzed and structured, it has become easier for businessmen and behind-the scenes manipulators to structure their approach to merchandising music. The process of creating stars has become a routine and a formula as dry as an equation. (Landau 1972, 40)

Landau raises an important issue related to the source of nearly all of the anti-war and pro-war material. Nearly all of the recordings that made an impact, anti-war, pro-war, and those focusing on the plight of U.S. soldiers and their loved ones, were written by those outside of the 1960s version of the Tin Pan Alley scene: conspicuous is the absence of such figures as Carole King, Gerry Goffin, Cynthia Weil, Barry Mann, Howard Greenfield, Neil Diamond, and other Brill Building, songwriting factory figures. Numerous mass media theorists have suggested the progressive nature of the various media forms have encouraged a feeling of shared expertise, further taking corporate bodies out of the picture, and making most of the music studied in the present book a kind of folk music. Indeed, the reader may sense and the listener may hear in much of this material a kind of grassroots spontaneity. When that spontaneity was perceived as missing from recorded performances, critics were quick to note its absence.

Radio, too, was changing around the time that the Vietnam Conflict was being addressed by songwriters. In reference to the days before the 1960 payola scandals that rocked the American radio and record industries, media researcher Paul Hirsch quotes a record promoter, who worked closely with radio stations trying to get his label's single records on radio play lists in the 1950s and 1960s, as saying, "In those days you paid your money and got your hit. Today, nobody can predict what will be played on the air" (Hirsch 1969, 62). In the 1960s public demand, industry sales charts, likes and dislikes of individual disc jockeys all played a role in determining what was heard on the radio. In turn, the greater diversity in radio programming—since payola was not forcing product down the public's collective throat—allowed consumers more options in terms of what *they* would turn into the day's hits. In this sense the post-payola days of the relationship between the radio and record industries probably find the true public mood reflected in sales charts better than might have been the case before 1960. This is important to note as one considers the music of the Vietnam Conflict: hits that relate to the war were largely determined by the public and not so much by the music industry. (We shall see, though, that major record labels did heavily promote at least a few songs, such as SSgt. Barry Sadler's "Ballad of the Green Berets.") These hits, then, probably reflect the feelings of certain segments of the American public on the political issue of the war in Southeast Asia with a certain degree of accuracy.

As radio play lists came under less control from bribes, public reaction or the reaction of program directors or disc jockeys to controversial lyrics could influence the amount of radio airplay such controversial songs received. We shall see that recordings of songs including "Eve of Destruction" and "The Battle Hymn of Lt. Calley" were banned by some radio stations and by some radio networks, but managed to achieve commercial success, and in some cases *great* commercial success in spite of limited airplay. This seems to indicate that, again, such songs may have been touching a strong chord among certain segments of the population and generating a grassroots, almost folk appeal, supporting Landau's assessment of the popular music of the Vietnam era.

As we work through a study of the anti-war songs and pro-government songs, it will become clear that those on both sides of the Vietnam issue were largely propaganda devices, songs meant as rallying cries for people sharing the songwriter's views or possibly meant to try to convince those on the other side or those who might be swayed to accept the songwriter's views. Very few musical works even acknowledged the fact that there might be some legitimacy to another viewpoint. One of the few songs of the era to even acknowledge the complexity of the questions surrounding war in general, although the Vietnam Conflict is not explicitly mentioned, is The Moody Blues' song "Question," written by the group's chief composer and singer/guitarist Justin Hayward. Although Hayward espouses a sort of love-conquers-all philosophy, he does allow that people probably really have more questions than answers about war. I would submit that he is probably right in that regard, but he was certainly in the minority among songwriters of the 1960s and early 1970s who dealt with the issue of war, most of whom seemed to have more answers than questions. Interestingly, two other songs in particular, Mel Tillis's composition "Ruby, Don't Take Your Love to Town" and Loretta Lynn's "Dear Uncle Sam," each finds the protagonist considering (to some extent) the various questions surrounding service in the war. These songs will be studied in detail in the chapter "Pro-Government and Plight-of-the-Soldier Songs." Ray Stevens's "America, Communicate with Me" is one of the very few songs of the era to take extremists on both sides of the issue to task. Two anti-war songs, Buffy Sainte-Marie's "Universal Soldier" and Pete Seeger's "Bring Them Home," also known as "If You Love Your Uncle Sam (Bring Them Home)," also place war in context, both suggesting in their own ways that some wars may be worth fighting; the Seeger song suggests that the Vietnam Conflict simply was not one of them. The Sainte-Marie and Seeger works are detailed in the chapter "Anti-War Songs."

In any study of music of the Vietnam Conflict, the question of how the troops were affected by politically motivated popular music—just what did they listen to while on military bases in the United States, or while in the rice paddies of Vietnam—must arise. Throughout the course of the war, there was an official and an unofficial coffeehouse movement around military bases in the United States. The literature makes it clear that there was also an anti-war movement among some of the soldiers, and that these coffeehouses sometimes featured performers singing anti-war material in the folk revival style. There was also an active anti-war alternative press surrounding these coffeehouses.

Barbara Dane chronicled her work as a folksinger working these coffeehouses as part of an official, USO-sponsored tour in *Sing Out!*, the folk song magazine (Dane 1969-70). Dane's article suggests that the level of anti-war feeling among soldiers was higher than what the government had generally acknowledged. In fact, Dane released an album of material she (and the GIs) sang at some of the coffeehouses, *FTA!: Songs of the GI Resistance* (Paredon Records P-1003, 1971). While music may have played a propaganda role at the unofficial coffeehouses, and at least in Dane's case at official coffeehouses, there is significant evidence to suggest that active duty military personnel in the United States and in Southeast Asia simply continued to listen to the same styles of music by the same performers they enjoyed as civilians. Michael Herr's highly acclaimed book *Dispatches*, which documents the author's time as a war correspondent in South Vietnam, for example, suggests this to be the case (Herr 1978). Herr mentions soldiers enjoying country, rock, and soul, generally corresponding to obvious (or perhaps stereotypical) demographic, ethnic, and racial lines. He suggests, however, that hard rock music predominated, at least among the troops with whom he was associated. Sometimes familiar refrains or choruses of popular songs originally having nothing to do with the war elicited a response of major proportions from soldiers serving in Southeast Asia who yearned to return home: the title line of The Rolling Stones' song "Time Is on My Side," for example, as well as The Animals' hit "We Got to Get out of This Place," a composition by the Brill Building songwriting team of Barry Mann and Cynthia Weil. In fact, "We Got to Get out of This Place," a song that actually deals with a young couple's need to escape a life of poverty and pollution in the slums of the city, first caught on in the autumn of 1966 on military bases both at home and abroad. By mid-1967 it was one of the most frequently requested songs of performers entertaining at bases in Southeast Asia, sometimes being fitted with new, Vietnam-specific lyrics improvised by the performers (Randal 1967). I have confirmed the immense popularity of this song in informal conversation with veterans of the war who still recall the immense popularity of "We Got to Get out of This Place." Among the Vietnam-related recordings documented to have been among the most popular with the U.S. troops in Southeast Asia were Creedence Clearwater Revival's "Who'll Stop the Rain" (Pratt 1998, 179) and Glen Campbell's "Galveston" (Greenway 1970, 853).

2

ANTI-WAR SONGS

BACKGROUND

At the time of the arrival of the first U.S. military advisors in Vietnam in the late 1950s, up to approximately the time of the first U.S. bombings of North Vietnam in late summer 1964, most of the anti-war songs were fairly generic, in that they expressed either a desire for universal peace or a general anti-war sentiment not explicitly aimed at the growing tensions in Southeast Asia. In this respect they followed very much in the tradition of Ed McCurdy's "Last Night I Had the Strangest Dream," a Korean War-era song. Counted among the more general anti-war type songs of the pre-1965 era are "Blowin' in the Wind," "I Ain't Marching Anymore," and "Where Have All the Flowers Gone?" While the main catalyst behind these songs might have been the Cold War between the United States and the Soviet Union, once the Vietnam Conflict started to escalate in late 1964 and throughout the remainder of the war, they could be understood in a specifically anti-Vietnam Conflict context. That they were sung at rallies against American involvement in Vietnam suggests that their general nature made them easily adaptable to a very specific situation. Also used at anti-war rallies throughout the conflict were such traditional folk songs as "Down by the Riverside" (also known as "I Ain't Going to Study War No More") and "We Shall Overcome." The lead sheets for many of these revived folk songs are contained in *Songs of Peace, Freedom, and Protest* 1970. The first protest songs to actually mention Vietnam began to appear in 1963, but these generally received little radio airplay, little, if any, commercial success, and were generally only heard when they were performed live by singer/songwriters of the folk genre. A large number of these songs, as well as the more general anti-war songs, were published in lead sheet form in *Broadside*, the "official" protest song magazine. While these songs in the broadside tradition, a tradition reaching all the way back to sixteenth-century England, may have had relatively little exposure among members of the general public, they greatly influenced many in the anti-war movement, as we shortly shall see in the discussion of several of the specific songs. *Sing Out!*, which tended to include more in the way of true folk material than did *Broadside*, was also a significant source for Vietnam-related protest music. The reader should keep in mind the fact that chart standings, radio airplay, and sales of singles and albums do not tell the entire story of the anti-war songs: performers such as Phil Ochs, Joan Baez, Tom Paxton, Malvina

Reynolds, Pete Seeger, and others performed their repertoire in front of thousands and thousands of people at peace rallies, going back to the very start of the 1960s. Only a few of these songs were on commercially successful singles or albums, but many were heard and were found to be meaningful to thousands of anti-war activists.

The reader might note that newly composed, pre-1965 songs come completely from the so-called "folk" music or folk revival style. Purists would argue that they are not truly folk songs: folk music is by definition anonymously composed and passed along through oral tradition. The relationship between true folk music and topical protest songs written by, credited to, and copyrighted by identified, living composers had grown so close, especially in the 1940s through the 1960s, that the lines had been permanently blurred in the public consciousness between true folk music and music by singer/songwriters working in an acoustic, "folk-sounding" style.

The years 1965-69 saw the birth of a heavier type of protest music, largely spawned by P. F. Sloan's composition "Eve of Destruction." The intensity of the rhetoric in the songs' lyrics had been anticipated by Bob Dylan's "With God on Our Side," and especially by his "Masters of War." The lines between folk, rock, and the hybrid folk-rock would become blurred. The Sloan and Dylan works and the merging of rock and folk changed the overall approach to the mood of protest music on the pop charts. As B. Lee Cooper and Wayne Haney write, "The gentle early 1960s folk criticism by The Kingston Trio, and Peter, Paul, and Mary escalated into full-throated screams for the warring to end from Barry McGuire, Bob Dylan, John Fogerty, Phil Ochs, Edwin Starr, and Neil Young" (Cooper and Haney 1997, 335).

Even considering the famous anti-war songs of the Vietnam Conflict, and there certainly were a number of highly memorable ones, commentators have noted the relatively small number of anti-war rock songs, in light of the huge number of rock songs composed during the 1965-75 period and given the widely held notion that most rock musicians were against the war. Historians Kenneth J. Bindas and Craig Houston write, "On the subject of the Vietnam War, one of the most important events of the sixties, rock music and its musicians were noticeably silent. Only when the American public altered its opinion toward the war did the record industry and prominent musicians redirect their music by marketing songs with antiwar themes" (Bindas and Houston 1989, 1). The authors go on to show a major spike in the number of anti-war songs making *Billboard*'s weekly top 100 in 1968, coinciding with the high point in the number of U.S. troops stationed in Vietnam and the pivotal point when public opinion polls first detected more "doves" than "hawks." Another spike occurred in 1970, at the time when anti-war demonstrations reached their highest levels of violence. Even then, contrary to widely held beliefs, "antiwar rock songs comprised less than 1.5 percent of the approximately 1000 singles to make *Billboard*'s yearly top 100 chart, 1965-74" (Bindas and Houston 1989, 3). Yes, there were non-single, album cuts, but again, rock and pop musicians wrote and recorded relatively few songs dealing with the Vietnam War. John Lennon of The Beatles was asked at a press conference when The Beatles were going to record some anti-war songs. He has been widely quoted as saying, "All of our songs are antiwar." Part of the reason for the relatively small number of *specifically* anti-Vietnam Conflict songs might well be that so many of the songs of the era were *generally* pro-youth, pro-love, pro-experimentation, and anti-status quo: perhaps in the minds of the musicians, there was not a need to be specifically anti-war when the general nature of their material made an unspoken statement against violence and against a society that sponsored violence in the form of warfare.

It is also known that a number of artists' managers went so far as to forbid even mention of the war in press conferences: The Beatles' manager Brian Epstein, until his untimely death in 1967, was among them. Perhaps, too, part of the reason for the relatively low number of anti-war rock songs and the reluctance of musicians to support the anti-war cause rests with problems within the movement itself. When asked why big name bands did not play for anti-war rallies, Country Joe McDonald said, "They don't trust them. The Left Wing has alienated itself from them. I don't blame them [for not appearing at the rallies]" (Silber 1968, 21). In the interview McDonald goes on to say in rather graphic terms that if he had not been surrounded by and deeply interested in politics since his childhood, he would eschew the left-wing political scene as a musician, just like many of his colleagues.

Curiously, both right-wing and left-wing politicos found common ground on one other possible reason for the relative apathy of many young people during the 1960s and early 1970s: recreational drug use, the subject of numerous songs, and the inspiration for countless others, especially in the rock genre. Nearly all of the right-wing writers who dealt with music, including Noebel 1966 and Garlock 1971, expressed the opinion that the use of drugs such as marijuana and LSD were having negative effects on American youth—actually most of these writers went much further and accused rock musicians who, through their music and lifestyles, led youths into the use of these drugs, of either wittingly or unwittingly being part of a Communist conspiracy. Left-wing writer, folk musician, and publisher Irwin Silber suggested that drug use, especially of LSD, and the "tune in, turn on, and drop out" attitude of Dr. Timothy Leary was effectively taking young people out of the protest movement. Silber wrote that "if I were working for the CIA in some executive capacity, and if Dr. Timothy Leary did not exist, I would recommend a grant to bring him into being. They don't care how you support the War in Vietnam—by carrying a gun or dropping out of protest against it" (Silber 1967a, 33). In one of his non-Vietnam-related songs, "Outside of a Small Circle of Friends," Phil Ochs expressed similar thoughts, suggesting in one stanza that marijuana was dulling young people's ability to put any compassion and desire for social justice that they might feel into positive action.

Taking a cue from Plato's *Republic*, right-wing critics generally blasted the anti-war songs of the Vietnam era. Not only were the lyrics considered by such writers to be un-American, pro-Communist (Noebel 1966), and blasphemous (Garlock 1971), the rhythm, metrical structure, use of simple harmonies, and repetitive melodies of rock and folk-rock were also criticized by right-wing writers. Especially in retrospect, some of the attacks might seem extreme, such as Gary Allen's *American Opinion* article "That Music: There's More to It Than Meets the Ear" (Allen 1969). Allen quotes a Dr. Joseph Crow as suggesting that composers and performers of rock music use rhythm, melody, and harmony to try to "sell attitudes and concepts" (Allen 1969, 59). According to Crow, "By changing the rhythm within a musical piece you can have a strong impact on the listener and the subliminal effect is to push the 'message' much more strongly. Some people actually have a physiological response when, for instance, a beat is switched from three-four to five-four time. Pop music now does this type of poly-rhythms [*sic*] all the time, because it accentuates the message. We were taught never to do this in music school, but we were not trying to use music for mind conditioning" (Allen 1969, 59).

Crow's assertion that some songs may be attempts to influence the attitudes and beliefs of listeners very well may be true. Evidence exists to suggest that music is one effective means of affecting such changes. One major problem with his argument is the very imprecise, even inaccurate use of musical terminology and the "expert's" suggestion that pre-rock-era composition students were taught never to change meters. Apparently Dr. Crow's composition teachers also instructed him to look for inspiration only in the pre-twentieth-century European art music repertoire, as the changing meters of Igor Stravinsky, Béla Bartók, and others working as early as the 1910s quickly became accepted in twentieth-century art music circles. Aaron Copland's well-known ballet scores of the 1930s and 1940s are filled with mixed meters. In fact, even the politically and musically conservative American art music composer Howard Hanson used the type of metrical structures that are associated with a Communist plot in the Allen book. Allen/Crow's assertion that poly-rhythms are used *because* they accentuate the message is also misleading for the following reasons: (1) when Crow refers to poly-rhythms, he is actually talking about mixed meters (something altogether different); and (2) even if he really were referring to poly-rhythms and cross rhythms as his terminology suggests, true poly-rhythms and cross rhythms are an important part of most late nineteenth- and twentieth-century dance-based music, message or not; indeed, words or no words. Those rhythms are used because they make people want to move, *not* because they are designed to help convince teens to go out and buy Chairman Mao's *Little Red Book* as the quote from Gary Allen's book suggests. Another more fundamental problem with the argument is that nearly every well-known anti-war song is in quadruple meter throughout and simply does not utilize metrical changes from triple to quintuple meter as Dr. Crow claims to find in abundance. Granted, there are a few instances in the anti-war corpus, such as Bob Dylan's "Blowin' in the Wind," in which asymmetrical phrase structures are used, but it should be noted that at least one ultra-right-wing song, Harlan Howard's "The Minute Men (Are Turning in Their Grave)," does likewise. Would Gary Allen and Dr. Crow paint the Harlan Howard number as the devil's music? I doubt that they would.

Given the kind of argument presented by right-wing critics of anti-war material such as Gary Allen, it is interesting to note that a number of the musicians most closely associated with the anti-war movement expressed a greater interest in the artistry of their music than in the political messages contained in the lyrics of their songs. Richard Fariña, singer/songwriter and writer on folk music, mentions this tendency specifically in reference to Bob Dylan and Joan Baez (Fariña 1969). Phil Ochs, whose career featured a hefty amount of topical "folk" material with left-wing ideology, is quoted as having said in November 1965, "I'm at the point in my songwriting where I give more consideration to the art involved in my songs rather than the politics. As bad as it may sound, I'd rather listen to a good song on the side of segregation than a bad song on the side of integration" (Kemp 1997, 34).

It is also interesting to note that a number of the major players in the musical peace movement eventually withdrew from writing and singing political music, including Donovan Leitch, who performed many topical protest songs early in his career and had a 1965 hit with Buffy Sainte-Marie's "The Universal Soldier," and Bob Dylan, who wrote some of the most important anti-war material of 1962 and 1963. Leitch, quoted in an UPI dispatch of 2 November 1969, said that by late 1969 the "best writers" had "evolved to the point" where they "left protest behind and beauty" found its way into their work (Rodnitzky 1971a, 47): Leitch himself largely had ceased writing and performing overtly political material by the mid-1960s. Moving into an impressionistic, essentially non-political (or at least not overtly political) songwriting style as early as 1964, Bob Dylan was quoted as telling topical songwriter Phil Ochs that "the stuff you're writing is bullshit, because politics is bullshit. Just look at the world you're writing about and you'll see that you're just wasting your time" (Scaduto 1971). According to Arlo Guthrie, best known for his "Alice's Restaurant Massacree," "You don't accomplish very much singing protest songs to people who agree with you. Everybody just has a good time thinking they're right" (Woody's Boy 1966, 110). Indeed, seemingly contrary to the organized mass brainwashing scheme that many right-wing writers claimed was taking place, some of the left-wing singer/songwriters, like Guthrie, felt that they were simply, to use an old cliché, "preaching to the choir," while others, like Dylan and eventually Ochs, grew disillusioned with music's potential to end the war.

Another problem with the right-wing arguments against protest music, of both the acoustic, folk type and of the rock genre is that the evidence suggests that lyrics were easily misinterpreted by listeners and that lyrics generally did not play a pivotal role in teens' responses to songs. I shall cite studies by Denisoff and Levine 1971 and Edwards and Singletary 1984 in discussion of the controversial song "Eve of Destruction," both of which demonstrate that lyrics simply did not play as important a role in shaping young people's attitudes as some of the right-wing writers would have had one believe.

By 1969, the well-known, well-respected rock critic Greil Marcus was also lamenting the death of the protest song, writing, "There is a reason for that: protest songs, when they were bad, were preaching songs, instant pulpit, instant Billy Graham. They refused to allow the listener to make any decisions; they took away his freedom by telling him that if he liked the song he was right, and if he didn't like it he was wrong" (Marcus 1969, 127). In a similar vein Jerome Rodnitzky attributed the decline of protest music between 1966 and 1971 to the fact that "it is no longer stylish or profitable to sing directly about social evils. Muckraking lyrics now often insult an audience's intelligence" (Rodnitzky 1971a, 44). He adds that "whereas in 1967, topical singer Phil Ochs could fire up sophisticated radical activists, by 1969 Ochs was incapable of firing himself up" (Rodnitzky 1971a, 49). Despite the pronouncement of the death of the anti-war protest song made by such writers of Rodnitzky and Marcus, successful, potent examples can be found through the end of the war, as the reader shall see later.

It should be noted that some AM radio program directors and disc jockeys did not appreciate the protest movement being played out on the airwaves when the first very specific anti-government-policy records came out in 1965. One disc jockey was quoted as saying that "there are dozens more of these records that you don't hear simply because we don't choose to play them" (Battle of Ideologies Set to Music Meets Deejay Resistance Movement 1965, 63). By the late 1960s, FM radio provided the principal medium for left-wing politically oriented material.

U.S. military officials were concerned throughout the war with the possible harm to the morale of the troops that might be caused by anti-war songs. In early 1966 military authorities "cracked down on the disks, banning them from sale in U.S. military post exchanges throughout Europe, and from exposure on U.S. military radio stations," such as the Armed Forces Network (Anderson 1966). We shall see later, however, that it was not only anti-war material that fell under the censors' scrutiny; "The Battle Hymn of Lt. Calley," a popular song among conservatives was also banned, but for very different reasons.

Let us now examine some of the specific anti-war songs of the entire Vietnam era in approximately chronological order of their first appearance or the appearance of their most well-known recording.

THE SONGS

Pete Seeger's 1961 composition "Where Have All the Flowers Gone," in addition to being the first of the great songs of the Vietnam Conflict, provides an important link to the earlier history of protest and folk music. The basic cycle-of-life narrative of the text and the tune seem to be based on a Civil War-era song. In the best folk tradition, Seeger adapted the earlier material to make it more current. Seeger, however, kept his song general enough that it is stands as an expression of the futility of war, any war. The fact that it is so general in its anti-war message, yet appeared at a crucial time in the course of the growing tensions between South Vietnam and North Vietnam—the best-known recording appeared at about the time President Kennedy made the first major increase in the number of U.S. military advisors in South Vietnam—has enabled the song to be at once "perhaps the best-known song of Vietnam" (Sheehan 1988) and an enduring expression of solidarity in the face of the inevitable end of the cycle-of-life story.

Seeger's adaptation of earlier non-attributed, folk material and its subsequent copyright and publication represents an important trend during the folk revival of the late 1950s and early 1960s, although in the case of Pete Seeger, this freezing of older material goes back to his work with the Weavers in the 1940s. Folklorist B. A. Botkin noted two seemingly contradictory trends during the folk revival: (1) "the tendency to substitute for the folk exchange of songs in a social situation, rote learning of songs from records, radio and television" and (2) "the compensatory desire of the singer to make a song his own by changing it to suit his taste or whim, and often for no other reason than to make it his own" (Botkin 1967, 96). Seeger not only adapted earlier material for his "Where Have All the Flowers Gone," his copyrighting of the finished song, and the song's subsequent publication, represents the second part of Botkin's description. The song was such a popular success in several early recordings by The Kingston Trio and Peter, Paul & Mary that it also was very much a part of the first of Botkin's trends: numerous musicians copied these widely distributed recordings, freezing not only the now-copyrighted melody, harmony, and lyrics, but also freezing the early influential musical arrangements. Incidentally, the controversy surrounding the copyrighting of material based in whole or in part on folk sources was played out in some of the popular folk music magazines of the time. Those interested in reading more about this are encouraged to read Botkin's book as well as Lloyd 1962 and Seeger 1963-64.

That "Where Have All the Flowers Gone?" came to be seen, and is still seen, as a nearly universal song of solidarity for those Americans primarily in their twenties is evidenced by its inclusion in the 1991 episode of the television program *Columbo*, "Death Hits the Jackpot." In this special episode of the Peter Falk detective program, friends of the murdered Freddy Brower gather in the victim's apartment and sing the song accompanied by an acoustic guitar. Used in this context, the song is stripped of the anti-war interpretation of the 1960s and becomes a purer, more universal, cycle-of-life narrative.

The first commercially successful recording of the song was the single by The Kingston Trio, which made its chart debut in January 1962. As mentioned previously, this coincided with the Kennedy administration's increase in the number of U.S. military advisors stationed in South Vietnam to 4,000. The recording reached #21 on the *Billboard* pop charts and remained on the charts for over three months. The recording falls neatly in line with Jerome Rodnitzky's assertion (Rodnitzky 1971b) that recordings of the period 1960-63 emphasized the understandability of the lyrics as consumers and musicians alike became more interested in the lyrics: The Kingston Trio recording is exceptionally clean and clear, with sparse accompaniment by acoustic guitars and bass.

Perhaps due in part to the clarity and cleanness of The Kingston Trio's Capitol Records release, and perhaps due to the fact that this ensemble enjoyed much greater commercial success in the late 1950s and early 1960s than other folk revival performers, some folk traditionalists heavily criticized the group. In response to an article by Stephen Fiott expressing support for The Kingston Trio and other commercial folk groups as important performers who brought the acoustic style back into prominence (Fiott 1962-63), Dan Armstrong wrote the following: "I said Pete Seeger was traveling and singing and absorbing and creating from what he experienced. The Kingston Trio are panty-raiders on a weekend vacation in Dad's Rambler. John Lee Hooker is letting go on Sat. Nite in a gin mill. The Kingston Trio is a milkshake and 15¢ hamburgers" (Armstrong 1963, 21). According to Armstrong, "Conformity was introduced into folk music by The Kingston Trio" (Armstrong 1963, 22). To be fair to the ensemble, it should be pointed out that part of the stylistic discrepancies between the Trio, which developed in the San Francisco, California, folk scene (two of the original members were in fact from as far west as Hawaii), and the singers who were either from New York or Midwesterners who moved into the New York folk scene comes from general differences of approach between musicians of the two coasts. In a very mild sense, this bicoastal competition suggests the real bicoastal war that developed in the rap music world in the 1980s and 1990s, without the physical violence associated with the bicoastal rap wars. It also should be noted that some of the east-coast protest musicians did indeed give the Trio its due. In a 1968 interview in *Broadside*, Phil Ochs credited The Kingston Trio and Joan Baez with being strong artists who, through their ability to win over audiences, acted as "translators" for the late 1950s and early 1960s folk song movement (Interview with Phil Ochs 1968, 13). Baez herself has been widely quoted as saying that The Kingston Trio was one of her early inspirations for becoming a folk musician.

Shortly after the successful 1962 recording by The Kingston Trio and the popularity the song itself attained, Phil Ochs wrote that "one good song with a message can bring a point more deeply to more people than a thousand rallies." Ochs went on specifically to cite "Where Have All the Flowers Gone?" as a song that had affected and led to political activism even in those who "do not consider themselves involved in politics" (Ochs 1963, 6). That it was an important part of anti-war activism at the time of its initial popularity can be seen in Agnes Friesen's report that on a peace walk April 6-12, 1962, from McGuire Air Force Base in New Jersey to the United Nations building in New York City, marchers sang traditional folk songs, such as the "We shall live in peace someday" stanza of "We Shall Overcome" and "Down by the Riverside" and the newly popular "Where Have All the Flowers Gone?" (Friesen 1962).

Pete Seeger's song certainly did not exist in only one definitive version, however. Peter, Paul & Mary included an acoustic rendition of "Where Have All the Flowers Gone?" on their first album, and the song made it back into the top 40 in October 1965 when rock and roll singer Johnny Rivers's recording was released on the Imperial label. On the charts from October into December, the Rivers single followed the spring 1965 bombing raids on North Vietnam, the introduction of U.S. ground troops in Southeast Asia, and the start of organized anti-war demonstrations. It was a most timely release of the gentle anti-war song.

The Johnny Rivers recording falls into the folk/rock genre—the development of this sub genre of rock will be discussed a bit later—with the use of rock drum set, electric guitars, and electric keyboards; however, note that the tempo of the Rivers recording is easily within the range of the earlier versions, just the orchestration and emphasis on rhythm has changed substantially. Rivers adapts the material somewhat to his own vocal style by singing a slight melodic variant in each stanza, suggesting his work in his even better-known recording of the song "Secret Agent Man." The Rivers recording also includes a repeat of the first stanza at the end of the song, taking some of the emphasis away from the inevitability of death contained in Seeger's story, but also bringing the story more obviously full circle. Rivers also heightens the anti-war message of the song by asking about the fate of the soldiers and when *they* specifically might ever learn in the improvised coda on the song's studio fade out. Based on the photographs on the album *Johnny Rivers Rocks the Folk*, which contains the Seeger opus, Imperial seemed to be marketing Rivers to a college-aged audience, or possibly at those in their early twenties. From his relatively clean-cut appearance, and from the type of material he was recording at the time, it is almost as if the same people who would have purchased The Kingston Trio's recording but might now be developing an appreciation of the rock styles of The Beatles, say, might be the target audience for Johnny Rivers.

Even in the jungles of Vietnam, "Where Have All the Flowers Gone?" was part of singers' repertoire. A report in the *New York Times* from February 1968 indicated that in the midst of a night "when more than 1,000 rounds hit Khesanh," soldiers were ordered to sing songs to pass the time. Lance Corporal Richard Morris played the guitar for some of his favorite songs, including the Seeger tune. According to the report, "a hard emphasis accompanied the part that went: 'Where have all the soldiers gone? To the graveyard every one. Oh, when will they ever learn? Oh, when will they ever learn'" (Folk Music in Vietnam 1968).

The power of "Where Have All the Flowers Gone?" as a means of gently focusing a collective psyche on the futility of war and on the inevitability of death can be seen in its spurts of popularity surrounding specific events. The song is not just narrative poetry; however, it is a musical setting of that poetry. Harmony and melody very clearly support the structure of the lyrics and are a near textbook example of the use of repetition and contrast in musical construction.

A very different sort of anti-war, actually anti-draft, song also hit the pop charts in early 1962 when The Four Preps' "The Big Draft Medley" was issued. The vocal ensemble impersonates other vocal groups, including The Platters, The Four Aces, Dion and The Belmonts, and The Highwaymen in this medley of "I'll Never Smile Again," "Love Is a Many-Splendored Thing," "The Mountain's High," "Heartaches," "Michael, Row the Boat Ashore," and "Runaround Sue." In between the humorous parodies of their contemporaries, they musically beg the draft board to draft the other groups, both to give The Four Preps less competition and because all of the members of The Four Preps are 1-A for the draft! All in all, this is a good-natured dig at the draft and a record that probably shows as well as anything else that for some Americans at least, the Vietnam Conflict was still viewed as a police action not to be taken too seriously. As the reader might suspect, then, this medley faded from the airwaves fairly quickly, especially as the buildup in the war effort by 1965 made the draft less and less of a laughing matter.

Folksinger Mark Spoelstra dealt differently with the draft in his 1962 song "We've Got to Find Another Way." The song, published in lead sheet form in *Broadside #5* (May 1962), presents strictly a pacifist message about the need for young men to fill out the necessary forms to become conscientious objectors. Spoelstra uses a simple pentatonic tune, similar in many respects to old British and American folk songs, to set his appeal to his contemporaries.

While Mark Spoelstra may have composed new material modeled on Anglo-American folksong in his "We've Got to Find Another Way," Ewan MacColl in his "The Dove" and Pete Seeger in "The Flowers of Peace" stayed even closer to tradition. MacColl's gentle pro-peace song, which uses the metaphor of the dove representing peace, utilizes the traditional folk tune "The Cuckoo." Seeger's text is set to an adaptation of the tune "Will Ye Go, Lassie Go?" as sung by Francis McPeake, Jr. of

Belfast, Ireland. Seeger poses rhetorical questions related to peace and war in a manner suggesting his own "Where Have All the Flowers Gone?" and Bob Dylan's only slightly later composition "Blowin' in the Wind." Indeed, this seemed to be a very workable format for the 1961-62-era protest singer. We shall see that these gentle, rhetorical-question-laden songs soon disappeared as the war continued to grow in scope. "The Dove" was published in *Sing Out!* 10/4 (December-January 1960-61) and "The Flowers of Peace" appeared in *Broadside* #3 (April 1962) and *Sing Out!* 12/3 (Summer 1962).

Bob Dylan's "Blowin' in the Wind" represents classic folk material to a large extent. The beginning of the tune is based on a nineteenth-century anti-slavery song that Dylan reportedly learned while on his early travels. This kind of adaptation of earlier material, whether lyrical or musical, has been part of the folk tradition ever since the Middle Ages in Europe and was quite common in the American folk singing tradition in the nineteenth century. Both music and lyrics have elicited a great deal of comment, and at least three well-known recordings of "Blowin' in the Wind" came into prominence during the course of the Vietnam Conflict.

In terms of phrase structure, the song is built in stanzas with the following scheme (based on Dylan's recording of the piece): *a* (eight measures), *a*^{l} (eight measures), *a* (eight measures), *b* (seven measures), *b* (instrumental answer—eight measures), with the *a* phrases ending on tonic in most performances but being melodically open, ending on the fifth scale step; the *a*^{l} phrase ending on a half-cadence; and only the *b* phrases ending both melodically and harmonically closed. Generally, harmony is limited to tonic (I), subdominant (IV), dominant (V), and submediant (vi), with the submediant being used only in the *b* phrases. Although Wilfrid Mellers describes the melody as consisting of a "nagging pentatonic tune and reiterated ostinato" that helps the composer "build up a cumulative fury" (Mellers 1969, 185), it is really the *a* and *a*^{l} phrases that heavily emphasize the pentatonic: the melody actually eventually includes all of the tones of the diatonic major scale, although the full complement of tones do not come into play until the *b* phrases of each stanza.

Text and melodic phrase compliment each other well in "Blowin' in the Wind," with each of the *a* and *a*^{l} phrases consisting of a question and the *b* phrase of each stanza replying that, as the title of the song suggests, the answer to each question is "blowing in the wind." While not all of the questions deal with the issue of war, a number of them do, and led to the song's importance within the anti-war movement. In dealing with the issue of war, Dylan uses a mixture of specific references (mentioning cannonballs, for example) and metaphorical references (using the dove to symbolize peace). Dylan's 1962 and 1963 manner of writing song texts as political messages has not met with universal approval from those who study the protest music genre. The prolific writer on music and society Serge Denisoff, for example, characterizes this type of rhetorical song as one "which stressed individual indignation and dissent but did not offer a solution in a movement" (Denisoff 1972a, 18). Similarly, Jon Landau criticizes the Dylan of "Blowin' in the Wind" and "Masters of War" as a "one-dimensional moralist" (Landau 1969, 219), stressing that not only did Dylan fail to offer solutions, but that he also failed to allow for alternative views or alternative interpretations of his lyrics. That Dylan did not offer solutions to the problems about which he complained certainly was not unique to his way of songwriting: most of the pre-1965 anti-war protest songs were strictly propaganda devices for the peace movement and found songwriters working in a similar, one-dimensional lyrical vein.

A song that has been performed and recorded by a large number of musicians, Dylan's own version of "Blowin' in the Wind" was featured on his album *The*

Freewheelin' Bob Dylan; Peter, Paul & Mary recorded probably the best-remembered 1963 hit single version; and Motown singer and multi-instrumentalist Stevie Wonder took the song to #9 in the *Billboard* pop charts in 1966. Let us examine each of these recordings in detail to see how Dylan's message of protest could be given differing sympathetic treatments, each of which found appeal among audiences.

Bob Dylan's own recording of "Blowin' in the Wind," first found on the 1963 album *The Freewheelin' Bob Dylan*, remains firmly in the acoustic American folk tradition, with Dylan singing, accompanying himself on guitar, and providing harmonica solos to answer the *b* phrase in each stanza. Dylan's performance of a seven-measure *b* vocal phrase and an eight-measure instrumental answer is unusual in terms of common-practice concert music and probably even more unusual in American popular song. Such asymmetrical structures can be found in traditional American folk music, especially in the work of some of the early rural blues performer/composers, such as Robert Johnson. In my own listening to "Blowin' in the Wind," I find that the asymmetrical phrase structure, the perceived truncation of the *b* phrase, tends to make me pay more attention to the composer's performance. Like the seven-measure opening phrase in Paul McCartney's "Yesterday," or the rhythmic/metric anomalies in the Jimmy Webb composition "MacArthur Park," popularized in 1968 by actor/singer Richard Harris, or the occasional three-beat measures in Blondie's new wave/disco hit "Heart of Glass," Dylan's phrasing, although found in the folk and rural blues repertoire, is so unusual in a pop song that it tends to capture the listener's attention. Whether or not it was Dylan's intent to heighten the listener's attention through this phrase structure, the heightened attention caused by the phrasing can sharpen the listener's appreciation of the text and its anti-war ramifications. That having been said, it should be emphasized that the piquing of the listener's interest possibly caused by the unusual phrase structure can in no way be equated with the type of rhythmic anomalies for brainwashing purposes supposedly found by Gary Allen's expert, Dr. Crow in contemporary protest and rock music.

The reader should note that even early on in his career, young people took Bob Dylan very seriously, especially because of the poetry of his lyrics. Wilfrid Mellers, one of the few musicologists who gave serious attention to music of the rock era—his *Twilight of the Gods*, a book about the music of The Beatles, is considered seminal in Beatles scholarship—noted that in sharp contrast to the way in which they listened to pop groups like The Beatles, young people listened in silence to Dylan, latching onto his every word (Mellers 1969, 185).

Bob Dylan's version of probably his best-known composition was an album cut, but did receive some radio airplay and was well known, at least among folk music fans. Folk cognoscenti, incidentally, also knew the song from its publication in lead sheet form in *Broadside* #6 (late May 1962) and *Sing Out!* 12/4 (October-November 1962). The generally more widely known renditions were those that made it into *Billboard*'s top 10 singles charts: the 1963 recording by folk artists Peter, Paul & Mary, and the 1966 version by Stevie Wonder.

Peter, Paul & Mary's recording of the Dylan song not only reached #2 on the *Billboard* pop singles chart, the album on which it was featured, *In the Wind*, was #1 on the magazine's pop album charts for five weeks and remained on the charts for eighty weeks. Although albums were not as important as sales vehicles as were 45 rpm single records in 1963—pop musicians would generally shift their focus to albums later in the decade—the sales success of *In the Wind* should not be taken lightly. That this album was the top-selling collection in the nation for over a month, coupled with the success of the single during its fifteen weeks on the charts, and the large amount of radio airplay top

10 singles such as this received meant that millions of Americans were exposed to Bob Dylan's subtle anti-war message.

The Peter, Paul & Mary recording uses a folk-derived, acoustic guitar and bass accompaniment, holding to the general instrumental style of Dylan to a large extent, minus the harmonica. Where the trio's rendition differs is in the three-part setting of the song and in the significantly greater use of texture and dynamic shading to highlight certain parts of the text. Probably the most apropos example of this text painting occurs in the stanza asking how much longer in history cannonballs will continue to be used. The trio crescendo for this particular stanza, and then drop back considerably in volume as they conclude that the answer can be found in the wind. To my ear this clearly places the question relating to warfare on a higher plane, on a higher level of importance. I find that the rapid diminuendo that follows the question lends a greater sense of futility to our search for questions about war and peace than I feel when I listen to Bob Dylan's considerably more evenly modulated version of the song.

Peter, Paul & Mary also change texture throughout the song, with some solo lines, some three-part chorale-like harmony, and just about every permutation short of complex polyphony. While the vocal arrangement does not necessarily seem to be meant to highlight particular kinds of text in a systematic way, these changing textures can have the affect of holding the listener's attention better than a solo performance. Of course, changing textures can draw the attention of some listeners away from the text and focus it more squarely on what is taking place musically. From my experience in talking with college students in classes in which we discuss the effect of texture on what we get out of performance, I conclude that it is largely a personal matter. To my ears, Peter, Paul & Mary's subtle texture changes in the Dylan piece tend to drawn me more fully into the text than do the more constant textures of the other performances detailed here.

Stevie Wonder took the song to #9 in the *Billboard* pop charts after the sixteen-year-old's single version had its chart debut in July 1966. Still recording in the Motown corporate style at this stage in his career, Wonder's recording utilizes many of the same instrumentalists and the same instrumental style heard on contemporary recordings by other Motown Records acts such as The Temptations and The Supremes. I refer to the stylistic feel as "Motown swing," which features electric rhythm guitar chords on beats two and four, a moderate tempo swing or shuffle feel, and a horn section; incidentally, the rhythm guitar style heard on Wonder's recording, especially, immediately identifies this as a Motown product. The reader might note that Wonder's recording was released on the Tamla label; however, Tamla was a subsidiary of Berry Gordy's Motown. Not that Stevie Wonder's recording is generic: Wonder's vocal stylings are uniquely his own. Another interesting feature of the Wonder record is his call and response work with an unidentified second male singer; this gives the performance a feel of spontaneity, of improvisation. As the reader will see later, by the time of Stevie Wonder's recording of "Blowin' in the Wind," most anti-war, and indeed most pro-government songs had become more pointed, even angry. Wonder's recording of an already familiar song probably achieved its success in part due to the fact that it pointed out the questions that were continuing to build concerning the expanding war, but in Dylan's subtle, and somewhat vague way; it was probably a needed break in the extreme rhetoric that was building after the introduction of U.S. ground troops in spring 1965.

Probably best remembered for her song "Little Houses," recorded and popularized by Pete Seeger, folk singer/composer Malvina Reynolds was also active in producing a number of anti-war songs throughout the Vietnam Conflict. Reynolds's "The Little Generals," one of the earlier songs related to the growing conflict, was published in

Broadside #13 (September 1962). In a move unusual in a folk-styled song, the composer uses the four-chord sequential string A7, D7, G7, C at the cadence points. The use of the string of two secondary dominant chords, A7 and D7, to precede the key of C major's dominant-seventh chord, G7, suggests Tin Pan Alley-era American popular music more so than music of the folk revival. The text of the Reynolds song comments on how difficult it is for generals to get a war started today. Obviously she believed that the Americans stationed in Vietnam were still acting in an advisory role and would likely be brought home soon.

Phil Ochs, who made the Vietnam Conflict the principal focus of his early songwriting career, made a similar miscalculation in his "Vietnam," one of the earliest published compositions to mention the country by name. Published in *Broadside* #14 (October 1962), the Ochs piece, which was written at a time when there were approximately 10,000 U.S. military advisors in South Vietnam, asks listeners to contact their congressmen and express their anti-war feelings so that the United States might soon withdraw from southeastern Asia. Little did he imagine the course that the war would take. Ochs did make a point of stating that South Vietnam was being ruled by a one-family dictatorship, a point that a number of anti-war songwriters would echo throughout the Diem rule.

Ochs's "Vietnam," written in the key of D major, is fairly rich harmonically, using six different chords. The tune bears some resemblance to the American folk song "She'll Be Coming 'Round the Mountain." Although I have seen no evidence to suggest that it was the case, the tune of "Vietnam" very well could have been inspired by the folk song. Folk revival songwriters created their material in several standard ways: (1) fitting new words to existing public domain folk tunes; (2) writing songs using entirely original words and music; (3) doing minor adaptations to folk material and then securing a copyright; and (4) basing melodic material on earlier songs, but taking the pre-existing material as a starting point for original work. Songwriters also did just about every conceivable permutation of these *modus operandi*, so it should come as no surprise that a folk revival protest song like "Vietnam" might not overtly copy but closely resemble an earlier folk song.

Although Phil Ochs was just building a following at the time of the publication of "Vietnam," very soon thereafter a campus cult of sorts developed around Ochs and his music. According to Ray Pratt, "Ochs helped catalyze a generation's peace activism" (Pratt 1998, 175). I will cite further examples of this a bit later, as they start to appear within our chronology.

Like its near contemporary "Blowin' in the Wind," Bob Dylan's "Masters of War" provides another link to the classic tradition of folk material usage. The tune basically is that of the Appalachian folk song "Nottamun Town," as Dylan learned it from Appalachian singer Jean Ritchie during his travels before settling into the New York City folk music scene (Kingman 1998, 19). In true, classic, topical folk singing style, Dylan adapted the music slightly and fit the tune with his own words, much the same way folk musicians had been working for centuries. That Dylan's version of the tune is based on one that he learned by means of the oral tradition, of course, neatly fits the traditional definition of true folk music. The difference here was that by then copyrighting and recording a definitive version of the song, Dylan essentially froze the song's lyrical content, as well as the tune, causing "Masters of War" to cease to be true folk material. Incidentally, other songwriters were doing the same sort of thing as they wrote material for the growing anti-war movement: Russ Farrell's 1964 song "I've Got No Use for the

Army," as published in *Broadside* #120 (July-August 1972), is just one example, as it uses the late nineteenth-century cowboy tune "I've Got No Use for the Women."

Dylan's "Masters of War," published in lead sheet form in *Broadside* #20 (February 1963) and in *Sing Out!* 13/3 (Summer 1963), is as pointed as "Blowin' in the Wind" is subtle. Ray Pratt suggests that "while critical minorities on the left might have given voice to similar sentiments [as those found in "Masters of War" and Dylan's slightly later "With God on Our Side"], Americans had never heard anything like these bitter comments on aspects of their nation's history and wars issued on commercial recordings" (Pratt 1998, 173). Pratt further writes that those who purchased Dylan's albums listened to these songs, along with "A Hard Rain's Gonna Fall," particularly intently and repeatedly.

So just what are these left wing sentiments that so captivated listeners of Dylan's early albums? Dylan blames the U.S. military-industrial complex for designing and building weapons and starting the wars that others must fight, all for the sake of corporate profits. The songwriter states that there will be no forgiveness from on high for these warmongers when they die, and he expresses the hope that he will have the chance to see their deaths and burials. These sentiments would be taken up by a fair number of songwriters subsequent to "Masters of War," but probably most literally by the heavy metal band Black Sabbath in their song "War Pigs."

In its harmonic and melodic simplicity, "Masters of War" resembles rural folk music—Dylan did not alter the basic nature of the folk material on which the song is based—basically using only two differing melodic phrases, the first of which is repeated several times. The melody itself, in the key of E minor, uses only the notes E, G, B, and D. The harmonic scheme of each stanza is an E minor drone for 24 measures, followed by quick single measures of G major, A9, C major, and E minor chords for the cadence. With the degree of harmonic stasis, the simplicity of the melody, and the simplicity of Dylan's acoustic guitar accompaniment on his recording of the song on the album *The Freewheelin' Bob Dylan*, the emphasis is clearly on the words, which are sung by the composer with a hint of a sneer.

Published in *Broadside* #27 (June 1963) and in *Sing Out!* 13/5 (December-January 1963-64), and originally recorded by its composer, Bob Dylan, on his 1964 album *The Times They Are A'Changin'*, "With God on Our Side" (sometimes given as "With God on Your Side") calls into question the belief that God is on our side in war, whomever "we" may be. The songwriter points out that those on both sides of a two-sided conflict could (and still frequently do) make such a claim, thereby rendering the claim void as a justification for war. The lyrics make it clear that Dylan cannot accept such a justification for war, finally concluding that if God is truly on our side, He will not even let the next war begin; the theme of the mutual incompatibility of war and religion harkens back to Dylan's "Masters of War." The lyrics mark this a general anti-war song, chiefly influenced by the Cold War: clearly the next war Dylan fears is a thermonuclear war. The song, however, is one of those general songs that could be understood, and was understood by audiences, as referring to some extent to Vietnam. It should be noted, though, that none of Dylan's anti-war songs actually mentions the Vietnam Conflict; by leaving out specific references to Vietnam, Dylan created propaganda for peace that could be relevant in many situations.

Melodically and harmonically, the song resembles true folksong in its simplicity. Dylan's use of triple meter, found more frequently in folk music than in pop music, also suggests indebtedness to the folk tradition. Unlike the songwriter's previous anti-war songs, "With God on Our Side" seems to consist entirely of newly written material.

With the emergence of folk-rock, rock and pop bands began covering the Bob Dylan songbook later in 1964 and over the course of the next several years. The British pop group Manfred Mann recorded "With God on Our Side," releasing it as a single in England; the record made no chart impact in the United States. The Manfred Mann recording features gospel-tinged piano, acoustic guitar, and a march-like snare drum part played with brushes. With each stanza the song's instrumentation grows, with electric bass guitar, bass drum, and eventually a separate lead piano part entering.

Like Dylan's "With God on Our Side," Tom Paxton's satirical "What Did You Learn in School Today?" (sometimes given as "What Did You Learn in School?") was published in lead sheet form in *Broadside* #27 (June 1963); the Paxton number was published one issue earlier than the Dylan song in *Sing Out!*, appearing in 13/4 (October-November 1963). Paxton may be best known today for his children's songs, but in the early 1960s he was a potent force in the protest song movement. "What Did You Learn in School Today?" finds the composer questioning the honesty of politicians, the necessity of war, and the hatred of groups of people based on how they look. He also suggests that the glamour of war is learned and is deliberately taught to children. Although Paxton does not specifically mention Vietnam, his song suggests that an atmosphere of war is in the air and that teachers seem to be preparing children to fight in that war in the very near future.

The Paxton song has a melodic range of a major 9th, making it fairly easy to sing, and the use of just three chords, C, F, and G7 in the key of C major, makes instrumental accompaniment possible even for those with very rudimentary guitar skills. The phrase structure, too, is very straightforward: Paxton's form is a (with a half cadence), a^1 (perfect authentic cadence), b (in the secondary key of F major), b^1, a^1. Despite the apparent simplicity of the song—the simplicity seems to be especially befitting a song featuring a child as the main character—"What Did You Learn in School Today?" finds Paxton doing some subtle text painting, emphasizing the irony of the song. He incorporates syncopation in the rhythm in setting the word "school," giving the word and the concept of the place a sense of fun. That the lessons given in school are those of hatred and war make Paxton's rhythmic setting of "school" all the more ironic.

A contemporary of "What Did You Learn in School Today," Tom Paxton's "The Willing Conscript" was published in *Broadside* #28 (late June 1963). The song shares many traits with the other Paxton work, including an emphasis on war as learned behavior; melodic, harmonic, and formal simplicity; and a cutting sense of irony brought forth by the songwriter's combination of text and music.

The autobiographical song, based on Paxton's two months at Fort Riley, Kansas, in 1960, begins with a new draftee telling his sergeant that he will need to have lessons in killing because he has no previous experience. The novice enumerates in each stanza the requisite skills that his superior will need to cover to help prepare the young man to be a killer. Finally, in the last stanza the soldier thanks his sergeant, telling the officer that he now has the necessary skills to kill the enemy. The subtext of the transformation of the draftee is that the blame for molding the innocent into killers rests on military officers: the foot soldier is a pawn of sorts. Bob Dylan had stated this sentiment explicitly in his "Masters of War." Paxton allows the listener to discover it. It is interesting to note that Vietnam is not specifically mentioned. In fact, one stanza finds the draftee telling his sergeant that the enemy looks just like he looks, suggesting that the enemy is white, like Paxton. This interpretation would certainly be in keeping with the composer's experience at Fort Riley in 1960: before the build up in Vietnam, the principal enemy was thought to be Soviet. In light of the song's appearance in *Broadside* in mid-1963 and especially in light of its appearance on Paxton's 1965 album *Ain't That News!*, released at a time at which the abstract enemy was more likely to be North Vietnamese, the stanza takes on a new, metaphorical meaning: under the skin, all people look alike.

"The Willing Conscript" has an octave melodic range, easily singable for most people, and uses only the chords, C, F, G7, and the secondary dominant D7, making it, like the previously discussed Paxton song, easy to accompany on the guitar. The form is *aaba¹*; very much standard in popular song literature. Here, the simplicity of structure and materials helps to emphasize the nature of Paxton's protagonist: the draftee is a young man of simple upbringing, lacking education in the skills necessary for his new job. Paxton's Pete Seeger-influenced performance on "The Willing Conscript" on *Ain't That News!* finds the musician singing in an almost child-like, singsong manner, emphasizing even more the unsophisticated innocence of the protagonist.

For his successful performances of self-composed protest songs such as "The Willing Conscript" and "What Did You Learn in School Today," light-hearted children's songs, and traditional folk material, Paxton was praised by *New York Times* critic Robert Shelton, who called the singer/songwriter "a superb melodist, using tunes that ring original and familiar" (Shelton 1963).

Published in *Broadside* #32 (September 20, 1963), Phil Ochs's "Talkin' Vietnam Blues" received its premiere at a September 1963 hootenanny in New York City. The piece represents an important folk music form, used by musicians on both sides of the political spectrum to great effect throughout the Vietnam era. Basically, the talking blues consists of a recitation over a repeating accompaniment figure, usually played on the acoustic guitar, but sometimes including a more elaborate instrumentation. As a recitation, not necessary in verse or rhyme structure, the talking blues is one of the vocal music forms most open to improvisation.

Christian fundamentalist writer David Noebel, writing in his book *Rhythm, Riots, and Revolution*, referred to "Talkin' Vietnam Blues" as a "perversion," and Ray Pratt wrote that this song in particular "struck home with [Ochs'] small, but politically astute (and soon-to-be-influential) college audience" (Pratt 1998, 176). Pratt further stated that Ochs "helped catalyze a generation's peace activism" through his compositions and his tireless performing on university campuses and at numerous peace rallies. Just what was it about "Talkin' Vietnam Blues" that caused Noebel to label the song a "perversion" and caused Pratt to consider it one of its composer's more influential works?

The text includes elements of sharp satire and biting social commentary, with the principal recipients being (1) the U.S. government, for claiming that the 14,000 to 15,000 (at the time of the song's writing) Americans stationed in South Vietnam were "trainers" or "advisors" helping the South Vietnamese fight for democracy; and (2) the Diem family, the rulers of South Vietnam, seen by Ochs, and by most in the anti-war movement, as a one-family dictatorship, and definitely *not* leaders of a democracy. Among the examples of intolerance in the South Vietnamese government cited by Ochs is the intense discrimination against Buddhists: this song was written at the time (mid-1963) when the infamous suicides by fire committed by Buddhist monks protesting government repression first took place. Because of the timeliness of songs such as "Talkin' Vietnam Blues," which frankly only fully functions in the context of 1963 and 1964, Robert Shelton, writing in the *New York Times*, called Phil Ochs "a musical editorial writer" (Shelton 1963). Indeed, one needs to be familiar with all of the topical references in the song in order to "get it."

By the time of Ochs's performance of "Talkin' Vietnam Blues" at the 1964 Newport Folk Festival, the text had evolved somewhat—perfectly in keeping with what a topical talking blues does at its best—but still retained all of its earlier caustic humor and biting political commentary. Recall that at this time approximately 20,000 Americans called Southeast Asia "home" but that U.S. ground troops had not yet been deployed, and neither had the massive bombings of North Vietnam started. In addition, since the song's publication in *Broadside*, Diem had been overthrown in a military coup on November 1-2, 1963, and General Duong Van Minh, who had taken over in the November coup, himself had been deposed on January 30, 1964. The Newport Folk Festival performance, recently issued on compact disc, finds the audience audibly responding to the humor and the biting political commentary of the song: this is a crowd that obviously agrees with Ochs's assessment of the situation in South Vietnam.

Phil Ochs was not by any means the only protest songwriter to take on the Diem family's opulent lifestyle and repressive political stances. *Broadside* #34 (November 5, 1963), ironically printed before the coup that toppled the Diem but dated three days after the coup, contained Bonnie Day's "What Can We Do for Madame Nhu," a newly written set of words to be sung to the tune of "Skip to My Lou." The text lampoons the ruling family, especially Madame Nhu and her extensive collection of fine clothing that she wears despite the fact that the peasants of her country are literally starving. Incidentally, the fitting of new words to pre-existing musical material dates back to the unfortunately labeled parody Masses of the Middle Ages and the work of the French troubadours. While today we might better remember the humorous parody songs of the 1980s and 1990s by "Weird Al" Yankovic, protest singers were fitting sometimes humorous and sometimes not-so-humorous words to traditional folk songs. As we shall see later, protest songwriters also added new, anti-war lyrics to some of the contemporary pro-government hits of the 1960s.

After the November 1963 coup, topical protest songwriters naturally dealt with the event. Bill Frederick's "Two Brothers—A Nhu Version," printed in *Broadside* #36 (December 10, 1963), uses the traditional folk tune "Two Brothers." Frederick's new text comments on the army coup that toppled the Diem government and on how the peasants' desires for land reforms were never met by the old government. He also details how the peasants gradually became more and more disenchanted with the Diem government when their requests for land reforms were met with their being given uniforms to fight the North Vietnamese. Fredericks comments too on the irony that while peasants are starving and dying, millions of U.S. dollars are being pumped into the South Vietnamese military.

A fifteen-year-old writer sent an open letter to Phil Ochs, published as a letter to the editor of *Broadside*, saying "I feel and believe in what you voice in your songs" (E.D. 1964). The young man was writing in response to Ochs's 1964 album *All the News That's Fit to Sing*, a record containing the anti-war song "One More Parade," written by Ochs and Bob Gibson. The song, printed in lead sheet form in *Broadside* #50 (September 22, 1964), represents an interesting compositional process, one that was used fairly commonly by musicians active in the folk revival movement. The folk musicians frequently participated in formal songwriting workshops and informally helped each other in an almost communal spirit. In 1961 Bob Gibson, an established folk singer who was headlining at Faragher's in Cleveland, Ohio, gave his young opening act (Ochs) a tape of melodies, encouraging the budding songwriter to hone his skills by writing words to one of Gibson's tunes. According to Ben Edmonds, "One More Parade" was the result of that process (Edmonds 1997, 73). As such, the song is one of the earliest anti-war songs directly related to the growing possibility of war in Southeast Asia. I have placed discussion of the song here as its 1964 publication in *Broadside* and release on Och's debut album gave the song its widest exposure three years after its composition.

"One More Parade" takes on the glorification of the military and the glorification of war in American society. Gibson's D minor music, which uses a fairly rich harmonic vocabulary, including the D minor, F, E7, G, A, and A7 chords, hints at the dorian mode at times. The snaky, fairly difficult-to-sing melody, which includes some unexpected chromaticism, has a tendency to move upward in pitch at the endings of phrases, a melodic motion unusual in Anglo-American folk tunes. In Phil Ochs's performance on *All the News That's Fit to Sing*, the combination of Gibson's surprising music and Ochs's text, implying that the next parade to war is clearly on the horizon, create a sense of urgency. That the song was not released on vinyl until 1964 does nothing to diminish this urgency—if anything the later date increases the topicality of the song—as the number of U.S. advisors stationed in South Vietnam had risen from less than 4,000 at the time of the song's writing to something in the neighborhood of 15,000, and the record's impact was being felt in the peace activist community right at the time of the alleged August 1964 attacks on the USS *Maddox* and USS *C. Turner Joy* by the North Vietnamese. It should be noted that while Ochs's album made little impact commercially—none of his albums ever made it into the *Billboard* top 100 pop charts—those who followed Ochs's music felt passionately about it, like the fifteen-year-old quoted earlier.

As tensions and the size of the U.S. advisory force in South Vietnam both grew, a number of songwriters took Tom Paxton's "What Did You Learn in School Today?" one step further and dealt with the issue of the growing popularity of the toys of war among American children. Malvina Reynolds's "Playing War" was printed in lead sheet form in *Broadside* #50 (September 1964). The song suggests that the toys of war are being used deliberately and subconsciously by corporate America to prepare young boys to fight in Vietnam, which is mentioned by name in the text. Although the music is newly composed, the simple melodic and harmonic schemes closely resemble traditional Anglo-American folk music. Tom Paxton's "Buy a Gun for Your Son," which dates from approximately the same time period, features a rollicking tempo and some traditional country-western guitar picking on the composer's recording on the album *Ain't That News!* The melodic and harmonic style of the Paxton number reflects the country tradition as heard in earlier twentieth-century recordings of groups like the Carter Family. Paxton's sentiments align closely with those of Malvina Reynolds: taking the voice of a corporate toy salesperson, Paxton sarcastically gives parents reasons for buying various toys of war to help prepare their sons for future warfare; however, while Reynolds's song specifically deals with the growing conflict in Vietnam, which at the time was on the verge of seeing the introduction of U.S. ground troops and the beginnings of massive bombings of North Vietnam, Paxton's piece suggests that war toys are preparing children for the upcoming, inevitable thermonuclear war. Paxton does not mention Vietnam. In this sense Reynolds's song represents the new trend in the protest song movement—to specifically protest the war in Vietnam—while Paxton's song reflects the older, more generally cold war-related style protest song of the earlier part of the decade.

The protest movement saw a number of rollicking, satirical, anti-war songs specifically aimed at the desire to avoid military service; the earlier "Big Draft Medley" of The Four Preps was never a significant part of the peace movement. The first prominent example is the 1964 Phil Ochs composition "Draft Dodger Rag"; as we shall see, later examples include Arlo Guthrie's "Alice's Restaurant Massacree" and Country Joe McDonald's "I-Feel-Like-I'm-Fixin'-to-Die Rag." The Ochs song, published in lead sheet form in *Songs of Peace, Freedom, and Protest* 1970, *Broadside* #53 (December 20, 1964), and *Sing Out!* 15/1 (March 1965), was performed to great effect by the composer at the 1964 Newport Folk Festival and was included on Ochs's 1965 album *I Ain't Marching Anymore*.

Historian Ray Pratt describes "Draft Dodger Rag" and its contemporary "I Ain't Marching Anymore" as quickly having achieved "anthem status" in the peace movement. Pratt also writes that Och's albums *All the News That's Fit to Sing*, containing "One More Parade," and *I Ain't Marching Anymore*, containing both "Draft Dodger Rag" and the title song, became "essentials of the record libraries of activist students and early opponents of the war" (Pratt 1998, 176).

"Draft Dodger Rag" consists of several stanzas, each constructed of two identical eight-measure phrases, in which the singer details a litany of ailments and perversions he has that, he hopes, will make him unfit for military service. The "Rag" is actually misnamed; it contains no classical ragtime syncopations at all. What it does contain is a boom-chuck style guitar accompaniment (in Ochs's recordings of the song) suggesting the left hand part of a piano rag, and the type of dotted rhythms found in the post-ragtime, early jazz piano work of Jelly Roll Morton. In terms of the anti-war movement and the war resistance movement, the song's appearance coincides with the first of the publicized draft-card burnings related to Vietnam and the start of mass attempts to avoid the draft by seeking Conscientious Objector status and various types of deferments. The history of this resistance movement is detailed in journalist/draft resister Roger Neville Williams' book *The New Exiles: American War Resisters in Canada* (Williams 1971).

Easily Phil Ochs's best-known and best-remembered composition on the subject of the Vietnam Conflict, "I Ain't Marching Anymore" found a home at numerous anti-war rallies from 1965 through the end of the war. Ochs's magnum opus was printed in *Broadside* #54 (January 20, 1965) and *Sing Out!* 16/1 (February-March 1966). While right-wing writers called the song "notorious," "un-American propaganda" (Noebel 1966, 225, 226), and "subversive" (Allen 1969), a presumably left-wing writer in a letter to *Broadside* stated, "Phil Ochs speaks more than any other American I know of today for a segment of American youth which is discontented and restless and can not find the channels through which to register their discontent and bring about needed changes" (O.S. 1965, 12). Ironically, at about the time of the publication of "I Ain't Marching Anymore," Ochs himself told a *Village Voice* interviewer, "I'm writing to make money. I write about Cuba and Mississippi [and presumably Vietnam] out of an inner need for expression, not to change the world. The roots of my songs are psychological, not political" (Eliot 1979, 93)

Despite the reasons for Phil Ochs's songwriting, despite the deep feelings some listeners had about songs like "I Ain't Marching Anymore," despite the concern expressed by right-wing writers over the politics of Ochs, and despite the commercial popularity of folk revival and folk-rock in the early and mid-1960's, even an anti-war classic like "I Ain't Marching Anymore" made virtually no commercial impact. In the case of Ochs, context reigned supreme, and the context for Ochs's music was live performance, primarily at peace rallies. The more politically charged the atmosphere when Ochs performed his anti-war songs, the better they were received. As noted rock critic Greil Marcus writes, "That's why when Phil Ochs gets up to sing protest songs to people getting ready for a demonstration, telling them that they are right and that their opponents are wrong, he always sounds flat and empty compared to the singing that begins when the cops move in" (Marcus 1969, 91-2). By the time of "I Ain't Marching Anymore," Ochs was supplanting Bob Dylan as the favorite protest singer of the anti-war movement. As sometimes *Broadside* contributor Paul Wolfe wrote in reviewing the two musicians and their impact in the protest movement, the comparison between Ochs and Dylan at the time was "meaning vs. innocuousness, sincerity vs. utter disregard for the tastes of the audience, idealistic principle vs. self-conscious egotism" (Wolfe 1972, 148).

"I Ain't Marching Anymore," an up tempo protest number, usually sung by Ochs to his own guitar accompaniment, finds the musician picking out various American snapshot battles of the past, the Battle of New Orleans, the German trenches of World War I, the dropping of the atomic bomb, and so forth, responding that with what he has learned about the futility of war, he has decided that he will not march anymore. The song's chorus clearly paints war as a generational issue, with the older generation always being responsible for initiating wars, and the younger generation always suffering the deaths associated with those wars. The song was important not only at the more general peace rallies, but played an important role in the early resistance movement, voicing the feelings of draft resisters and military deserters.

As mentioned earlier, Bob Dylan was quoted as telling topical songwriter Phil Ochs, "The stuff you're writing is bullshit, because politics is bullshit. Just look at the world you're writing about and you'll see that you're just wasting your time" (Scaduto 1971). Dylan did indeed leave behind the writing of explicitly political material by 1964; however, his 1964 song "It Ain't Me, Babe" was widely interpreted as an anti-war statement. Actually, the song could be, and was, interpreted on a number of strata, including the following: (1) a rejection of a former lover in a relationship that had gone bad; (2) Dylan telling "his thousands of worshippers to look elsewhere for someone to walk on water" (Wolfe 1964, 11); and (3) Dylan telling the military to draft not him, but someone else.

Whether or not Dylan intended "It Ain't Me, Babe" to be an anti-war song, we will probably never know. It is clear that the surface message, that of the rejection of a former lover, is worded in such a way, with references to strength, protection, and the like, that it easily can allow the deeper, anti-war interpretation to come though. That this interpretation quickly became widespread, at least among those active in the anti-war movement, is evidenced by the fact that the chorus, which includes the song's title in its lyrics, was sung at numerous anti-war rallies. On the other hand, it should be noted that The Spokesmen, a musical ensemble that supported the U.S. involvement in Vietnam in their self-penned "The Dawn of Correction," recorded the Dylan song on their 1965 album *The Dawn of Correction*. In the context of the title song of The Spokesmen's album, "It Ain't Me, Babe" can only be understood as a folk-rock style song (the folk-rock style will be discussed in detail later) about a failed interpersonal relationship.

When The Turtles covered "It Ain't Me, Babe" in 1965 as the title song for their first album, context again played a significant role. *It Ain't Me, Babe* features much in the way of folk-rock material, no pro-U.S. involvement in Vietnam songs, and includes the notorious anti-war song "Eve of Destruction," a work to be discussed later. In *this* context Dylan's composition can easily be understood as a thinly veiled anti-draft anthem.

Although active as a performer in the folk revival movement, Buffy Sainte-Marie was far more influential in the 1960s and 1970s as a songwriter, composing works made popular by other singers. A 1963 composition that the composer recorded in 1964, "The Universal Soldier" (also commonly given as "Universal Soldier), is one of the more curious songs of the Vietnam era in terms of the way in which Sainte-Marie's message was either misinterpreted or incompletely understood, apparently even by recording artists who included the song in their repertoire. In his liner notes for Sainte-Marie's album *It's My Way!*, on which "The Universal Soldier" first appeared, Maynard Solomon writes that the piece is "a song of war and peace, but mainly a song of personal responsibility which cries out not against the 'little guy' but against those the 'guy who knows better,' against those who work or fight in an unjust cause, who turn their heads or shut their eyes or cross to the other side of the street" (Solomon 1964). The lead sheet for this song is included in the collection *Songs of Peace, Freedom, and Protest* 1970, and was also printed in *Sing Out!* 15/1 (March 1965). The song is best known through two 1965 recordings of the song, one by American country/pop singer/guitarist Glen Campbell, at the time a well-respected, although somewhat anonymous studio musician, and the other by Scottish folk (and later psychedelic) singer/composer/guitarist Donavan Leitch.

Campbell's recording, which hit the charts in autumn 1965, eventually reached #45 during its seven weeks on the *Billboard* pop singles charts; the record spent eight weeks on the *Cash Box* singles charts, peaking at #61 in the final week of its run. The single was subjected to a ban by some disc jockeys who were uncomfortable with the anti-war implications of the song (Battle of Ideologies Set to Music Meets Deejay Resistance Movement 1965, 63). Campbell either did not understand the pacifist implications of the song, or he had undergone a change of heart regarding the growing conflict in Southeast Asia between the time when the song was recorded and when his recording was released, as he was quoted as saying at the time of his recording's popularity, "If you don't have enough guts to fight for your country, you're not a man" (Protest Disker Hits Draft Vandals 1965, 60). The other possibility that has been suggested is that this was simply a record made to make money: the anti-war implications were perhaps deemed to be *au courant* with recording-buying young people and the song was put "in the can" in order to make a likely profit. In any case, Glen Campbell's statement denouncing the very movement that had embraced "Universal Soldier" was unusual: most artists who recorded songs like this were, at least for a time, committed to the cause.

Whatever the cause for the conflict between Campbell's politics and Sainte-Marie's intended message, Glen Campbell sounds genuinely angry with the universal soldier as he sings with an uncharacteristic (for him) aggression in his vocal timbre. The tempo is also downright aggressive, with its four-beat feel clocking in at approximately 200 beats per minute. Stylistically, the Campbell recording is fairly standard folk-rock fare, with acoustic and electric guitars, electric bass, rock drumming, tambourine, and a heavy metric emphasis on beats two and four; however, a hint of the Glen Campbell of the later 1960s can be heard in the country style guitar finger picking, presumably played by the singer/guitarist himself.

Despite the fast tempo and the folk-rock style, Campbell may have been influenced in his vocal delivery by Buffy Sainte-Marie's earlier recording of "The Universal Soldier." Like the song's author before him, Glen Campbell crescendos noticeably and simultaneously takes his voice into a more aggressive timbre when he gets to the stanza concerning how Hitler and Caesar would have been nothing without the help of their soldiers.

It should be noted that "The Universal Soldier" never appeared on any Glen Campbell album, despite the mild success of the single. Of course, there could be any number of explanations. While Campbell was a well-established session musician and had toured with The Beach Boys, played guitar on some of The Monkees' first recordings, and had released several unremarkable recordings under his own name, he was not yet well defined in terms of his musical and audience niche. This can be seen in the B-side to "The Universal Soldier," an instrumental pop number with a Spanish influence, musically bearing no resemblance to the A-side. He had worked in surf, country, and pop, but had not quite made the big time. By the time Campbell became famous for his so-called countrypolitan style, the folk-rock of "The Universal Soldier," not to mention its political message, simply did not fit.

On the *Billboard* pop singles charts at precisely the same time as Glen Campbell's recording of "The Universal Soldier" was Donovan's version, which did not achieve quite the same degree of sales success as the American's #45 rendition, reaching only #53 on the *Billboard* pop charts; however, Donovan's rendition reached a high point of #45 during its eight-week run in *Cash Box*'s charts, suggesting that while one might have been more likely to purchase the Campbell recording, the Donovan recording was the preferred version when one had a quarter to put in a juke box. According to Sy and Barbara Ribakove, writing in their 1966 biography of Bob Dylan, teenagers in the 1965-66 period were greatly affected by "the anti-war songs of England's [*sic*] Donovan Leitch" (Ribakove and Ribakove 1966, 120). Since "The Universal Soldier" was the singer's only anti-war single of the period to make the charts in the United States, I presume that this must be one of the recordings to which they refer.

"The Universal Soldier" is a very different song in the hands of Donovan than in the hands of his American contemporary, with the Scottish singer accompanied by acoustic guitar, playing his guitar in a slower-tempo, two-beat feel very similar to Buffy Sainte-Marie's version. Donovan's resigned-sounding style and considerably more static dynamic level differentiates his reading of the song from both the composer's and Glen Campbell's recordings. Donovan's is easily the subtlest of the three recordings and in many respects the most successful; the manner in which Sainte-Marie and Campbell spit out some of lines seems more affected than appropriately expressive.

Country singer Autry Inman covered "The Universal Soldier" on his 1968 album *The Ballad of Two Brothers*. The bulk of this album consists of patriotic material, such as the title song, "The Ballad of Two Brothers," and "Must We Fight Two Wars?" In this context, the Sainte-Marie song's support of the soldier as a necessary part of society (for at least as long as society insists on solving problems through warfare) seems to be emphasized and the song tends to moderate some of the more one-sided material. In particular, the end of the song, in which the composer suggests that perhaps the universal soldier's role could, or should, become unnecessary in the future, gives Inman's package the overall feel of a complete support for military personnel, a complete, unquestioned support for American involvement in Vietnam, but tempered with a hope that someday war will be obsolete.

Buffy Sainte-Marie's opus generated some controversy, to the extent that it became the subject of a minor legal battle. Capitan Richard Rote of the West German Army became upset that "The Universal Soldier" debased professional soldiers, and sued Peer Music Publishers, holders of the German copyright, in an attempt to have the song banned (Universal Song 1966).

I have previously noted that some of the pre-"Eve of Destruction" anti-war songs, in their subtleties, were open to differing interpretations. "The Universal Soldier" seems to have been particularly susceptible as R. Serge Denisoff and Mark Levine documented that more than 60 percent of teenagers polled either misinterpreted or did not full understand Buffy Sainte-Marie's lyrical intent (Denisoff and Levine 1971). Yes, for a time the song sounds like a tribute to the soldiers of the world's history. If one hears only the first two-thirds of the song, that might be the interpretation; however, in the last several, crucial lines, Sainte-Marie quickly expresses the futility of fighting for peace, blames the universal soldier for fighting all of these futile wars, and blames everyone who, actively or tacitly, gives the soldier the order to kill for the continuation of war.

Another early anti-war recording by Donovan was his take on the Mike Softley song "The War Drags On." The recording had no chart activity in the United States and in fact only received anything resembling wide distribution at least a couple of years after the initial recording sessions. This is very much a Bob Dylan-styled performance, complete with harmonica answers to some of the vocal phrases and a Dylanesque, clipped vocal phrasing. The song itself involves a soldier who is stationed in Vietnam. The soldier has an apocalyptic dream in which the war in Southeast Asia leads to a thermonuclear holocaust, a theme found in several pre-1966 anti-war songs. The song is notable for the title line in the chorus, which features a melodic descent from the lowered (mixolydian) seventh scale step. The melodic descent itself is not necessarily remarkable. What *is* remarkable is the fact that a half-decade later John Lennon would mirror this melodic motion in a line also containing the word "on" in the chorus of his "Instant Karma." Probably the most notable feature of the song is the fact that it was one of the first recorded anti-war works to deal expressly with the Vietnam Conflict.

Better known in recent years for his children's material than for his protest music, Tom Paxton, as has already been suggested, was one of a handful of solo singer/songwriters working in the 1964-66 period who left several memorable anti-war songs for posterity. "Talking Vietnam Pot Luck Blues" finds Paxton combining anti-war sentiment and humor, while he weaves what he claims to be a true tale of how illicit drugs brought together American and Viet Cong troops.

Composed in the rural talking blues style used by musicians on every side of the political spectrum during the Vietnam Conflict (see the previously discussed "Talkin' Vietnam Blues" by Phil Ochs and Kris Kristofferson's "Vietnam Blues," discussed in the next chapter, for example), Paxton performed "Talking Vietnam Pot Luck Blues" at the 1964 Newport Folk Festival and at numerous concert appearances throughout the 1960s. His album *The Compleat Tom Paxton Recorded Live*, a 1970 effort, finds the audience obviously enjoying the subtle anti-war, pro-marijuana message. On the 1970 recording, as in most talking blues performances, the instrumental accompaniment is totally subservient to the rhythmic intonation of the text—the "rap" as it were.

Paxton tells the story of an American squad on patrol in South Vietnam who set up camp on a bed of marijuana plants. The first-person protagonist at first observes his comrades smoking, getting high, and going into various outlandish antics: the captain chanting the "Hare Krishna" mantra, for example. Suddenly some Viet Cong soldiers, also high on marijuana, show up armed not with guns, but with their own sash of the drug. The Communist troops share their special brand of Vietnamese marijuana with the Americans.

Paxton never makes an overtly anti-war statement in the text, nor does he explicitly state that marijuana use should be condoned. By telling the tale as he does, he allows the listener to interpret the story in several possible ways. One could cite this story as an example of the evils caused by recreational drug use: obviously not the composer's intent, but an interpretation that I could very easily imagine reading in a right-wing article on the evils of protest music. One could appreciate Paxton's yarn purely as a humorous war story, a sort of "boys will be boys" tale. This song, however, does not exist in a vacuum, nor was it a work enjoyed by a mass audience like such top 40 singles as "Eve of Destruction," "Blowin' in the Wind," or "The Ballad of the Green Berets." This song, like J. B. Lenoir's "Vietnam Blues" or much of the work of Phil Ochs, was meant for audiences that, by virtue of the fact that they were at a live performance by a particular singer/songwriter, most likely shared the musician's political views: these songs were far more important in the context of a live performance than on record. A Paxton audience member, then, would more likely come away from their experience with "Talking Vietnam Pot Luck Blues" hearing a anti-war subtext suggesting the absurdity that these soldiers should get back to their jobs of killing each other the day after their communal intoxication.

The subject of drug abuse among soldiers in Vietnam continues to arouse controversy. Various sides in the various debates have cited drug abuse to make just about every point imaginable, from the government using it as a way of attempting to de-emphasize or to discredit anti-war statements made by returning Vietnam veterans (particularly in the late 1960s and early 1970s) to those in the anti-war movement using it to support their claims that this war was entirely unfightable without the aid of mind-altering substances, so horrible was it. On the page of *The Vietnam Songbook* on which the text of the Paxton talking blues in printed, Barbara Dane quotes G.I.s who have recently returned home from Vietnam as saying, "We couldn't make it sane without grass. It costs 3¢ a joint, or you can trade a $1.49 bottle of whiskey from the PX for an ounce. Probably between 50-80 percent of the guys use it regularly and heavily" (Dane and Silber 1969, 124).

Julius Lester, another stalwart of the folk revival and protest song movement, also contributed a talking blues, "Talking Vietnam Blues," to the anti-war cause. Lester's work, published in *Broadside* #56 (March 10, 1965), takes on President Johnson, suggesting that the President, a Democrat, behaves more like a typical Republican warmonger. Lester cites the credibility gap created by the conflict between Johnson's famous autumn 1964 statement that "we seek no wider war" versus the reality of the escalation of warfare in Southeast Asia. As we shall see, both Tom Paxton and Phil Ochs followed Lester in composing songs dealing with this credibility gap: their songs on the subject were published in *Broadside* in the autumn of 1965. Lester's "Talking Vietnam Blues" wins out in terms of topicality, as its publication in the protest song magazine coincided with the first massive U.S. bombings of North Vietnam with napalm and came less than a month before the introduction of U.S. ground troops into the conflict.

As previously mentioned, one of the functions served by protest songwriter/singers was that of musical editorial writer. Left-wing musicians were constantly on the lookout for news stories painting the war in a negative light, and used these reports as the basis for anti-war songs. Tom Parrott's "Hole in the Ground" was written in response to an incident in which a young South Vietnamese boy unwittingly sold out his Viet Cong father for candy given to him by U.S. advisors and South Vietnamese troops. The incident, which took place in December 1964, was given brief mention by the U.S. press (*see* Boy, 10, Leads Viets to Father's Hideout 1964). Parrott found the incident fodder to illustrate the cruelty of the soldiers in using a child in this way; the troops never bothered to tell the boy that his father was dead and how it was that the Viet Cong soldier had been found. "Hole in the Ground" was published in *Broadside* #58 (May 15, 1965). Ruth Jacobs' "Letter from Vietnam," a slightly later song seeing publication in *Broadside* #64 (November 15, 1965), represents another topical song, in this case dealing with a true incident in which an American soldier unwittingly shot and killed a baby when he fired on the gun-toting wife of a Viet Cong soldier the American had just killed.

Topical songs like Tom Parrott's "Hole in the Ground" have generally fallen into obscurity, partly due to the very nature of topical songwriting—outside of the context in which the songs were written, they tend to lose their meaning—and partly due to the fact that most of these songs were either not commercially recorded or found themselves on recordings that sold few copies, were quickly deleted from record company catalogs, and have not been reissued since. Parrott's opus was reissued in 2000 on *The Best of "Broadside," 1962-1988*, a multiple compact disc set. Unfortunately, "Hole in the Ground" is an exception in this regard. Among other anti-war songs published in *Broadside* and/or *Sing Out!* in 1965, but currently unavailable, are works such as the following: (1) "The New 'MacNamara's' Band," a text to be sung to the tune "MacNamara's Band," written by students Judy Halperin, Joan Halperin, Susan Perkis, Susan Warshau, George Phillips, and Happy Traum on a train to Washington, D.C. for the April 17, 1965, peace march; (2) Malvina Reynolds's "Napalm," a newly written text set to the tune of Woody Guthrie's "Slipknot," and published in *Broadside* #60 (July 15, 1965), in which the songwriter takes digs at Luci Baines Johnson, daughter of the President, for having fun at school and going about her life blissfully unaware of the hideous results of the napalm attacks upon North Vietnam ordered by her father; (3) Bill Frederick's "Hitler Ain't Dead," a song published in *Broadside* #61 (August 15, 1965) in which the writer suggests that Nazi leader Adolf Hitler is still alive, but that now he talks with a southern drawl, an obvious reference to President Johnson; and (4) Malvina Reynolds's "Peace Isn't Treason," a song published in *Sing Out!* 15/4 (September 1965), and most notable for the composer's use of the Neapolitan triad, a harmony quite uncommon in folk revival-style songs, but found in European art music since the Baroque era.

The spring 1965 bombings of North Vietnam and the introduction of U.S. ground troops prompted topical singer/songwriters to focus even more on the credibility gap created by President Johnson's now often-questioned statement that "we seek no wider war." By summer a number of songs addressing the issue, some newly composed and some written before the 1964 presidential election but now found to be more relevant, were making the rounds, with several eventually finding their way into the folk song magazines, including Mortimer Frankel's "The Ballad of L.B.J.," published in *Broadside* #62 (September 15, 1965). Frankel points out what he sees as the hypocrisy of the President's statement in light of the napalm bombings of innocent North Vietnamese women and children, and in light of the introduction of ground troops based on naval attacks by boats that were not even there. Of course, the official government line at the time was that North Vietnamese had prompted the Gulf of Tonkin Resolution by attacking, or at least trying to attack two U.S. Navy vessels in August 1964. To suggest that the attacks never took place was certainly a minority opinion in 1965, although this unfortunate fact eventually would be confirmed with the 1971 release of *The Pentagon Papers*.

Like the Mortimer Frankel song, Tom Paxton's "Lyndon Johnson Told the Nation" was published in *Broadside* #62 (September 15, 1965); as the title suggests, the piece deals with the same basic subject matter. The Paxton work, which easily is the best-known song about the credibility gap, was also published as a lead sheet in Dane and Silber 1969 and *Songs of Peace, Freedom, and Protest* 1970. "Lyndon Johnson Told the Nation," with its opening march-like rhythms suggesting a snare drum cadence, goes beyond the "we seek no wider war" theme: Paxton's other main point is that the United States now finds itself in the unenviable and highly ironic position of trying to save Vietnam from the Vietnamese. The song has an almost classical structure, with an $aa^l bb^l$ form in which the end of the b^l phrase is identical to the end of the a^l phrase.

Phil Ochs contributed "We Seek No Wider War" to the list of credibility gap songs. Published in *Broadside* #63 (October 1965), the triple-meter song has an almost through-composed structure, certainly highly unusual in American popular music, and rare, although not unheard of, in the folk-related repertoire. "We Seek No Wider War" provides an excellent example of how many of the lead sheets published in *Broadside* came into being. The Phil Ochs three-compact disc collection *Farewells and Fantasies* contains a previously unreleased recording of the song made at the New York City apartment of *Broadside* publishers Gordon Friesen and Sis Cunningham. When lead sheets were not already published, Friesen and Cunningham would transcribe informal performances such as this, smoothing out the rough edges for publication in the magazine.

At one time a member of the fairly obscure surf group The Fantastic Baggys, and later associated as a songwriter with The Grass Roots, P. F. (Phil) Sloan was nineteen years old when he wrote one of the most notorious songs of the mid 1960s, "Eve of Destruction." It should be noted that although Sloan's name alone is typically listed, there have been suggestions that Sloan's former songwriting partner and former fellow Fantastic Baggy, Steve Barri, played a role in the song's creation (Holdship 1991). Barry McGuire, former bass singer with The New Christy Minstrels, recorded the best-known rendition of the song. The recording, which featured the instrumental backing of the original members of The Grass Roots and an angry, gravelly vocal from McGuire, reached #1 on *Billboard*'s "Hot 100" singles chart after an August 21, 1965, debut. Writing on political propaganda in the *New Mexico Quarterly* less than a year after the release of the single, Michael Orth describes the record as a "powerful musical setting" (Orth 1966). Although American involvement in the Vietnam Conflict is not explicitly mentioned, and although the singer's complaints deal with other issues, the nuclear arms race and racial discrimination chief among them, the song is clearly anti war in nature. Let us now examine the musical setting; the controversies surrounding the song, both from the political and religious right and from musicians closely aligned with the political left; and issues revolving around radio airplay and audience perception of P. F. Sloan's magnum opus.

The spring and summer of 1965 saw the emergence of a new style of popular music in America, folk-rock. The Byrds' recording of Bob Dylan's "Mr. Tambourine Man" debuted on the *Billboard* pop singles charts on May 15, spending thirteen weeks on the charts and eventually reaching #1. The recording featured the jangling electric guitars and drums of Beatles-influenced rock music married to the poetic imagery of folk musician Dylan. Four of the five members of The Byrds had experience in folk revival ensembles such as The New Christy Minstrels and the Chad Mitchell Trio. In July 1965 Dylan himself created a sensation when, at the until-then-acoustic Newport Folk Festival, he strapped on an electric guitar and sang accompanied by a rock band: folk purists booed him and Pete Seeger reportedly tried to cut the cables leading to the amplifiers. Incidentally, possibly the earliest hint of the possibilities offered by a combination of folk and rock, and one that is often overlooked in the literature, was The Animals' 1964 rock recording of the nineteenth-century American folk song "House of the Rising Sun."

"Eve of Destruction," which chronologically was wedged between the two events described above and The Byrds' even more successful recording of Pete Seeger's "Turn! Turn! Turn! (To Everything There Is a Season)" (which had its chart debut in late October 1965), fits the Byrds-defined folk-rock style to a tee. The accompanying instrumentalists mirror the timbre of The Byrds' electric guitars, although absent the unique character of Byrd Roger McGuinn's twelve-string electric guitar, and Sloan's harmonic scheme incorporates the now-cliché suspended fourth moving to a root position tonic triad in the introduction and at the end of each section of the piece. I describe the figure as "now-cliché" because the suspended fourth to tonic rhythm guitar figure quickly grew to become one of the defining (and stereotypical) musical motifs in folk-rock style.

Structurally, the song, with its verse-by-verse detailing of the various ills in (primarily) American society, narrow-range melody, and use of simple harmonies is similar to such earlier protest songs as "Join the CIO" and "We Shall Overcome." According to R. Serge Denisoff and Mark Levine, the main difference between these earlier protest songs and "Eve of Destruction," as recorded by Barry McGuire, is that while the earlier songs were typically hymn-like in their treatment in performance, the McGuire rendition of "Eve of Destruction" is "rhythmical dance music" (Denisoff and Levine 1971, 119).

Composer Sloan includes some obvious text painting similar to that found frequently in western music as early as the Renaissance (more isolated examples can be found in the Middle Ages and even in Gregorian chant). In a song with stanzas featuring different words but the same music and a repeated refrain phrase that includes the same words and music each time, one might expect to find text painting, the setting of particular words or phrases to music that highlights them (a rising melodic line for the word "higher," for example), in the refrain phrases. This is exactly what Sloan does in his three-fold repetition of the word "over," within a descending pitch line, suggesting the frustration felt by the singer with the character to whom the song is addressed, a character who seems quite insistent that all is basically all right with the world.

The lyrics, with their list of social ills, naturally aroused considerable controversy. Conservative, fundamentalist Christian writer David A. Noebel, writing shortly after the height of the song's popularity, stated that some of the lyrics of "Eve of Destruction" "and similar expressions are constantly being used to induce the American public to surrender to atheistic, international Communism" (Noebel 1966, 229). The song as an agent for international Communism was denounced from pulpits and at civic meetings throughout the country. Others would argue that Sloan was just chronicling, in a fairly pointed way, some of the important issues of the day and the fear that a number of these, including the war in Southeast Asia, the threat of thermonuclear holocaust, racism, and increasing violence in the streets, might very well lead to global destruction. Did "Eve of Destruction" have an effect upon its audience? Certainly Noebel's statement suggests a strong fear that the song would affect young people in a particular way. Sy and Barbara Ribakove, writing in their 1966 biography of Bob Dylan, reported that young people were deeply affected by the Sloan opus (Ribakove and Ribakove 1966, 120). Given all of this controversy surrounding the lyrics of the song, it is fascinating to note Denisoff and Levine's findings that 41 percent of teens polled about the meaning of the song either did not fully or correctly interpret P. F. Sloan's intended message (Denisoff and Levine 1971). In the same light, it is interesting to note that Emily Edwards and Michael Singletary, in their study of the relative importance of lyrics in the complete song, found that only 25 percent of teens primarily liked a song because of the lyrics (Edwards and Singletary 1984, 23).

Naturally, politicians and religious leaders expressed concern about some of the more fatalistic aspects of "Eve of Destruction." One might assume that it was only politicians aligned with the right wing and possibly fundamentalist Christian religious leaders who protested the song. Others found the popularity of the song to be a rallying point as well. In his Yom Kippur sermon, for example, Rabbi Richard Rubenstein of the Beth Shalom Synagogue in Pittsburgh chided young people for sitting on the sidelines, waiting for "destruction," when they should be preparing for the future and all of the problems they might some day solve (Rabbi Chides Folkniks on "Destruction" Fears 1965).

The radio industry, too, took note of the controversial lyrics of "Eve of Destruction." Jack Williams, program director at Chicago radio station WIND, called the lyrics "sick," saying "Eve of Destruction" is "not the sort of record we want to play for our audience" (Sternfield 1965, 12). Twenty of the fifty largest radio markets in the United States banned the song from play lists, with the American Broadcasting Company banning it from all of its network stations. Interviews with disc jockeys conducted shortly after the radio network banning of the song revealed that some stations in smaller markets banned the song "because the big markets did" (Orth 1966, 78). The huge popularity of the McGuire recording—it spent thirteen weeks on the *Cash Box* jukebox charts, including one week at #1; and spent eleven weeks on the *Billboard* top 100 pop chart, and one week at #1—not to mention issues of free speech, made it impossible to achieve a full-blown nationwide ban of the song and some disc jockeys "played it safe by allotting equal air time to 'The Dawn of Correction,' an 'answer song' intoned by the Spokesmen" (Music 1965, 102). Perhaps somewhat related to its radio exposure and perhaps somewhat related to the demographics of the major American cities of 1965, the McGuire single showed signs of regionalism in its commercial success: it sold best in the large coastal cities of Los Angles and New York, somewhat less well in the mid-western Chicago, and even less well in smaller cities and towns. Given the organized efforts to suppress the recording, its success in the various charts and in a variety of markets is remarkable.

Incidentally, three years after the initial success of and controversy surrounding "Eve of Destruction," near the apex of the Vietnam Conflict, the controversy continued. The University of Buffalo Marching Band, led by Director of Bands Frank Cipolla, performed a show entitled "Give Peace a Chance" during halftime of the fall 1968 nationally televised football game between the University of Buffalo and Holy Cross University. The television network objected to the anti-war theme of the halftime show, with its centerpiece "Eve of Destruction," and censored the band's performance (Bewley 2000).

The question also arises as to whether "Eve of Destruction" is a truly honest, artistically successful piece of protest music. In fact, it may surprise the reader to discover that the song, blasted by right-wing critics because of its indictments of American society, aroused a significant amount of negative criticism from those of other political persuasions as well. Perhaps aware that P. F. Sloan had been writing such innocuous and absolutely apolitical material as "Tell 'Em I'm Surfin'," only about a year before "Eve of Destruction," some critics suggested that the composer was less of a legitimate voice in the protest movement than a commercially successful chameleon who could cash in on current trends. Indeed, Sloan's statement in an interview that "I know we have to stay there [in Vietnam], but I don't know why particularly" (Music 1965, 102) does not seem to be reflective of someone deeply committed to the anti-war cause. Some musicians and critics also took exception with the artistic quality of the song and Barry McGuire's performance. In a *Broadside* interview, Phil Ochs referred to the McGuire recording as "a bad introduction" to protest music. Ochs also praised The Beatles and The Rolling Stones for raising "the quality of the Top 40." According to Ochs, speaking just after "Eve of Destruction" had made its major chart impact, the McGuire record did nothing to raise the quality of Top 40 music (Cunningham and Friesen 1965). The reader might note that this is the same Phil Ochs who practically made a career out of the peace movement and other progressive causes, but also the same Phil Ochs who said, as quoted earlier, "As bad as it may sound, I'd rather listen to a good song on the side of segregation than a bad song on the side of integration" (Kemp 1997, 34). In reference to "Eve of Destruction," Tom Paxton said, "The fact that there has been a response by the young to these protest songs is no cause for rejoicing. Anyone who asks of these idols that they probe a bit deeper will be disappointed, because these songs never intended to tell them anything more than Mom and Dad don't understand them" (Denisoff 1990, 83). The influential blues guitar player and teacher Dave Van Ronk called "Eve of Destruction" "an awful song" (Van Ronk 1966, 21). Others, too, have found P. F. Sloan's attempts, for example, to create rhymes out of such locations as Selma, Alabama, and Red China to be awkward and have suggested that McGuire's angry delivery, the use of harmonica at the end of the song (in overt reference to Bob Dylan), and the aping of folk-rock style to be somewhat affected. To put it even more bluntly, it has been suggested that the song was simply a poorly constructed experiment meant to cash in on the folk-rock craze (Holdship 1991).

Despite criticism from songwriters of the political left, from writers of the Christian religious right, and despite all the faults that might be found in Barry McGuire's definitive performance of P. F. Sloan's best-known composition, "Eve of Destruction" obviously, evidenced by its #1 standing in the charts, touched a chord with young people; showed that those same young people were willing to accept dance music with thought-provoking, politically charged lyrics; reflected the social concerns of its time, particularly in light of the growing U.S. presence in Vietnam; and started the trend of heavy-duty, nonsubtle anti-war songs in the fall of 1965.

For those of the Woodstock generation, those who either attended the 1969 rock music festival in upstate New York, or those who were old enough to see the motion picture synopsis of the Woodstock festival, or buy the multi-album recording of highlights of the event at the time of its initial release, probably *the* most memorable anti-war anthem of the Vietnam Conflict was Country Joe McDonald's "I-Feel-Like-I'm-Fixin'-to-Die Rag." A 1965 composition, "I-Feel-Like-I'm-Fixin'-to-Die Rag" was generally preceded by the "Fish" cheer. Although called the "Fish" cheer, perhaps because the word "fish" is spelled out on the initial commercial release of the song on vinyl, at anti-war rallies and at concerts Country Joe and his group The Fish usually spelled out and publicly used the word "fuck." This was considered to be a rebellious, counterculture political act demonstrating free speech rights in the mid-1960s, but an act that largely has lost its shock value as well as its political ramifications today.

"I-Feel-Like-I'm-Fixin'-to-Die Rag," which was published in lead sheet form in *Sing Out!* 16/3 (June-July 1966), mirrors the humor of Phil Ochs's "Draft Dodger Rag" and makes use of the same sort of dotted rhythms. Country Joe and The Fish's recorded performances generally make use of all sorts of humorous, homespun sound effects from horns, kazoos, and the like, in sharp contrast to Ochs's acoustic-guitar-accompanied performances of his "rag." In this respect the Joe McDonald piece better represents the free form, hippie side of the peace movement. This psychedelic approach is confirmed by County Joe and The Fish's 1967 album *I Feel Like I'm Fixin' to Die*, the cover of which resembles that of both The Beatles' *Sgt. Pepper's Lonely Hearts Club Band* and The Rolling Stones' *Their Satanic Majesty's Requests* with the group dressed in costumes: a fool, a wizard, a bandito, and so forth. *The Fish Game*, which was packaged with the album, continues the psychedelic theme, with the players accomplishing such goals as "scoring a joint" (obtaining a marijuana cigarette).

"I-Feel-Like-I'm-Fixin'-to-Die Rag" evokes images of the military recruiter as a carnival barker and includes a chorus in which a new draftee sarcastically expresses his cluelessness about what he is fighting for and his belief that he is about to die. The satire of this song resembles some of the more politically motivated satirical songs of Tom Lehrer; the listener can also hear a hint of Tom Paxton's "The Willing Conscript" in

McDonald's lyrics. It is a song that simply must be heard, both in its original version and as it was performed and recorded several years later at Woodstock, in order to be appreciated. Even then, like the very specifically Vietnam-oriented songs of Phil Ochs, the Joe McDonald song was probably so much of a song of its era that its impact at the time would not be self evident by listening to it today.

Country Joe McDonald used the Vietnam Conflict as a musical and political focus throughout and beyond the Vietnam era. One of his other most notable songs related to the war was his 1967 "Untitled Protest #1," published in *Sing Out!* 18/3 (August-September 1968). This work, which concerns the bombing of innocent children with napalm, contains some outstanding visual and metaphorical poetic imagery, and in that regard is about as different from the straightforward satire of "I-Feel-Like-I'm-Fixin'-to-Die Rag" as probably any two songs could be. As is often the case when a songwriter is primarily known for one famous work, Joe McDonald's composition range has been under appreciated. Comparison of the two pieces reveals a songwriter capable of expressing his message of peace effectively in the most eclectic of ways.

With folk-rock still a new sub genre of top 40 music in mid-1965, The Byrds turned their attention to Pete Seeger's "Turn! Turn! Turn! (To Everything There Is a Season)," which featured lyrics adapted from the Book of Ecclesiastes. Although the song is primarily known through the efforts of The Byrds, Seeger had actually written the song in 1962; it was printed in *Sing Out!* 14/4 (September 1964). The Byrds' single made its chart debut on October 23, 1965, right in the middle of the first major build up of the war. The single was extremely successful, spending fourteen weeks on both the *Cash Box* and the *Billboard* pop singles charts; on the *Billboard* charts it held the #1 position for three weeks. The Byrds' recording of the Seeger composition, featuring the beautiful vocal harmonies of David Crosby, Roger McGuinn, and company, along with McGuinn's distinctive twelve-string electric guitar playing, is one of the most frequently reissued songs of 1965 on compilation albums and continues to be used in films and television shows, often in support of cycle-of-life story lines. Judy Collins released a recording of the song in 1969, coinciding with the escalation of violence in what were becoming almost daily clashes between anti-war protesters and police across America, which itself was somewhat successful from a commercial standpoint.

The familiar lyrics of "Turn! Turn! Turn!," which indicate that there is a time for both peace and for war, have been set by Seeger in such a way as to indicate that he feels that this is the time for peace. In view of the date of the piece's composition and events of 1962 in the nuclear arms race, Cuban Missile Crisis, the growing tensions in Southeast Asia, and other skirmishes around the world, Seeger seems to be begging for a cooling off period.

A somewhat unusual anti-war song, Paul Simon's "A Simple Desultory Philippic (Or How I Was Robert McNamara'd Into Submission)" originally appeared on Simon's rare 1965 solo album, which was released exclusively in Great Britain. By the time Simon renewed his association with Art Garfunkel in 1966, Simon had changed some of the text to reflect the times. The song is one of the few recorded at the time to actually mention U.S. government figures (other than the President) by name. At the same time, the song is a tongue-in-cheek parody of Bob Dylan.

Simon mentions novelist and pro-government spokesperson Ayn Rand, U.S. Secretary of Defense Robert McNamara, and American Ambassador to South Vietnam General Maxwell Taylor in his list of people who seem to bother him. "A Simple Desultory Philippic," performed in the acoustic guitar and harmonica-accompanied style of early Bob Dylan, and with Simon's lead vocals incorporating some convincingly

Dylanesque *Sprechstimme*, mentions Dylan as one of the hip, new voices of Simon's generation; this is a song that finds Simon paying tribute to Dylan, parodying Dylan, and dismissing the pro-Vietnam Conflict politicians and spokespersons with some caustic humor. It is also, because of its very specific references, the kind of 1965 anti-war song that has not remained part of public consciousness. Another Paul Simon work, "The Side of a Hill," written under the pseudonym Paul Kane, is one of those early 1960s, relatively gentle peace songs that may have survived had it not been later suppressed by the composer when he rejected some of his early, less mature works. The song finds Simon asking about the value of the life a child killed in wartime, while the soldiers, who have long since forgotten why they are at war (and who killed the innocent child), continue to fight on.

Beginning in mid-1966 the importance of rock as a related genre within the folk music scene became clear with the first appearance of advertisements for electric guitars in the folk song magazine *Sing Out!*, as well as the first appearances of advertisements for rock criticism publications: *Crawdaddy Magazine*, in particular. That a simplistic anti-war rock song should appear in a folk-related publication at this time, then, is probably not too surprising. Such was the case with the publication in *Sing Out!* 16/2 (April-May 1966) of Tuli Kupferberg's "Kill for Peace." The song, recorded by Kupferberg's group The Fugs, shares much in common with that garage band/punk classic "Louie Louie," as recorded by The Kingsmen.

The tune for the chorus of "Kill for Peace," the only part of the music printed in *Sing Out!*, is a simple, four-note tune, Mi-Fa-Sol-Fa; the recorded performance by The Fugs (a thinly veiled mutation of the famous four-letter word spelled out by Country Joe and The Fish in their "Fish" cheer) on their self-titled debut album reveals that the music for the stanzas is the same as that of the chorus. The recording has a raw quality, from the simple, somewhat unprepared-sounding instrumental work to the brittle recording quality itself. The black and white album cover art, too, exudes rawness, looking like a major source of inspiration for the cover art used by British punk rock bands like The Sex Pistols, The Clash, and The Damned a decade later. The photographs of the band members show them looking dangerous, with angry expressions. In fact, The Fugs, somewhat like the MC5 later in the decade, were truly a revolutionary-oriented group. According to noted beat poet Allen Ginsberg, "when they scream 'Kill for Peace' they're announcing publicly the madness of our white haired crazy governments" (Ginsberg 1966).

The highly satirical, even sarcastic, lyrics of "Kill for Peace," written from the standpoint of a stereotypical ultra-militaristic, racist American, spout reasons that everyone who does not agree with our lifestyle or political beliefs should be killed, referring to the Vietnamese by the highly offensive, racist term "gooks," and stressing that the release one feels when one kills is similar to the ecstasy of sexual orgasm. This is the musical equivalent of the revolutionary political theater of Jerry Rubin and Abbie Hoffman, something that probably would never win over any converts to the cause but that helped to galvanize the most radical members of the anti-war movement.

The racist overtones of the U.S. involvement in Vietnam were also taken up by Phil Ochs, but in a very different manner. "White Boots Marching in a Yellow Land," published in *Broadside* #68 (March 1966) and included in Dane and Silber 1969, finds Ochs using a simple *aa¹* phrase structure, with the first phrase cadencing on the submediant and the second on tonic. By 1966 Ochs was receiving the same kind of criticism Bob Dylan had received about his 1963-era protest songs: noted jazz and folk music critic Nat Hentoff wrote that Ochs's lyrics, "a few ballads excepted, are flatly prosaically polemical. They are one-dimensional and drearily dated in style, though not in their areas of commitment" (Hentoff 1967, 13). While "White Boots Marching in a Yellow Land" may fit Hentoff's description to some extent, the song is significant in that it provides us with one of the few examples available today on compact disc reissue of a mid-1960s song to take on the issue of the racism that was a background part of the Vietnam Conflict.

Whatever subtlety "White Boots Marching in a Yellow Land" might have lacked, Ochs's "Is There Anybody Here?" made up for. The song, called by Ben Edmonds an uncharacteristically restrained Vietnam-related work by Ochs (Edmonds 1997, 78), finds the composer exploring the sense behind the war and the possible reasons that some Americans would be willing to die for what seems to Ochs to be an indefinable cause. He does this by asking a series of rhetorical questions, each beginning with the title line of the song. The flow of the text finds the subtle anti-war message of the song being gradually developed in such a way that the listener must hear at least the first half of the song to really know how the composer feels about war; if one were to listen to the first two stanzas only, one might think that this is a simple tribute to those who are willing to die for their country. That Ochs does not mention Vietnam in the lyrics and uses the subtle method of developing his theme through rhetorical questions places this song stylistically alongside "Blowin' in the Wind" and other 1962 and 1963 pro-peace songs. Perhaps by this point in his career, Ochs was searching for a more effective way to express his anti-war message and reverted back to the style of the recent past as an anchor.

We have seen examples of pro-peace songs from the Vietnam era related to or inspired by several folk traditions, but most frequently Anglo-American folk song and African-American folk, spiritual, and work song. Richard Kohler's "Beware: Here Come Friends," printed in *Broadside* #71 (June 1966), indicates that occasionally other less obvious folk music sources were exploited by the protest musicians. The piece uses the traditional, nonattributed calypso melody "When Dolly Hear the Sound of the Drum," fitted with new words by Kohler. As implied by the song's title, the text deals with the irony that the U.S. government, claiming to be a friend of the Vietnamese people and involved in the conflict only to help them, is in fact killing hundreds of thousands of them: by the end of the war the Viet Cong and North Vietnamese body count would surpass 3,000,000. Certainly the use of a Caribbean rhythmic style was unusual in a 1966 American anti-war song—Jimmy Cliff's 1969 reggae song "Vietnam" is one of the few other songs to do the same—and for some listeners the syncopation and the extra-musical stereotypical associations of this style with a particular place easily could lessen the impact of the lyrics.

A model of simplicity, adherence to the structural traditions of American folk music, and sincerity, Pete Seeger's "Bring Them Home" is one of the true classics of the anti-war movement. Published in *Broadside* #71 (June 1966) and *Sing Out!* 16/6 (January 1967) under the moniker "If You Love Your Uncle Sam (Bring Them Home)," the song is a simple, two-part call and response form owing a structural debt to the African-American work song and spiritual, with a melody largely outlining the tonic, C major triad and also containing stepwise descending motion through the C major scale; the entire melody is only eight measures in length.

The gist of "Bring Them Home" is that it is the patriotic duty of Americans to bring the troops home from Vietnam; U.S. troops are fighting an unwinnable war against the wrong enemy. According to Seeger the true enemies to the development of a democratic Vietnam are poverty, a lack of education, and hunger. The composer also suggests that

U.S. troops are in for a formidable battle, since the Vietnamese will defend their homeland with all of their might: he obviously subscribes to the belief that *all* of the Vietnamese considered the entire Vietnam peninsula their homeland.

Interestingly, "Bring Them Home" is one of the few anti-war songs that is not strictly pacifistic in nature. In fact, Seeger writes that if the United States were to be invaded, he would be found fighting on the front lines. He clearly sees the defense of one's homeland as justifiable warfare, but does not seem to believe that U.S. interests are truly at risk in Vietnam. By making a patriotic anti-war plea, pro-United States, pro-soldier, but anti-current government policy, Pete Seeger constructed one of the most even-handed peace songs of the entire Vietnam era. Perhaps because of this even-handedness, Seeger was permitted to perform the song on the short-lived television program *The Music Scene*, even though he had been under an on-again, off-again ban from radio and television for years due to his leftist affiliations.

Seeger released a live recording of "Bring Them Home" on his 1969 album *Young vs. Old*. The singer receives several spontaneous outbursts of applause on the recording. Significantly, the first such outburst occurs when Seeger espouses his right to sing the song, an obvious reference to the censorship under which he had suffered in the 1950s and 1960s. The second major burst of applause happens when Seeger indicates that he is not a pacifist, that he would be the first to defend the U.S. against invasion. Seeger's vocal on the song represents exuberance from start to finish: he exudes sincerity.

As we have already seen, some traditional folk songs were refitted with new, anti-war lyrics to create new songs for the peace movement. Rarely were new lyrics published for non-folk songs. Pete Seeger's "Bring Them Home," due to its simplicity and its adherence to the nineteenth-century folk tradition, was an exception to the rule: additional verses to the song were written by some seventy-five GIs from Fort Hood on their way to Houston, Texas, for a joint GI-civilian peace rally in 1969. These additional verses were published in *Sing Out!* 19/4 (Winter 1969-70).

Although Seeger performed "Bring Them Home" on network television in late 1969, he had been banned from performing his composition "Waist Deep in the Big Muddy" two years earlier. The song actually told the story of a disastrous army training mission that took place in Louisiana in 1942. In the mid-1960s, however, the "big fool" mentioned at the end of each verse, the platoon commander who leads his soldiers into a river and to their eventual drowning, was interpreted as symbolizing President Lyndon Johnson, especially with the extra final stanza added by Seeger, in which he specifically mentions that he is concerned every evening when he reads the news and sees that the "big fool" is still having the troops press forward. When Seeger was scheduled to perform the song on *The Smothers Brothers Comedy Hour* on September 12, 1967, CBS objected to the last verse and refused to allow him to perform the song. Incidentally, television censorship of anti-war material was not limited to the United States. The BBC banned British group Manfred Mann's performance of the Paul Jones (lead singer of the ensemble) composition "Paul's Dream" on the *Gadzooks* program in early 1966, saying that the song, which dealt with U.S. government double-talk, was not light hearted enough (Paul's Dream 1966).

Seeger's "Waist Deep in the Big Muddy" appeared in print initially in 1963. By the time of its publication in *Broadside* #74 (September 1966), the final verse, that which clearly identified President Lyndon Johnson as the current "big fool," had been added. It is also included in lead sheet form in *Sing Out!* 16/6 (January 1967). The song clearly owes a debt to the nineteenth-century African-American work song, both in terms of its form and its blues inflections.

Seeger's recording of the song, included on the 1967 album *"Waist Deep in the Big Muddy" and Other Love Songs*, is notable for producer John Hammond's exceptionally clean production. Also notable is the cover art, which features a picture of a globe oriented in such a way as to show both North America and Asia, a position that helps to bring home the anti-Vietnam Conflict message of the song and the album. Note that this technique was also used on Victor Lundberg's contemporary album *An Open Letter* for an entirely different effect: the Lundberg collection uses the globe to help promote its pro-government action message, showing just how close the United States was to the domino that we were trying to keep from falling.

One of the more unusual peace compositions of the 1960s, Paul Simon's 1966 work "Seven O'Clock News/Silent Night" consists of the duo Simon and Garfunkel singing the Christmas hymn "Silent Night" to Simon's acoustic guitar accompaniment over a backdrop of a reading of the nightly news. The news items focus on the war in Vietnam, and specifically on government projections that the war could drag on for several more years unless the number of ground troops is increased substantially.   I find the juxtaposition of the carol and the backdrop of an almost clinical analysis of the war on the nightly news to be a most effective means of exposing the immorality and inhumanity of war. While not all writers have agreed with his assessment, noted pop music critic Ralph J. Gleason, in the liner notes for the Simon and Garfunkel album *Parsley, Sage, Rosemary and Thyme*, wrote of the song: "My first hearing of it brought chills to my spine and tears to my eyes. It is one of the most effective statements about the world today that I have heard" (Gleason 1966).

Paul Simon and Art Garfunkel collaborated to write another sort of composite composition in the form of the 1966 song "Scarborough Fair/Canticle."   The song represents a variation on the traditional folk *modus operandi* of fitting new words to traditional music in order to create a "new," topical song. In this piece, which gained its widest popularity in 1968 when it was finally issued as a single to coincide with its use in the film *The Graduate*, Simon and Garfunkel have written an anti-war countermelody that is performed in counterpoint to the traditional words and music of the British folksong "Scarborough Fair." In the weaving together of the two melodies, the duo emphasizes the traditional song; the new anti-war countermelody is somewhat obscured in the recording's mix so as to give the listener vague, impressionistic snippets of an anti-war "feel."

In part, the success of "Scarborough Fair/Canticle" relies on the listener's understanding of the subtext of the original folksong, in which a young man makes impossible demands on a young woman in order that she might prove her love. She responds with equally impossible requests of him. It is not a happy song, as we know that "she *once was* a true love" of the young man; in other words, it sounds as though the relationship did not stand up to the impossible requests that were part of it. In the context of these impossible demands and how they appear to have destroyed a relationship, the newly written anti-war material takes on a heightened meaning, even with its impressionistic nature. The entire package of text seems to imply that war itself seeks to do the impossible; killing for peace is the ultimate impossibility. Simon and Garfunkel's "Scarborough Fair/Canticle" was tremendously popular in the 1966-69 period and has retained its popularity to a much greater extent than most of the songs presented in this study, perhaps because the anti-war message is so impressionist and general, and because the traditional folk material is the focus of the recording's mix.

Showing the continuing topical nature of the *Broadside* protest songs, Jacqueline Sharpe's "No More War," which appeared in *Broadside* #75 (October 1966), was built on the theme of Pope Paul VI's October 4, 1965, United Nations speech in which he pleaded for "No more war, war never again." The controversy aroused by the Pope's message and the ironies it put in the spotlight—that the leader of the Roman Catholic Church was denouncing war in general and the Vietnam Conflict in particular, while bishops and priests in the Church were both actively and tacitly blessing the activities of the troops in Vietnam—became fodder for a number of songwriters. A 1967 song that I will nevertheless detail here because of its related theme, Tom Paxton's "The Cardinal" takes on Cardinal Francis J. Spellman, who had told GIs to "kill Communists for Christ." After the unnamed Cardinal of the song tells the U.S. troops that Jesus would lead them into battle if he were with them in Vietnam, Paxton has the Cardinal encounter a Jewish soldier who asks why he should fight if this is a Christian war. The Cardinal then encounters some Viet Cong Christians who also express confusion about what they should do, since they obviously cannot join the U.S. Army. Eventually, the Cardinal gives the U.S. soldiers a dispensation absolving them in advance of the mortal sin of taking a human life; only after this official "blessing" is given do the troops rally for the slaughter. The Cardinal explains to the soldiers that they should ignore the Pope's plea for peace, saying that obviously the Pope has become nothing more than a brainwashed, Communist pawn. The lead sheet for "The Cardinal" was included in Dane and Silber 1969.

Also printed in Dane and Silber 1969, Jacqueline Sharpe's "Honor Our Commitment" clearly provides a link between the protest songs of the 1960s and early American patriotic songs. The rhythm, with some use of syncopation, and the shape of the melody resemble early American war songs, especially calling to mind William Billings' Revolutionary War hymn "Chester." The composer uses an unusual aa^1a^2b form to tackle the issue of the Vietnam Conflict possibly leading to direct conflict with the Soviet Union or China, and thermonuclear war. Sharpe points out the absurdity of sending candy and treats to the remaining Vietnamese to try to show them how friendly Americans are as we wipe out millions, and she deals with the irony of talking about our desire for peace talks while we continue to bomb the North Vietnamese. This would turn out to be one of last songs to link Vietnam with global nuclear war: the war seems to have taken on a life of its own within the peace movement by 1967.

I mentioned earlier that some protest singers took some of the popular pro-government songs of the Vietnam era and set new lyrics to them. Such is the case with Grace Mora Newman's text "The Fort Hood Three's Answer to the Green Berets," to be sung to the tune of SSgt. Barry Sadler and Robin Moore's "The Ballad of the Green Berets." Newman, the sister of one of the "Fort Hood Three," a group of soldiers who made headlines around the country for their refusal to kill and for their subsequent jailing, wrote the text, published in *Broadside* #76 (November 1966), to chronicle the plight of these anti-war draftees. The text to Newman's opus is also included in Dane and Silber 1969. The Sadler and Moore song would also be parodied in Leda Randolph's "Green Berets," in which the U.S. troops are presented as a superior race, trained to scorn those with darker faces. The entire text for the Randolph parody can also be found in Dane and Silber 1969. Pete Seeger used the traditional folk melody "Peter Amberly" to set his text "The Ballad of the Fort Hood Three," a song printed in *Sing Out!* 16/6 (January 1967). Seeger's text covers basically the same ground as Grace Mora Newman's text.

Carrying a 1966 copyright, Arlo Guthrie's "Alice's Restaurant" made its print debut in *Broadside* #80 (April-May 1967) and was expanded in *Broadside* #81 (June 1967), at which time the title was also expanded to "Alice's Restaurant Massacree." That Guthrie would end up writing one of the best-known works of 1960s anti-war, counterculture movement probably came as no surprise.   The son of folk/protest legend, singer/songwriter Woody Guthrie, Arlo had been exposed to protest music for literally all of his life, hearing the songs of his father and all of the major figures in folk and protest music at his home in New York City, traveling as a teen to the Newport Folk Festival with Phil and Michael Ochs, and so on.

The 18½-minute song consists of a catchy chorus that recurs from time to time and a long, rambling monologue spoken over the chord progression of the chorus. The chorus was originally an advertising jingle for Guthrie's friend Alice's eating establishment, while the spoken monologue tells the story of Guthrie's misadventures trying to dispose of the restaurant's trash on Thanksgiving. The incident eventually leads to Guthrie's arrest and his being judged unfit to serve in the military in Vietnam. The anti-war aspect of the song is slow to evolve, but clearly emerges at the end; what one hears throughout the song is a tale of the polarization of young versus old, status quo versus the counterculture.

Arlo Guthrie's album *Alice's Restaurant* made its chart debut in *Cash Box* in November 1967, and graced the charts for twenty-five weeks. It returned to the charts in October 1969 for twenty-three more weeks when a film based on the song "Alice's Restaurant Massacree" was released. Although numerous other albums sold more copies than Guthrie's magnum opus, *Alice's Restaurant* was a staple of the counterculture in the last few years of the 1960s.

Incidentally, "Alice's Restaurant Massacree" was first performed at a songwriting workshop. As mentioned earlier, the folk revival found established performer/composers assisting younger artists one on one, and found a mixture of established and up-and-coming songwriters helping each other at more formal workshops. The songwriting workshops were essential components of the various festivals, including the important Newport Folk Festival. Workshops, such as the Newport happening at which Arlo Guthrie first performed his masterpiece, provided composers with instant feedback and suggestions from colleagues. The story behind the Guthrie song is that it was so well received at the workshop that the singer was invited to perform it at an afternoon concert for an audience of 3,500; the afternoon performance proved so successful that Guthrie was invited back for the featured concert that same evening, at which time he performed it for 9,500 people.

In the definitive recording of "Vietnam Blues," the composer, blues musician J. B. Lenoir sings, accompanied by himself on guitar and by a drummer who plays rather sparsely and quietly. Recorded in late 1966 or early 1967, the song is one of the earliest recorded statements on the war by an African-American musician. Lenoir was certainly no stranger to dealing with questions of war and politics in a blues context: his "I Got My Questionnaire," a Korean War-era composition, was reworked in 1965 to apply to the Vietnam Conflict and his "Eisenhower Blues" of the 1950s achieved notoriety when it was studied by the House Committee on Un-American Activities.

Segregation in the south and the racial discrimination Blacks found throughout the nation formed the principle focal point for marches, demonstrations, and works of art, including musical compositions, among all of the social issues of the late 1950s and early to mid-1960s for the majority of African Americans. Lenoir successfully weaves the issues of discrimination and the Vietnam Conflict together in a rather sophisticated way in this blues form piece. Indeed, Lenoir was notable among the blues musicians of his time for addressing such issues. The liner notes to the album *J. B. Lenoir*, which pulls together some of the musician's rare single releases, quote a nonattributed article correctly claiming that "possibly J. B. Lenoir however [*sic*] is the first blues artist who has included and incorporated the social and political situation of the contemporary negro in his work" (Liner notes to *J. B. Lenoir* 1970).

Lenoir begins his piece by contrasting the uproar about the Vietnam Conflict with the relative quiet that greeted the murder of Blacks in Mississippi church bombings and lynchings throughout the south. He continues by praying that God will help his brothers fighting in Vietnam because they may be killing *their* own brothers whom they do not recognize. Due to the way Lenoir phrases his plea to God, it is not entirely clear if he is concerned about the possibility that U.S. troops are accidentally killing other U.S. troops through "friendly fire," (a term not used by Lenoir, but one which I enclose in quotation marks because of its dubious meaning) or if the composer perhaps is suggesting a sort of universal brotherhood of humankind: the lyrics could be understood both ways. Lenoir then closes off the piece by revisiting the issue of the active and tacit acceptance of racism at home by suggesting that those who cry about peace must also work to achieve peace in their own house and by calling upon President Johnson to also show more concern with the plight of the disenfranchised at home.

Due to the sparse accompaniment and slow tempo of the piece, Lenoir is able to treat the melody somewhat freely, highlighting certain aspects of the text. He also changes vocal timbre, showing a depth of mood found in many of the great rural-style blues. Although "Vietnam Blues" is a difficult-to-come-by recording, it is well worth the search, if only to experience these expressive qualities. Due to the obscure nature of this recording, and the generally small sales of this type of rural-style, acoustic blues during this period in the United States, J. B. Lenoir's "Vietnam Blues" probably had negligible impact on any segment of the U.S. population. In all likelihood, Lenoir's producer, Willie Dixon, was aiming the song at the growing anti-war movement in Europe, where Lenoir had achieved a fairly high level of popularity among the blues cognoscenti (Pratt 1998, 181). What it did in the United States, however, was to reflect the kind of thoughts that were undoubtedly on the minds of many African Americans, especially as the anti-war forces mobilized increasingly larger forces while the civil rights of Blacks were still routinely violated and with comparably little outcry. As word spread, rightly or wrongly, and the point is still the subject of much debate due to varying interpretations of the salient statistics, that Blacks were over-represented numerically among the U.S. forces stationed in South Vietnam, African-American songwriters grew ever more openly critical of the war itself: J. B. Lenoir represents one of the artists who, in his own way, anticipated this trend of 1969 and 1970.

A song popularized at the 1969 Woodstock Festival, and by means of the subsequent album and film from the event, Richie Havens' "Handsome Johnny" was initially recorded by the singer/guitarist three years earlier. Havens and Louis Gossett, Jr. jointly composed the folk-revival song. Featuring Havens's distinctive-sounding "open E" guitar tuning, in which the guitar strings are tuned to an E major triad (E, B, E, G-sharp, B, E) instead of the instrument's standard tuning (E, A, D, G, B, E), the 1966 recording on the album *Mixed Bag* finds Havens singing a passionate anti-war message. Lyrically, "Handsome Johnny" resembles Phil Ochs's "I Ain't Marching Anymore," in that Gossett and Havens take the listener through a series of wars, specific battle sites and the corresponding weaponry in each of the stanzas. The form of the first part of the song is as follows: (1) a stanza about Handsome Johnny fighting at Concord; (2) the second stanza, which finds the title character at Gettysburg; (3) the chorus, which describes the hardness of war; (4) a stanza in which Johnny is at Dunkirk; (5) a stanza concerning Korea, in which Havens sings an improvised melodic variant; (6) a repeat of the chorus;

and (7) a stanza finding the soldier in Vietnam. The eighth and ninth sections of the song present a "kicker." Following Johnny's appearance in Vietnam, Havens sings about the character fighting in the streets of Birmingham, a reference to the struggle of Havens's African-American brothers and sisters for civil rights. In the final stanza the singer asks what it will take for Americans to listen to and understand the message of his song—that we must find a way for wars to cease—perhaps the dropping of a hydrogen bomb?

By structuring the song as they do, Havens and Gossett force the listener to undergo a series of shifting reactions and take the listener from a veiled anti-war message to a pointed call to action to end war once and for all. The first five stanzas could easily be taken as a tribute to the soldiers of U.S. history and to the sacrifices they made. If there is an anti-war message in this part of the song, it is similar to the subtle message of "Blowin' in the Wind" and "Where Have All the Flowers Gone?" The stanza that finds Handsome Johnny in Birmingham suggests both that America is at war within—just like America was at war with Germany at Dunkirk—and, on a deeper level, that the struggle for equality is perhaps ultimately behind *all* war. The final stanza, much more pointed than those at the start of the song, seems to be directed to the American consumer of music, as Havens seems really to ask, "With all of the millions of anti-war protest records that have been purchased, and with all of the performances by protest singers at peace rallies and concerts, what will it take for you to listen, really pay attention, and *take action* based on what we sing?" Writers have found the approach to be most effective, with *All Music Guide* critic Jim Newsom calling "Handsome Johnny" "a classic anti-war ballad, stoked by the singer's unmistakable thumb-chorded guitar strumming" (Newsom 2000).

Best known for their recordings of pop songs like "Never My Love," "Along Came Mary," "Windy," and "Cherish," The Association contributed "Requiem for Masses" to the anti-war corpus in 1967. The song, composed by group member Terry Kirkman, juxtaposes quotes from Gregorian chant from the Mass for the Dead, folk-styled anti-war stanzas using contrasting colors (black and white; red, white, and blue) metaphorically to symbolize the losses of war and the lack of clear answers to a soldier's questions about war, and instrumental sections in which a mournful French horn and military snare drum seem to call a funeral to a close. "Requiem for the Masses" is a rarity as an anti-war song from a top 40-oriented group before such songs became fashionable. The song received a great deal of exposure as the B-side of the hit single "Never My Love" in autumn 1967; "Requiem for the Masses" itself touched the singles charts, hitting #100 on the *Billboard* charts about a month after the debut of the A-side. As the final song on The Association's album *Inside Out*, "Requiem for the Masses" abruptly reminds the listener that the world of 1967 was not just about love songs and incense.

Late 1967 also saw a quickly issued response to Victor Lundberg's commercially successful recording of "An Open Letter to My Teenage Son" (a song to be discussed in the next chapter) barely make it into the charts. Bill Dean and Ron Marshall's "A Letter to Dad," as recorded by Every Father's Teenage Son, was that response. This talking song, backed by acoustic guitar, electric organ, and some light rock-style drumming, finds the speaker addressing each of the points mentioned in "An Open Letter to My Teenage Son," including questions of men wearing beards and long hair, the existence of God and the role of organized religion, and the morality of past wars. The young man expresses his pacifism and finishes by indicating that if he decides to burn his draft card, it will be his father that has to burn the son's birth certificate, because he will never stop calling his father "Dad." The final coda of the song is a harmonized vocalization on the final phrase of "America."

While "A Letter to Dad" attempts to make an even-handed response to a somewhat harsh letter the young man has received from his father, it tends to come off as an attempt to cash in on the commercial success of "An Open Letter to My Teenage Son": even the name of the supposed group, Every Father's Teenage Son, seems to be part of the cash in. The public evidently questioned the integrity and sincerity of this anti-draft recording: after making its chart debut on November 25, 1967, the record only made it to #93 on the *Billboard* pop singles charts.

Backed by acoustic guitars and by a brass ensemble playing arranger/conductor Peter Schickele's funeral-like, minimalist dirge, singer/songwriter Joan Baez included the song "Saigon Bride" on her 1967 album *Joan*. The song, cowritten by Baez and Nina Dusheck, finds a soldier saying goodbye to his Saigon bride as he ventures off into battle; Baez takes the role of the soldier in her performance of the song, following an Anglo-American folk music practice of stripping characters of their gender by allowing women to sing material associated with male characters and *vice versa*. The composers base the melody on the repeated expansion of a short ascending motive contrasted by a static final phrase in each stanza and use the metaphors of time and of a wave in the soldier's explanation for why he must fight in Vietnam. Baez and Dusheck also hint at the inherent racism in the war in their use of color metaphors. To me, "Saigon Bride" symbolizes in an anecdotal way the extent to which album tracks and even songs known primarily through their live performance by singer/songwriters could greatly impact the lives of Americans during the Vietnam Conflict. One of my colleagues at Mount Union College mentioned this song as among the most meaningful anti-war ballads of the era for him, significant to note due to the relative lack of commercial popularity of the song compared with, say, a "Eve of Destruction" or "Where Have All the Flowers Gone?"

The reader undoubtedly will have noticed that the vast majority of anti-war songs focus on the immorality of war in general, the immorality of the Vietnam Conflict in particular, and the tremendous amount of killing that was going on in Southeast Asia. Those anti-war songs that dealt with particular groups of people naturally focused on soldiers, civilians killed by soldiers, and the loved ones and friends and relatives of soldiers. "Saigon Bar-Girl," which was printed in *Broadside* #87 (December 1967), chronicles the problems faced by a young woman with hungry children at home, whose only hope for survival is to serve, or perhaps to service, American soldiers. Composers Gail Dorsey and Emilie Gould point out that the United States has not provided anything tangible, like food, that the woman needs, and that the only advantage she can get from U.S. involvement in her land is what she obtains by prostituting herself, if not in the physical sense, then at least emotionally.

Two 1967 songs, Peggy Seeger's "L.B.J." and Norman A. Ross's "Who Killed Vietnam," use a similar approach to delivering their messages of blame for the still-expanding war. The Seeger work, printed in *Sing Out!* 17/2 (April-May 1967), uses a traditional Scottish tune to set a text that describes in each stanza how people from different occupations, a miner, a weaver, a doctor, a farmer, and so forth, contribute to the war effort, the killing of the people of Vietnam, and the destruction of the land. The lead sheet for "Who Killed Vietnam?" was printed in *Broadside* #88 (January 1968). Composer Norman Ross directs the performer to "ad lib freely on the notes given or make your own tune." The notes given, E, G, A, B, C, and D, have a sort of generic A minor quality; because no F-sharp or F-natural is used, one cannot define which minor-type mode this is. Stanza by stanza the improvisatory song places the blame for the killing of Vietnam on each of the following: the eighteen-year-old soldier, President Lyndon Johnson, General William Westmoreland, U.S. Secretary of Defense Robert

McNamara, Secretary of State Dean Rusk, and the silent majority, represented by the writer's next-door neighbor, making this one of the blunter songs of the war in terms of placing blame. Another 1967 protest song, Ewan MacColl's "The Fields of Vietnam," published in *Sing Out!* 19/6 (June-July 1970), details the Vietnamese struggle for independence through long-term battles with the Japanese, the French, and now thirteen years of domination (since the 1954 Geneva Accord) by the U.S. Army.

That a noticeable, significant change was taking place in the established order of the protest/folk movement in 1967 can be seen in Israel Young's article in the April-May 1967 issue of *Sing Out!* in which he reports that The Kingston Trio is breaking up, that Donovan has given up protest music for the time being, and that Phil Ochs now "makes fun of those madcap Free Speech things and Mississippi peace marches he made a reputation on" (Young 1967, 35). In the same issue of *Sing Out!*, Larry McCombs reported on a "lost" Joan Baez album, a rock album that was left unreleased by the folk singer. Baez is quoted as saying, "I'm trying to grow up. That involves eliminating, not adding to, what's in your head." She further explains that, following the philosophy of Gandhi, she wants her art now to "elevate the spirit"; the songs on the album apparently did not all accomplish that goal (McCombs 1967, 49).

In studying musical trends, especially involving a large number of composers, some of whom had the ability and the corporate resources behind them to immediately record new material, some of whom lacked the necessary backing to commit their work to vinyl immediately, and some of whom focused on live performance and possible publication of their songs in a magazine like *Broadside* or *Sing Out!* for further dissemination, it is nearly possible to establish an accurate chronology of who wrote what, and when, not to mention establishing a hierarchy of influences, one writer to another. In looking at recording release dates and article and lead sheet publication dates, it appears that late 1967 saw the establishment of a new trend in anti-war songs: the declaration that war is over, at the same time both an anticipation of that day in the future when the Vietnam Conflict would end and a wishing away of the war.

Again, it is nearly impossible to establish a firm date for the start of this trend; however, we do know that Phil Ochs's June 1967 *Los Angeles Free Press* article "Have You Heard? The War Is Over!," given wider exposure in a November 1967 reprint in *Village Voice*, and the song he wrote and published at approximately the same time, "The War Is Over," caused others to take notice and may have influenced other songwriters to express similar sentiments. The article finds Ochs stating the case that he can make the absurd declaration that the war is over because it fits completely in line with the absurdity of the war itself. He writes, "Old America has proven herself decadent enough to be willing to sacrifice one of her finest generations into the garbage truck of cold war propaganda" (Ochs 1967, 38). Although the language is harsh, one could read a ray of hope into Ochs's declaration: he does seem sincerely to wish that he could make the declaration in the face of a new, peaceful reality. It was as though Ochs, and certainly others in the anti-war movement, both were fed up with the still escalating conflict and with the movement's inability to effect change, but needed to anticipate the end of the war in order to give them a clear focal point for their continued efforts. The "War Is Over" declaration was taken up by others in the anti-war movement: there were War Is Over pro-peace rallies right up to the actual end of the war; within a few years of Ochs's satirical declaration preceding the first War Is Over rally in Los Angeles, John Lennon would use "War Is Over If You Want It" as one of his prime rallying cries. Not only was the "War Is Over" declaration taken up starting in mid 1967, but a related rhetorical question, "What if they gave a war and nobody came?," also became a popular rallying cry at the time. Let us now examine a number of songs related to both.

The first to appear in print was "The War Is Over," with text by Lee Hays and music by Ruth Bernz. This song, with a simple, free rhythm and associated mixed meters, finds lyricist Hays suggesting that although the war still goes on, it is mercifully over for those who have died. This, of course, stops short of declaring the war to be over, although I suspect that the title of the song and the general "war is over" theme of the song may be related to the rallies of the same name. The lead sheet for the Hays and Bernz work was published in *Sing Out!* 17/4 (August-September 1967).

Although she never gained wide exposure or popularity, composer Jonna Gault, a classically trained musician, developed a style, self-named as "Symphonopop," which was meant to be a true blending of symphonic and popular music influences, in a way anticipating the symphonic or progressive rock of the 1970s. *Broadside* #89 (February-March 1968) contained the lead sheet for Gault's song "What If They Gave a War and No One Came?" The song, which in its harmonic richness and use of nonfunctional triadic relationships suggests French Impressionism, uses that famous rhetorical question and tends to wish the war away.

Like the Jonna Gault song, Phil Ochs's "The War Is Over" was published in *Broadside* #89 (February-March 1968); "The War Is Over" also appeared in *Sing Out!* 18/2&3 (June-July 1968). Certainly, Ochs's article "Have You Heard? The War Is Over!" and this song struck a chord with many in the anti-war movement; however, some, like folk musician Malvina Reynolds, had their doubts about how much good simply declaring the war to be over would actually do. Reynolds wrote in a letter to the editor of *Broadside*, "In reference to Phil Ochs's song 'The War Is Over' in #89, I wish I had Phil's confidence that I could merely tell the war to go away" (Reynolds 1968, 9). A read-through of the sheet music for the song, *sans* any reference to Ochs's actual recorded interpretation of "The War Is Over," very well could leave one with the impression that the song simply wishes the war away; however, with Bob Thompson's creative orchestration of the song on Ochs's album *Tape from California*, arranger and composer seem to be making the "war is over" statement on two levels: (1) wishing it away—the war certainly was anything but over in 1967 and 1968; and (2) anticipating a future in which the statement could be made legitimately and without satire. It is through the timbre and dynamic changes in Ochs's vocal interpretation and through Thompson's quotes of dark, minor key fragments of pieces such as Sousa's "The Stars and Stripes Forever" in the verses contrasted with the brilliance of the fanfares that back Ochs in the chorus when the singer actually declares the end of the war that give the song a depth lacking in the lead sheet.

Among the other features of the *Tape from California* version of "The War Is Over" that are notable are Bob Thompson's quote of Ochs's "I Ain't Marching Anymore" in the brasses during the song's fade out and Ochs's compositional tendency to set up the secondary key of A major in this C-sharp minor key song, only to have the E and E7 chords (the dominant of A major) resolve deceptively to F-sharp minor. The harmonic play of Ochs shows that the composer has moved outside of the box of the folk revival at least as much as Thompson's backing of Ochs with symphonic instruments does. Certainly Phil Ochs's most apropos performance of "The War Is Over" was not on *Tape from California*, but rather at the third War Is Over rally in front of more than 100,000 people in New York's Central Park on May 11, 1975; at that point, although the fall of Saigon was still several weeks away, the war finally was over.

By virtue of its having been featured both on an episode (the last episode of the last season, in fact) of the popular television program *The Monkees*, and on The Monkees' album *The Birds, the Bees & The Monkees*, Bill and John Chadwick's "Zor and Zam" achieved considerable exposure, although little radio airplay. The Monkees' recording finds singer Micky Dolenz seemingly imitating The Jefferson Airplane's Grace Slick in the phrasing, timbre, and intonation of his lead vocal. Musically, the song refers to folk-rock in its guitar parts and includes a military-style drum part. The lyrics deal with the preparations for war by the mythical lands of Zor and Zam; the war never takes place, answering that rhetorical question of the time, "What if they gave a war and nobody came?" The Monkees recorded another anti-war song, "War Games," written by group member David Jones and collaborator Steve Pitts. The song was not issued at the time of its 1968 or 1969 recording, not appearing until years later; however, it is interesting to note that it is one of the few songs from the Vietnam era to deal with the extensive media coverage given to the war.

Spring 1968 saw the release of The Doors' song "The Unknown Soldier" as a single. The recording reached #39 on the *Billboard* pop charts during its eight-week run, but made it to #22 on *Cash Box*'s charts; it remained on the *Cash Box* charts for ten weeks. In our study we have seen relatively few singles exhibiting this degree of difference between their chart standings in the two magazines. Since *Cash Box* dealt more with jukebox play than the more-consumer-sales-oriented *Billboard*, it would appear that listeners were more willing to use their coins to hear the song than to buy the record. The song reappeared in August 1968 on the album *Waiting for the Sun*, the group's biggest-selling collection, which held onto the #1 spot in *Billboard*'s pop album charts for four weeks.

"The Unknown Soldier" is highly sectional, exhibiting much textural, tempo, dynamic, and lyrical mood contrast. Like many of The Doors' pieces, particularly those written by singer Jim Morrison, it is highly theatrical in nature. The work begins as a mysterious, impressionistic, slow-paced tribute to the unknown soldier, that nameless, faceless individual who has made the ultimate sacrifice for his country. While each stanza of the song uses the same melody, the setting changes dramatically to alter the mood. The use of electronically manipulated keyboard, electric guitar, and voice in particular give "The Unknown Soldier" its mysterious, eerie quality. What turns this song into an anti-war statement is the triumphant celebration at the end, complete with a faster tempo, tolling church bells, and a cheering crowd, as singer Morrison proclaims that war is over.

The sense of celebration heard in The Doors' "The Unknown Soldier" and Phil Ochs's "The War Is Over" did not reflect the reality of the Vietnam Conflict in 1968. Perhaps the war had just reached the level of ugliness and even horror that the only way some musicians could cope was to project themselves into some sort of war-free future. The reality of 1968, a year in which the number of U.S. troops was still expanding, better can be found in Roberta Mase's "Is This What I Raised My Little Boy For," a heartfelt song about Mase's own experience—the composer's son had been fighting in Vietnam for several months when she wrote the song—that appeared in *Broadside* #91 (May 1968). Appearing in the same issue of *Broadside* was Jimmy Collier's "Fires of Napalm," a song that links the genocide of the Vietnamese to that of the Native Americans. Collier's theme had arisen in some of the early anti-war songs and would reappear from time to time throughout the war; as we shall see later, Holly Near revisited the theme of linking the genocide of Native Americans and that of the Vietnamese in one of her songs from 1971.

Before he had his Silver Bullet Band, and before he had achieved widespread fame, Bob Seger fronted The Bob Seger System. Seger composed the oddly titled "'2+2=?'," another of the large number of rock songs related to the Vietnam Conflict recorded in 1968. The gist of "'2+2=?'" is that the singer is not old enough to vote but is considered by the U.S. government to be old enough to kill, and he just does not understand why. He also does not understand why one of his friends had to leave his girlfriend and go to Vietnam where he was killed. The title of the song refers to Seger's desire to have a simple answer to these questions; he wants to ask "why war," but has been frightened out of making an inquiry, and seems to feel that there could be no satisfactory, black-and-white answer anyway. The riff-oriented structure of the song, the "freakout" style arrangement on Seger's recording, which finds the rock band's various instruments moving through the aural space from channel to channel, the fuzz-tone electric guitar, and the unison backing vocals from Seger's band mates all call to mind early Jimi Hendrix Experience material. Musically, the song is in fact practically a dead ringer for Hendrix's recording of "Fire." Does it therefore sound derivative? A listener familiar with Hendrix's work with The Experience hearing the Seger recording's backing tracks (everything except for Seger's lead vocal) unquestionably would say that "'2+2=?'" sounds like a complete rip-off of Hendrix's texture, tempo, style, form, and timbre. As a stand-alone expression of the singer's confusion, that is, in context (and safely away from the Hendrix work), "'2+2=?'" is highly effective.

Boston, Massachusetts, rock/jazz/country/bluegrass group Earth Opera made virtually no impact on American radio in the late 1960s and early 1970s, and had only one single that made it into *Billboard*'s pop singles charts (#97), but they did record the nearly eleven-minute opus "American Eagle Tragedy." It has been suggested by R. Serge Denisoff that perhaps because of the length of the song, "American Eagle Tragedy" received virtually no AM radio airplay, although it was heard on some progressive FM radio stations (Denisoff 1972a). With its mix of (slightly) avant-garde jazz reminiscent of Rashaan Roland Kirk, references to bluegrass in the form of band member David Grisman's mandolin, frequent tempo changes (the introduction, the stanzas, and the chorus are all in different tempi), screeching lead fuzz-tone guitar, lyrics that seem to be inspired by the impressionistic, metaphor-laden Bob Dylan of "All Along the Watchtower" and that recount the ironic discrepancies between the public lives of President and Mrs. Johnson and the reality of young men being sent off to the jungles of Southeast Asia, "American Eagle Tragedy" paints a picture of the near chaos that was 1968. Peter Rowan, guitarist, vocalist, and tenor saxophonist of Earth Opera, composed the piece, which in its complex structure and use of metaphor also recalls some of the contemporary works of Jim Morrison of The Doors. Rowan also wrote or cowrote most of the rest of the music on Earth Opera's album *The Great American Eagle Tragedy*. In his *All Music Guide* review of the album, Jason Ankeny refers to *The Great American Eagle Tragedy* as "an intriguing experiment which has stood the test of time" (Ankeny 2000).

David Crosby, Chris Hillman, and Roger McGuinn of The Byrds composed "Draft Morning," a song that is included on the group's 1968 album *The Notorious Byrd Brothers*. The song juxtaposes gentle folk-rock stanzas in which the singer indicates that he is going to take his time rising on this particular morning, as it is the day he will have to go and learn to kill, with a more aggressive, slightly distorted electric guitar-based instrumental section that is introduced by a bugle call in a dissonant key area and contains *musique concrète* recordings of the sounds of combat. The anti-draft message of the song takes on added significance when the song segues into the Gerry Goffin/Carole

King song "Wasn't Born to Follow"; the implication of the juxtaposition of the two songs being that the singer was not born to follow the sheep (draftees) into slaughter.

Probably the best known of the 1968 anti-war rock songs to incorporate *musique concrète* sounds of battle was Eric Burdon and The Animals' "Sky Pilot." Making its chart debut on June 1, 1968, the double-sided single—the song is spit into two parts on the single due to its eight-minute length—spent sixteen weeks on *Cash Box*'s pop charts, reaching #16, and fourteen weeks on the *Billboard* pop singles charts, hitting #14. According to Denisoff 1972a, the record received relatively little AM radio airplay due to its length, making its chart success all the more significant: the record industry of the 1960s considered radio airplay to be essential for insuring sales.

The over-riding theme of "Sky Pilot" is the exposure of the active and tacit support of war by organized religion. Throughout the song Burdon and The Animals use a variety of musical effects to support the lyrics. The title character of the song, a military chaplain, blesses soldiers as they prepare their weapons for battle in the song's first stanza. During the following chorus the electric guitars and voices are treated using a phase shifter, giving them an otherworldly quality. The second stanza finds the chaplain recognizing the fears of the soldiers and coming to the realization that those waiting for them back home will feel much anguish should the soldiers die. In the third stanza the chaplain says a prayer and smiles. The soldiers receive their orders to go into battle as the chaplain stays behind meditating. Here the implication is that the chaplain's prayers alone cannot protect the troops, nor can his meditation end the war. The chaplain's lack of action to stop the war, and his blessing of the troops, then, supports war as a means to achieve an end. This issue returns at the end of the song.

The troops go into battle in the fourth stanza while the chaplain feels satisfied that he has helped provide them with courage through his words. The fourth stanza is followed by a repeat of the chorus. The conclusion of the chorus is signaled by an electric guitar solo, which itself leads into the *musique concrète* sounds of battle. In addition to recordings of explosions, machine gun fire, and horrible screams, the electric guitar provides an imitation of an air raid siren in its distortion-drenched glissandi. After the fighting grows in intensity, bagpipes and their attendant drums overtake the sounds of battle; the sounds of a hard rock band have completely faded out.

The bagpipes effectively split the song into its two parts. The fadeout of the pipes and drums finds the electric bass guitar introducing the second part of the song: the aftermath of the battle. Part 2 of "Sky Pilot" is distinguished by a much cleaner timbre in the electric guitar parts, as well as by the use of string orchestra accompaniment. In the fifth stanza the chaplain places the fate of the country in the hands of the soldiers, telling them that God is on their side and that only time will tell if their sacrifice was worth the cost. In other words, only by winning the war can the soldiers validate the sacrifice of their comrades. The sixth stanza finds one young wounded soldier looking at the chaplain after his return and remembering the Old Testament commandment "Thou shall not kill." It is the soldier's questioning look at the Sky Pilot that points out the hypocrisy of this man of God: the soldier realizes that in stark contrast to the Old Testament teaching, the chaplain has actively encouraged the killing in which he, the soldier, has just participated.

After the young soldier's questions bring home the meaning of the entire song, a final statement of the chorus is heard. This time, no effects pedals are used in the guitar parts, the voices are free from electronic manipulation, and woodwinds, brass, and strings accompany Eric Burdon and The Animals for the first time. This orchestration is reminiscent of the work of George Martin in his 1967-68-era work with The Beatles. In fact, "Sky Pilot" is one of the few songs from the period to effectively juxtapose Jimi Hendrix-influenced electric-guitar based, American-style acid rock (part 1 of the song) and *Sgt. Pepper Lonely Hearts Club Band*, British-style acid rock, featuring elaborate orchestrations (part 2 of the song).

The stanzas of "Sky Pilot" have a notably simple structure, being essentially $aaaa^1$ with each being a two-measure phrase. Interestingly, the a^1 phrases end with half-cadences, which lead into either the next stanza or a statement of the chorus. The simplicity of the melody allows, or perhaps forces, the listener to pay attention to the progression of the story: one would not listen to "Sky Pilot" for the beauty of its melodic line. Although the text does not mention Vietnam, this is one commercially successful single that has not found a place on oldies radio stations, any more than it found a place on top 40 stations at the time of its popularity. It has become a memory, but one still vivid in the minds of those either in the peace movement or those concerned about loved ones stationed in Southeast Asia.

While The Beatles' composition and recordings of "Revolution" do not specifically deal with the Vietnam Conflict, the song makes an interesting comment on the revolutionary movements that were becoming part of some young people's lives in 1968. This is one of the few songs presented in this study that exists in multiple versions, each of which gives the listener a very different message, based primarily on musical style and tempo, but also on subtle text-related changes.

The two-album set *The Beatles*, commonly known as *The White Album*, contains the first version of the John Lennon composition "Revolution." The moderately slow shuffle finds the lead singer, Lennon, unsure whether he wants to be counted among those advocating and actively working toward revolutionary destruction. The single version, actually the B-side of "Hey Jude," was part of one of the biggest-selling 45-rpm records up to that time in history. "Hey Jude" remained at #1 on the *Billboard* sales charts for nine weeks in the autumn of 1968, while the B-side itself reached #12. The single version was recorded at a significantly faster tempo with greater dynamic emphasis on the electrified guitars and piano, all slightly distorted sounding, and on Ringo Starr's heavier drum effects. This time, however, Lennon declares definitively that he would like to be counted out of any violent opposition to the status quo. The song quickly became fodder for numerous writers dealing with the apparent conflict between the nature of the lyrics, in the form of Lennon's declaration, and the nature of the music.

Critic Greil Marcus discusses the irony of the single version of "Revolution" in his book *Rock and Roll Will Stand* (Marcus 1969). According to the writer, while Lennon declares himself out of a coming revolution, the song exudes revolution. In this case Marcus seems to feel that the musical sense of revolution overwhelms the text. Although Rodnitzky 1971b does not specifically mention "Revolution," he does confirm Marcus's take on The Beatles' song when he indicates that, beginning with the psychedelic revolution of 1966 and 1967, message songs were replaced by mood songs, in which the musical style and performance practice of the musicians themselves became the message. In his book on the relationship of rock music and American culture, Robert Pielke, writes that "as one facet of both the immanence and transcendence, authentic art will negate the established order, focusing on its fundamental values and the way they may be institutionalized. Of course, the negation must also involve a critical perspective on the historically conditioned embodiment of the revolution itself. The negation of art is total, all-encompassing. By far the best example of this is the ambiguous 'Revolution' by The Beatles" (Pielke 1986, 18).

The Beatles' "Revolution" is just one of a huge number of songs dealing with the general sense of conflict and the forebodings of a total revolution in the late 1960s and early 1970s. Another example, which again does not touch directly on the Vietnam Conflict but is concerned with the general sense of social upheaval caused in large part by the war and government reactions to protests of it, is Pete Townshend's 1971 composition "Won't Get Fooled Again," as recorded by his group, The Who. Neil Young's excellent "Ohio" deals specifically with the killing of four students by the Ohio National Guard at a Kent State University anti-war demonstration on May 4, 1970, and is an outstanding example of topical songwriting in the rock idiom: the Crosby, Stills, Nash & Young single made its chart debut less than two months after the incident that inspired it. One of the more interesting songs dealing with the possibility of armed revolution at the time was Thunderclap Newman's "Something in the Air." The song, a call to arms for an impending violent revolution, is curiously as tame musically as the single version of "Revolution," a plea *against* armed conflict, is oozing with revolutionary spirit. Among the other notable songs dealing with what appeared in the late 1960s and early 1970s as a full-scale revolution were The Jefferson Airplane's "Volunteers" and Chicago's four-movement suite "It Better End Soon."

Labeled by noted rock music critic Parke Puterbaugh as "a hypnotically pulsating number with a gospel undercurrent" (Puterbaugh 1993, 4), Tommy James and Richard Grasso's "Sweet Cherry Wine" reached #7 on the *Billboard* pop charts for Tommy James and The Shondells in spring 1969. One stanza of the song deals with the singer seeing one of his buddies march off to war with the implication that the friend was killed. James asserts that human beings do not have the right to decide who should live and who should die: that decision is for God alone. Although war is a part of the song, and although James clearly is against the very idea of warfare, "Sweet Cherry Wine" makes more of a statement about humans being part of a universal brotherhood and sisterhood than a specifically Vietnam-related statement. This kind of universalism would be popular in the rock/pop world for several years, culminating in 1973 with John Lennon's "Imagine."

Although given equal compositional credit when the song was recorded and published, Paul McCartney had little or nothing to do with the writing of "Give Peace a Chance." In fact, the composition by John Lennon, first recorded live at one of Lennon and wife Yoko Ono's infamous "Bed-Ins for Peace" in a hotel suite in Montreal, features simple melody and harmony and lyrics with a spontaneous quality: he refers to various personalities who were present at the recording in the one-chord, talking blues-inspired stanzas. A product of spring 1969, "Give Peace a Chance" was the only well-known song of its time in the traditional protest song format, "being repetitious, easy to sing, and stressing the word 'we'" (Denisoff 1972a, 23). The 45-rpm single recording reached #14 on the *Billboard* pop charts and became a prominent anthem for many of the peace demonstrations from summer 1969 until the end of the war. In fact, Charles DeBenedetti reported that participants in the November 15, 1969, Moratorium marches in Washington, D.C., chanted the chorus of the song for some ten minutes, led by singers Pete Seeger, Mitch Miller, and Peter, Paul & Mary (DeBenedetti 1990, 263).

After the song's prominent role at the Moratorium marches, Pete Seeger presented a transcription of the chorus of "Give Peace a Chance" in *Broadside* #104 (January 1970), noting that "several hundred thousand of us" sang it in Washington on November 15, 1969, the same "performance" mentioned by DeBenedetti. Interestingly, especially if one is familiar with the recording by Lennon, Ono, and friends, Seeger puts the squarely quadruple meter song into triple meter. Whether the song was performed in a metrically and rhythmically altered form at the November rally or whether perhaps it was notated that way so as to avoid legal difficulties surrounding unauthorized publication of copyrighted material is not clear. The song was not used exclusively at the Moratorium marches. According to Serge Denisoff, during the last several years of the war, the chorus of "Give Peace a Chance" was the only anti-war song to be sung *en masse* at rallies (Denisoff 1990, 91).

Although John Lennon's "Give Peace a Chance" become something like *the* anti-war anthem of the last years of the Vietnam Conflict—not bad for a melodically simple, two-chorded, four-measure phrase—the *Broadside* crowd of protest singer/songwriters continued to perform and publish new material for the peace movement throughout 1969 and 1970. Among these pieces was Tom Parrott's 1969 composition "Peace Is the Way," published in *Broadside* #104 (January 1970). Following the same sort of line as the Lennon song, Parrott's song makes the point that war can never lead to peace.

Shurli Grant's "Are You Bombing with Me, Jesus?," although written in 1968, received wider exposure through its publication in *Broadside* #98 (May 1969). Once again, we see the issue of the mixture of religion and war being explored as Grant's primarily mixolydian mode piece points out the irony of the airman praying for Jesus to be with him as he bombs innocent civilians with napalm. Perhaps just as graphic as the Shurli Grant song, but with quite different references, Andrew Wilde's "Song of the Sixties," also published in *Broadside* #98 (May 1969), describes the medals that the American dead earn in Vietnam as coming from Woolworth's, the discount department store of the era. The Wilde piece is notable for a fairly wide, octave-and-a-half melodic range, the way in which its heavy use of dotted rhythms suggests a march, and its modal ambiguity, moving somewhat freely between G minor and C minor.

In more than a few instances, jazz and blues record producers of the 1950s and 1960s supplied at least one cut on albums they were producing, especially if the producer (who typically did not act as a recording artist on the record date) was a talented composer and had significant clout with the artists and repertoire department at a record label. Indeed, some of the more noteworthy producers *were* the artists and repertoire departments for their respective labels. Producer Bob Thiele's "Vietnam" made the grade on blues singer/guitarist T-Bone Walker's 1969 album *Every Day I Have the Blues*.

In addition to T-Bone Walker singing and playing electric guitar, the recording of "Vietnam" features prominent session musicians, including guitarist Louie Shelton, and Max Bennett, a future member of the L.A. Express. (L.A. Express front man, saxophonist Tom Scott, is featured on several tracks on the album, but not on "Vietnam.") The musical style and rhythmic feel is archetypical moderate-tempo, electric twelve-bar blues, but the chorus-by-chorus format is somewhat unusual. The only full chorus of solo, played by Walker, is at the beginning of the song, allowing the entire text of the song to be developed without instrumental "interruption."

Taking the form of a letter from a soldier stationed in South Vietnam (portrayed by the singer) to his woman back home, the song begins by asking the female protagonist to write and to have all of her friends write letters to the President pleading with him to stop the madness of the war. The soldier suggests that if Congress and the President hear his plea, he will soon return home. The text then describes in a general manner what the soldier is experiencing: too much killing. In the next stanza he states emphatically that he is sick of the killing, is afraid of dying in battle, and has no desire to fight any longer. Through this progression, Thiele sets the stage for the letter and then allows the soldier's true frustration and fear gradually to emerge.

T-Bone Walker sticks pretty much to the same melody for each stanza, doing little vocal improvisation to heighten any particular stanza or particular words or phrases within any stanza. In performing the song in this manner, he allows the gradual transformation of the text to create its own effect upon the listener: the text is strong enough for this to work. Compared with the more expressive vocal style on J. B. Lenoir's blues form piece discussed earlier, Walker's seems a little understated. The production and the instrumental accompaniment are very clean, with producer Thiele allowing the text to be heard quite clearly in his composition.

T-Bone Walker's recording of "Vietnam" represents another step on the path leading to an African-American recording of an anti-war song that will cross racial boundaries in its appeal to the public—it was received by a significantly larger and more diverse audience than were the earlier Vietnam-related blues works of Lenoir and Johnny Shines—the breakthrough would come within a year in a rhythm and blues/funk song from Detroit's Motown record label.

According to John Kay, the German-born lead singer of the American hard rock band Steppenwolf, "I had my ides about the system, politics, and so on. It was people like Tom Paxton and Phil Ochs and Len Chandler and Bob Dylan and Buffy St. Marie and countless others. Like, they were our spokesmen" (Hey Brother! 1970, 3). Kay and Steppenwolf band mates Goldy McJohn and Larry Byrom contributed the song "Draft Resister" to the anti-war corpus of songs. This 1969 work, featured a hard rock, nearly heavy metal electric guitar-based sound, and Kay's characteristic, rather harsh vocal style, probably more familiar to many listeners from Steppenwolf's best-known song, "Born to Be Wild." Incidentally, Steppenwolf's studio recording of "Draft Resister" also uses marimba, an unusual instrument to be found in a rock song; among the few other groups ever to incorporate the marimba into a rock context are The Doors and The Rolling Stones. "Draft Resister," contained on the studio album *Monster*, and later included on *Steppenwolf "Live,"* deals primarily with the loneliness of the life of those tens of thousands who had fled the United States to avoid the draft; these men are painted as brave souls who have given up their homes, their friends, their families, their loved ones, and their beloved country in order to protest the unjust actions of a government and military that had gone completely out of control. The song is a tribute to those exiles. Given the counterculture nature of much of the band's material and the counterculture look of the *Monster* cover art, it can be reasonably assumed that Steppenwolf's audience included both those who are toasted in "Draft Resister" as well as those who might have been on the verge of joining their ranks.

Coincidentally, at approximately the time the Steppenwolf song was making the rounds on the #17 *Monster* and #7 *Steppenwolf "Live"* albums (*Billboard* pop album chart data), *Broadside* published a talking blues by someone identified only as K. C., a resister who had avoided the draft by escaping to Canada. His personal story of immigrating, having difficulties finding work as an immigrant, and the pain he felt in having to leave his friends and family, published as "Talking Draft Exile Blues" in *Broadside* #98 (May 1969), gives flesh and blood to the nameless draft resisters of John Kay and company's composition. The plight of "the new exiles," as writer Roger Neville Williams called them, draft resisters and deserters from the U.S. military, is well detailed in Williams' book *The New Exiles: American War Resisters in Canada* (Williams 1971). According to Williams, himself a draft resister, the election of Richard Nixon in 1968 and the 1968 Democratic National Convention debacle greatly increased the flow of American men of draft age into Canada and other countries: K. C.'s "Talking Draft Exile Blues" and Steppenwolf's "Draft Resister" were very much pieces of their time.

From late 1969 through 1970, three anti-war songs by the rock band Creedence Clearwater Revival enjoyed huge sales and extensive AM radio airplay, "Fortunate Son,"

"Who'll Stop the Rain," and "Run Through the Jungle"; all three songs were composed by the group's lead singer and lead guitarist John C. Fogerty.

Before delving into the messages of the three songs, let us examine the extent to which these recordings permeated America over the stretch of a little more than a year. Making its chart debut in late 1969, "Fortunate Son" reached #14 on the *Billboard* pop singles charts. The song was actually the B-side of "Down on the Corner," which went all the way to #3. Although certainly not unheard of, it was at the time rare that both sides of a single would make it into the top 40, let alone enjoy the success of this particular single. The album on which "Fortunate Son" appeared, *Willy and the Poorboys*, itself hit #3 on the *Billboard* pop album charts. Fogerty's "Who'll Stop the Rain," part of a double A-sided single with "Travelin' Band," hit #2 on the *Billboard* pop charts in early 1970, after a January debut. "Run Through the Jungle," part of a double A-sided single with "Up Around the Bend," made its debut on the *Billboard* pop singles charts in April 1970, eventually reaching #4. The reader should note that "Up Around the Bend" was clearly the more popular of the two sides, as evidenced by the disparities in the *Cash Box* chart rankings of it and "Run Through the Jungle." Creedence Clearwater Revival's two 1970 anti-war songs, "Who'll Stop the Rain?" and "Run Through the Jungle," were issued again in the summer of that year on the enormously popular album *Cosmo's Factory*, a disc that held on to the #1 position on *Billboard*'s pop album charts for a nine-week period.

The first of the three songs to appear, "Fortunate Son," has been described by *Rolling Stone* critic Paul Evans as "the most convincing political rock & roll before the Clash," the politically active British punk rock band of the 1970s and 1980s (Evans 1992, 167). The hard rock song takes on such topics as the following: (1) the ability of the wealthy and politically connected to avoid the draft legally, while the less fortunate are dying in war; (2) those who blindly follow the false "truths" doled out by political leaders regarding the necessity of the war in Vietnam; and (3) the ability of the wealthy to pay less than their fair share of taxes. Throughout the recording Fogerty sings passionately and plays the lead guitar lines with a bright, metallic timbre. "Fortunate Son" is truly one of those recordings that suffer through verbal description: one must hear it to appreciate it fully. It should be noted that, although clearly a song of wartime, Vietnam is not mentioned. The continued appeal of the song, as evidenced by its numerous reissues and its still frequent airplay on oldies radio stations, is due in part to the generality of Fogerty's message, in addition to the obvious: it is simply a great rock and roll song and performance.

Compared with the fury of "Fortunate Son," Fogerty's "Who'll Stop the Rain?" seems subtle and lyrically impressionistic. At the time of its issue, the title line of the song was understood as metaphorically asking the question "Who'll stop the war?" In fact, when Fogerty mentions "Bobby" in the lyrics, a reference to Senator Robert Kennedy, considered the 1968 presidential candidate most likely to end the war in Vietnam, it is clear that he is expressing a strong sense of loss: the peace movement has lost its greatest hope to an assassin's bullet, we are still very much at war in Southeast Asia, President Nixon does not seem to be ending the war as he promised, to whom can we turn? The moderate tempo, the relatively lush vocal harmonies, the slightly resigned quality of Fogerty's voice, and the sense of resignation or even sadness some (myself included) associate with the tonic to submediant harmonic oscillation used in the song's fade out all converge to create a beautiful expression of loss and near-complete resignation tempered with hope that someone will come forward who will put an end to the rain/war.

John Fogerty takes the listener into the jungles of Vietnam for "Run Through the Jungle," which begins with electric guitar feedback suggesting the sounds of military aircraft and other weaponry. The song is almost a rock version of a southern U.S., rural blues, consisting of one chord supporting a blues-infused melodic line, sung by Fogerty, whose voice is electronically manipulated with echo. While the lyrics do not make a clear anti-war or pro-government statement, the terror of the life of a soldier in the jungle, never knowing what or who lurks behind the foliage, hearing guns blazing and bullets whizzing by in the night, is well expressed. I believe this song fits squarely into the anti-war category, based almost entirely on context. Yes, it attempts to express something of what the soldier feels while fighting in a climate and land utterly foreign to Americans, but in light of the other Creedence Clearwater Revival songs dealing with the war that were circulating at the same time, the song seems to carry a strong anti-war subtext based on terror, almost as though the composer had decided to make the experience of a jungle war seem so horrible that "Run Through the Jungle" might further galvanize the calls to bring the troops home.

As mentioned earlier, the whole point of the original broadsides of William Shakespeare's time was to be topical, to respond to political and social events as they happened. Certainly, events of major proportion occurring throughout the Vietnam Conflict spawned such topical songs. Three songs in particular, Tom Parrott's "The Massacres of My Lai (Song My) and Truong Am, March 1968," Mike Millius's "Ballad of Song My," and Pete Seeger's "Last Train to Nuremberg," are outstanding examples of topical songs inspired by the revelations of the tragic massacres of hundreds of civilians, mostly women and children, by U.S. troops. The publication of these songs was spread out somewhat, with the Parrott piece appearing in *Broadside* #103 (December 1969), the Millius piece seeing publication in *Broadside* #105 (February-March 1970), and the Seeger work, although written the week that the massacres at My Lai were first made public, finally seeing publication in *Sing Out!* 20/2 (November-December 1970).

Tom Parrott's "The Massacres of My Lai (Song My) and Truong Am, March 1968" is structured in a somewhat unusual $abcc^{1}$ form, with the only authentic cadence occurring at the end of the c^{1} phrase. Although not necessarily intended for performance in a rock style, the song's scalar materials resemble many rock songs from 1965 forward, being based on a freely fluctuating mixture of the major scale and the mixolydian mode. Mike Millius indicates in the score that his "Ballad of Song My" is to be performed softly and slowly, which seems to be apt for the somber mood of the subject of the song. In fact, the rhythm of the transcription in *Broadside* suggests a very free, parlando approach. Interestingly, like the Parrott work, "Ballad of Song My" also freely mixes the major scale with the mixolydian mode.

Pete Seeger's "Last Train to Nuremberg" is in the style of an African-American spiritual or work song; even incorporating a blues-influenced flatted seventh scale-step against the V7 chord. Seeger's E minor work also uses only the tonic, subdominant, and dominant-seventh chords; again, in a characteristic scheme for a spiritual. In the text the composer sees President Nixon, Lieutenant William Calley, both houses of Congress, and other principals from the My Lai massacre on the train to Nuremberg, the site, of course, of the famous Nazi war crimes trials after World War II. In addition to placing the blood of the Vietnamese on the hands of the specifically named individuals, Seeger goes one step further and places the blood on the hands of all Americans who have not fought against the war.

In large part a vehicle for his extended, blues-based hard rock electric guitar solos, Jimi Hendrix's "Machine Gun" is based on a riff carried forth primarily by the electric bass. The text, sung in part to a machine gun, deals with how the gun is used in warfare. Hendrix's Band of Gypsys performed the piece at their famous, recorded New Years Eve 1970 concert, with Hendrix dedicating the song to all servicemen. In the course of the piece, Hendrix and drummer Buddy Miles each incorporate nine thirty-second-note and nine sixteenth-note figures in obvious imitation of the piece of weaponry to which the song refers. The music, as much if not more than the text, speaks to the terror of warfare and of the potential for destruction inherent in the machine gun, especially in some of the more feedback-laden passages in Hendrix's guitar solo. *All Music Guide* critic Sean Westergaard called Hendrix's solo on "Machine Gun" "arguably the most groundbreaking and devastating guitar solo ever" (Westergaard 2000). At the conclusion of the song, Hendrix tells the New Year's Eve crowd that the sound of the machine gun is one that "we" do not want to hear anymore.

Featuring lead singer Burton Cummings and guitarist Randy Bachman, the Canadian rock group The Guess Who had their biggest hit in 1970 with the ensemble-composed song "American Woman." The single entered the *Billboard* charts in March 1970, eventually holding the #1 slot for three weeks. This hard rock piece, based on a relatively simple rhythmic riff, and fueled by Bachman's sustain pedal-laden lead guitar and Cummings' powerful vocal, uses the character of an American woman for whom the group has great disdain as a metaphor for the various ills they see in U.S. society. Among the aspects of American society not appreciated by the Canadians is the military-industrial complex, which they hold responsible for the war in Vietnam (although they do not mention Vietnam by name). The song is still heard today on oldies stations in both the single version and in an extended, album version that features a long acoustic introduction ironically based to an extent on American rural blues. At the time of this writing, the song has lost most of its metaphorical bite; it has recently been used in television commercials to advertise designer clothing!

Wearing American flag, bowtie-shaped barrettes in the photograph on the back cover of her self-titled album, Melanie (Safka) wrote and recorded the spring 1970 hit "Lay Down (Candles in the Rain)." The song is the thematic centerpiece of the album and was issued as a 45-rpm single. The single reached #6 on the *Billboard* pop charts and, due to its jukebox popularity, hit #3 during its seventeen-week run in the *Cash Box* charts.

"Lay Down (Candles in the Rain)" exhibits an impressionistic quality in its lyrics, which best can be experienced by listening to the song on Melanie's *Candles in the Rain* album, on which the song is preceded by the spoken prelude/poem "Candles in the Rain." The singer/songwriter uses the metaphor of catching a disease for the need those in the peace movement feel to be activists. By using this particular word, Melanie cleverly shows both the infectious nature of activism and the dis-ease those in the movement feel with the ongoing war. The strongest metaphor in the song is that of holding a candle high in order to remain dry in the pouring rain, symbolizing keeping the hope for peace alive through activism. The reader might recall that John Fogerty's "Who'll Stop the Rain," which also used rain as a metaphor for war, was a contemporary of the Melanie work. Melanie sings passionately throughout and the arrangement features a strong use of dynamic and stylistic contrast to highlight her lyrics. Although it tends toward the general and makes a greater use of metaphor than some listeners might have liked, this gospel-tinged song, with a religiosity imparted by the featured Edwin Hawkins Singers, remains one of the best songs of hope of the period.

Melanie Safka would make the singles charts again in August 1970 with another parenthetically titled song, her "Peace Will Come (According to Plan)." The singer/songwriter, backed by acoustic guitar, bongo drums, electronic organ, and bass, expresses the hope that peace will eventually come as part of God's plan. "Peace" as used by Melanie in this song is quite general in nature; she could be singing of the absence of war or of an individual, inner peace.

As impressionistic, metaphoric, and even a little vague as Melanie Safka was in her peace anthems, longtime Motown songwriters Norman Whitfield and Barrett Strong were blunt in their "War." The song originally appeared in April 1970 on The Temptations' album *Psychedelic Shack*, a package that peaked at #14 during its twenty-two weeks on the *Cash Box* pop album charts. The potent track easily could have been issued as a single, had Motown's plans for The Temptations' next single not have been to release "Ball of Confusion (That's What the World Is Today)," a Whitfield and Strong song that, in the manner of "Eve of Destruction," rails against all of American society's ills, with a focus on the problems faced by African Americans. "War" was given to the lesser-known solo singer Edwin Starr.

Edwin Starr's recording of "War," which was produced by Norman Whitfield, represented the hardest core sound issued up to the time on a Motown-related record label. It was also a smash hit, being the first fully anti-war single record specifically dealing with the Vietnam Conflict to reach #1 on the *Billboard* pop charts; earlier #1 singles had either included the war as only a part of their message, like "Eve of Destruction," or were very general and non-Vietnam specific in their attention, like "Where Have All the Flowers Gone?" The record also reached #3 on the *Billboard* R&B charts, suggesting that both Black and White audiences purchased "War" in droves.

Some have questioned the motives of the Motown staff songwriters in suddenly putting out socially relevant material after years of near neglect of controversial issues. Historians Kenneth J. Bindas and Craig Houston write, "between 1970 and 1971 a majority [56%] of Americans viewed the war as a mistake and sixty-one percent advocated early withdrawal. Motown Records, the General Motors of rock, decided to cash in on the public's new outlook toward war and society" (Bindas and Houston 1989, 16). Whatever Whitfield and Strong's motivation, the Edwin Starr recording of "War" was one of the most musically powerful and rhythmically solid records of 1970. It remains a frequently reissued recording and one that well symbolizes the growing strength of the anti-war movement among Blacks at the end of the 1960s.

While I would tend to disagree with writers who suggest that Norman Whitfield and Barrett Strong concocted "War" wholly or primarily as a means to cash in on the popularity of anti-war sentiment sweeping the country—I find the song to be potent and honest sounding in its message—I do consider the composers' "Stop the War Now" to be little more than a crass attempt to cash in on the now-popular anti-war sentiment and on their own success with "War." Edwin Starr's recording of "Stop the War Now," also produced by Whitfield, reached #5 on the *Billboard* R&B charts, but only #26 on the magazine's pop charts. The brass and saxophone lines, rhythmic style, and even some of the text sound so suspiciously like a "War" outtake that one has to wonder if Whitfield and Strong would have sued for plagiarism had other writers composed "Stop the War Now."

According to Bindas and Houston, "realizing the vast consumer potential of antiwar material, record companies now [beginning around 1970] promoted 'schlock'" (Bindas and Houston 1989, 18). The authors cite Laura Nyro's composition "Save the Country," as recorded by The 5th Dimension, as one of the more offensive examples. Lyrically, the song resembles a hodgepodge of popular and nonoffensive pro-peace slogans, such as one might find on the bumper stickers of the time; it probably was one of the most banal "protest" songs of the era. Apparently the recording by the Black vocal group was most popular among post-teen, White audiences as it hit #10 on *Billboard*'s adult contemporary singles chart, but only #27 on the magazine's pop singles charts, and #41 on the R&B charts.   The recording is a highly commercial sounding, well-produced middle-of-the-road pop effort; however, the happy-go-lucky arrangement and performance style trivializes whatever seriousness might be found in Nyro's lyrics.

. Justin Hayward's "Question," released as a single by his group The Moody Blues in spring 1970 and on the hit album *A Question of Balance* in August 1970, does not deal directly with the Vietnam Conflict *per se*, but deals more abstractly with the concept of war. The song mixes two contrasting lyrical and musical styles in a way that gives the impression of a song within a song. "Question" begins at a quick tempo in a section that finds Hayward asking why people never seem to get adequate answers to the questions they have about war. He suggests as a conclusion that the questions are left unanswered because the truth would be too hard to take. Exactly what Hayward means by this is unclear; he could mean that war is simply inevitable, or that somehow war is outside of human control, being a result of fate or possibly in the hands of God. This second interpretation seems to be implied by the cover art of *A Question of Balance*, which suggests a higher being at work maintaining the delicate balance of the universe.

"Question" then moves into a slower section resembling an almost Elizabethan-style lute song, *sans* lute, but with the group's characteristic mellotron on a string setting. Hayward sings of being away from his homeland and his beloved. He does not specify why he is away, but the juxtaposition of this section, almost a song within a song, with the opening suggests that he may be away because of a war. The slow section is followed by a return to the fast, more rock-oriented material, again asking why answers to questions about war are not forthcoming.   On The Moody Blues' compact disc compilation *Anthology*, remastered from the original tapes, the closing sixteenth notes on the snare drum, starting just before and continuing through the song's fade out, are boosted in the mix and treated with added reverberation, suggesting a machine gun. While Justin Hayward is notably vague in "Question," the singer's plea for answers to his and the world's questions about war suggests a background belief that war is generally unnecessary; while the song is in no way referential to the Vietnam Conflict, it seems doubtful that even a vaguely anti-war song like this would have been found quite as relevant to the record-buying public had a controversial war not been taking place.

Fronted by lead singer Ozzy Osbourne, the British heavy metal rock band Black Sabbath included the group-composed "War Pigs" on their landmark 1970 album *Paranoid*. "War Pigs" equates generals with witches, wizards, and even Satan; Black Sabbath suggests that military commanders control the minds of their soldiers and derive pleasure from the plotting of the taking of life. The song paints politicians who support war as cowards who start wars, but force others to do the dirty work involved. And, on the Judgment Day, Satan will laugh as all of these War Pigs shudder in the shadow of God and become consigned to Satan's nether kingdom.   Every aspect of Black Sabbath's performance, including instrumental and vocal timbre, virtuosic lead guitar and drum work, the use of longish, twisting riffs, and the subject matter of the song itself make this a prototypical heavy metal performance—an early but fully mature example of the genre. In his book *Stairway to Hell*, critic Chuck Eddy rates Black Sabbath's *Paranoid* as the twenty-seventh best heavy metal album of all time (Eddy 1998, 26).

With a life story resembling a prototype, or better yet, a stereotype, of a southern, rural African-American bluesman, Robert Pete Williams contributed "Vietnam Blues" to the corpus of war-related songs in 1970. The song, sung by Williams to his own acoustic guitar accompaniment, was included on the 1971 album *Robert Pete Williams*. The fifty-six-year-old performer created an improvised, almost through-composed setting of a soldier's lament: he is stationed in Vietnam and sounds as though he would rather be anywhere else. Taken as an individual song, "Vietnam Blues" expresses the pain of the soldier and questions the U.S. role in the country; however, as a cut on the *Robert Pete Williams* album, the feeling inherent in the song is lost among other similar-sounding songs about different subject matter, illustrating the importance of context in conveying a musical message. The older blues style and the musician's age also work against the believability of his characterization.

Buffy Sainte-Marie's "Moratorium" stands as perhaps the greatest recorded document of the passion of the anti-war movement. Published in lead sheet form in *Broadside* #112 (March-April 1971), the song was issued on Sainte-Marie's album *She Used to Wanna Be a Ballerina*. Unlike nearly every other recorded song on any side of the Vietnam issue, "Moratorium" seems to be designed almost not to have commercial appeal. The composer sings in an impassioned, almost brutal voice of the loss experienced by a number of returning Vietnam veterans, then takes on the near-screaming voice of several anti-war protesters, backed by her poundings on a piano. Sainte-Marie proves that the human voice, unadorned by any electronic gadgetry and unsupported by any amplified instruments, captures the humanity and the depth of feeling of her characters better than any country or rock band, or any pop singer backed by the full resources of a major record label. The song is a near cinematic document with a through-composed, improvised quality, suggesting a musical counterpart to random shots taken by a television news camera at a peace rally, of a brutal, violent time period in which (1) the increasing flow of veterans back into the United States showed the public all too clearly their physical and emotional plights, and (2) the expansion of the theatre of operations and bombing campaigns symbolized an expansion of the war by an administration that had been elected on a pro-peace platform, thereby renewing and increasing the passions of the anti-war movement. Unfortunately, as a true product of its time, "Moratorium" teeters on the edge of sounding like a self parody of the singer/songwriter/folk revival movement; those who did not experience the way in which the Vietnam Conflict was ripping America apart in 1970 need to work a great deal to appreciate the intensity of the song thirty years later.

Unlike Buffy Sainte-Marie's "Moratorium," Gregory Perry, Angelo Bond, and General Johnson's "Bring the Boys Home," as recorded in 1971 by Freda Payne, is nearly the epitome of commercialism. Bindas and Houston 1989 mention "Bring the Boys Home" as one of the "slick" songs of the early 1970s intended to take advantage of the changing view of the Vietnam Conflict sweeping America. Payne's recording, with its Philadelphia Sound-style arrangement seemed to strike a chord, especially among Black audiences as the single reached #3 on the *Billboard* R&B charts, but only #12 on the pop charts. After its June 1971 debut, the single also reached #6 on the *Cash Box* Black contemporary charts. Curiously, the label on the 45 rpm disc indicates that the song is taken from Payne's album *Contact*; however, the song was not included on the album. In fact, the entire *gestalt* of *Contact*, from the fold-out, cut-out poster of Payne in a fancy evening dress to the songs contained therein represent nonpolitical pop music and marketing; the plea to bring the troops home and end the war would not fit, no matter what the commercial appeal of "Bring the Boys Home."

One of the complaints lodged against records like "Bring the Boys Home" is that the innocent, danceable pop musical settings, combined with the gentleness of the lyrical messages, tended to downplay the seriousness of the anti-war messages. Certainly Bindas and Houston 1989 considered one of the more generic-sounding pro-peace songs of the era to be Cat Stevens's "Peace Train." The single reached #7 on *Billboard*'s pop charts after its September 1971 debut. Yes, the song is a somewhat general call for a universal brotherhood and sisterhood of humankind based on the premise of peace and is performed in a commercially crafted manner; John Lennon's #3 pop single "Imagine" falls into the same general, hope-for-a-peace-based-utopia category, as does the Yoko Ono, Lennon collaboration "Happy Xmas (War Is Over)." Perhaps the naïve idealism of "Peace Train" and "Imagine" (which deals even more obliquely with warfare) was a reaction to not only the violence of warfare, but also the violence that had now been associated for a couple of years with the fight to end the war. Todd Gitlin, author and early president of the Students for a Democratic Society, refers to this late 1960s phenomenon as "violence shock" (Gitlin 1987, 317). Perhaps Cat Stevens and John Lennon showed that some were beginning to feel that only in the world of imagination could peace readily be found—a sort of extension of the "War Is Over" wishing away of the conflict dating from several years before. What some writers have failed to detect in "Peace Train," and in Freda Payne's "Bring the Boys Home" for that matter, is a real expression in the singer's voice—perhaps something short of raw passion, but a real sense of the artist's belief in the message nonetheless. "Peace Train" also features some expressive, Richie Havens-style guitar strumming that sets off several lines in Stevens's plea to end warfare. With the subtle vocal inflections and instrumental touches that give a sense of expression to "Peace Train" and "Bring the Boys Home," the songs stand on a middle ground between the truly generic 5th Dimension reading of the pastiche of clichés in Laura Nyro's "Save the Country" and the better Vietnam-specific songs of the anti-war movement.

As mentioned at the beginning of this book's Preface, Johnny Cash's statement that "the only good thing that ever came out of a war was a song" (Grissim 1970, 84), was understood as supporting both hawks and doves. Curiously, Cash's "Singin' in Viet Nam Talkin' Blues," written about the experiences of Cash and his wife June Carter Cash on a trip to South Vietnam just before the singer made that statement, also seems to walk the line between both sides of the Vietnam issue; although, ultimately Cash concludes with an anti-war message. The song was issued as a single, hitting #18 on the *Billboard* country charts, but only #127 on the magazine's pop charts.

As implied by its title, the Cash composition is a talking blues, with a longish ostinato accompaniment by guitars, bass drum, and acoustic bass in a country style (country-style finger picking in the guitars and archetypical root-fifth oscillations in the bass) backing up the narrative text. Cash's text tells the tale of a trip to South Vietnam to perform for U.S. troops. The tour found the Cashes in close proximity to shelling and seeing the wounded troops being brought back to base. Cash conveys the sense of terror he and his wife felt being so near to the heated nighttime battles. Eventually, Cash explains that the troops need to know that there are people back home who need them and love them. He acknowledges the differences of opinion about whether the United States should be involved in Southeast Asia, but states that as long as American servicemen are there, they should be told that those back home pray for their safe return. At the conclusion of the narrative, Cash expresses his hope that if he ever travels to Vietnam again, he will not find U.S. troops there, that they all would have returned; he expresses his hope for peace forcefully within a vocal crescendo.

What Cash manages to do in "Singin' in Viet Nam Talkin' Blues" is to leave the means to peace open to interpretation: we cannot be sure if he advocates early withdrawal or peace through victory. By promoting peace—something every side in the political debate wanted—but not specifying how he feels that peace should be achieved,

Johnny Cash manages to deliver a deeply personal story of a singer traveling to a dangerous foreign land, a plea for support of U.S. troops fighting abroad, whether they should have been sent there or not, all with a message of peace that all sides could interpret as supporting their view. Incidentally, it should be noted that Cash was one of the few performers of the 1960s and 1970s to have been considered a serious part of both the country genre and the folk revival, two frequently polarized forms from a political standpoint. "Singin' in Viet Nam Talkin' Blues" is probably one of the best examples of how he was able to work creatively and convincingly in the two genres simultaneously.

Johnny Cash's walking of the fine line between opposing political sides aside, the reader will undoubtedly have noticed the conspicuous lack of country songs among the anti-war corpus. The country chart success of Arlene Harden's recording of Garman, Hoffman, and Barr's "Congratulations (You Sure Made a Man Out of Him)" demonstrates the extent to which U.S. public opinion had turned against the war by the time of the release of the single in 1971.

"Congratulations" finds the singer addressing the U.S. military, sarcastically congratulating the military for making a real man out of her husband, who has just returned from serving in Vietnam. Uncle Sam's dubious "achievements" include: turning a root beer drinker into a drinker of gin; making a formerly loving husband cold to the touch; turning the singer's husband away from religion; making the veteran unable to talk about his emotional feelings, yet making him liable to cry for no reason at all; and emotionally distancing the formerly active, loving father from his children. In some respects this is a song about the plight of one soldier; however, the sarcasm of the lyrics and the blatant way in which the blame for the emotional demise of the singer's husband is placed on the U.S. military carries a potent anti-war message.

Musically, the Harden recording is an example of pure early 1950s pop, featuring strings, piano, and harp in its Bill McElhiney arrangement. In fact, although marketed as a country song and sold to country audiences, the recording contains no overt, stereotypical "country" musical references in instrumentation or in the singer's phrasing, inflection, or style. Given the utter disdain the woman expresses for the military and the musical style, the Arlene Harden recording's appearance on the country charts is amazing. In fact, comparison of "Congratulations" and Loretta Lynn's "Dear Uncle Sam" suggests the extent to which even country music audience members' attitudes toward the war had changed: gone are the patriotic, domino theory-inspired justifications for the war and gone is the understanding wife: the new soldier's wife is angry and is not afraid to express her bitterness. Harden exercises control over her character's emotions, allowing the song itself to tell of her resigned bitterness. Adding to the touching quality of the performance is an unresolved electric piano coda, suggesting that both characters will have to live with the results of post-traumatic stress syndrome for quite some time.

Although it peaked on *Billboard*'s pop singles charts at #73 in the summer of 1971, Graham Nash's "Military Madness" garnered a fair amount of radio airplay and was a central work on the singer's *Songs for Beginners* album. The autobiographical song tells of Nash's schooling—perhaps metaphorically referring to his introduction to the music industry in The Hollies—and his moving from England to the United States (when he formed Crosby, Stills, and Nash). Nash sings about how the madness of war had nearly killed the country of his birth during his World War II childhood and how war is now killing his new country. The barely two-minute song concludes with Nash's expression of hope that in the future someone may discover why humankind is so prone to war, so that war might be ended once and for all. "Military Madness" mirrors the reggae style of Bob Marley, from its use of echo on Nash's voice to the extensive use of the wah-wah pedal on the electric guitar, the shuffle rhythm, and the piano's eighth-note figures on beats two and four.   The plaintive singing and electric lead guitar breaks give the recording a high degree of believability; never do the infectious reggae rhythms overwhelm the story or the mood.

Probably most famous for the fact that they worked with The Beatles' former producer George Martin, the California group Seatrain managed to combine rock, traditional acoustic music, and hints of jazz on their album *The Marblehead Messenger*. The song "Marblehead Messenger," written by Seatrain members Andy Kulberg and Jim Roberts, hints at the contemporary sound of Jethro Tull, without the British band's heavily electric leanings. Kulberg and Roberts plead for the citizens of the world to heed the message of peace brought by the Marblehead Messenger. The message is fairly general—Vietnam is not mentioned—and the musical mix fairly eclectic, making "Marblehead Messenger" a song that, while undoubtedly a product of a time of warfare, can be fully appreciated in a time of peace.

Recorded by its composer Curtis Mayfield, "We Got to Have Peace" was the one anti-war single of the Vietnam era that was purchased almost exclusively by Black consumers; Mayfield's single release reached #32 on the *Billboard* R&B charts after a February 1972 debut but never made it into the magazine's pop top 100.   Mayfield, singing in his characteristic falsetto, calls for an equal chance for all people and states that peace is necessary for the survival of the world; he returns over and over to the theme that peace is needed for the sake of the children. "We Got to Have Peace" is very much an example of the slickness that can be found in post-1969 peace songs: a full string section and harp glissandi and arpeggios sweeten Mayfield's pop/soul performance.   The unusual demographics surrounding the sales of the record probably result from the fact that Mayfield was marketed primarily to Black audiences throughout his career: his pop chart success never rivaled his achievements on the R&B charts.

While the period between 1968 and the early 1970s saw a number of hard-rock and heavy metal groups record anti-war songs, and while we have seen that after 1970 even middle-of-the-road pop groups like The 5th Dimension jumped on the anti-war bandwagon, there was also a re-emergence of the topical songwriter with the new decade. In fact, the reader should probably note that 1970 marked the emergence of the singer/songwriter in American popular music; artists such as Carly Simon, James Taylor, and Carole King were among the musicians who made huge commercial inroads with songs featuring deeply personal lyrics and a musical style considerably more mellow than the hard-rock and heavy metal of the day. Holly Near was one of the leading new protest singers to emerge at this time.

Before she was widely known through recordings and for her concert work in support of a number of progressive causes in the later 1970s and 1980s, Near traveled to Southeast Asia in late 1971 with actors Jane Fonda and Donald Sutherland in an anti-war tour, and in 1972 and 1973 she toured with Fonda and progressive activist Tom Hayden as part of the Indochina Peace Campaign. According to the musician, she had always written based upon personal experience, and it was the deeply personal experience of performing in front of various types of audiences, young, old, military personnel, and anti-war politicos, that inspired most of the songs on her 1973 album *Hang in There* (Near 1974). According to *All Music Guide* critic William Ruhlmann, *Hang in There* "provided a snapshot of the American anti-war movement in its later days" (Ruhlmann 2000b). The critic describes it as a package of "frustration" with the ongoing war, as well as "extremism," combining to make the album "a historical curiosity with a few years of its release" (Ruhlmann 2000b). Although the entire album deals with the issue of the

Vietnam Conflict, I wish to focus on just four of the songs: "Hang in There," "No More Genocide," "G.I. Movement," and "Oh America."

In all of the songs, Near exhibits a vocal instrument that is quite refined, pleasant, capable of nuance, and well pitched; she compares favorably with the early 1960s protest singers in terms of her vocal instrument and her use of it. Near was, in fact, one of the few singers active in the protest movement to have actually studied voice formally; most of the singer/songwriters were self-taught vocalists and many simply did not possess the technique of a Holly Near.

Resembling an African-American spiritual in form and style, "Hang in There" leads off the album. The song is in call-and-response form, with Near's solo singing of the stanzas answered by a unison chorus, a response sung by some of the soloist's friends. In the tradition of a spiritual, occasionally a singer or two will join Near for a touch of improvised harmony or heterophony at the end of her solo stanzas. The text of the repeated chorus refers to the twenty-seven-year struggle for independence, referring of course to the period following the defeat of the French and the Geneva Accord of 1954, during which time Vietnam had been artificially cut in two.

"Hang in There" fades into "No More Genocide," in which Near asks why the United States does not just allow the Vietnamese to live as one people, as they freely would chose to do if there were no foreign intervention. Recall that this point had been revisited from time to time throughout the history of the protest song movement. It harkens back to the point made during the Eisenhower administration that, given the chance to vote on the matter, 80 percent of the Vietnamese people would favor being one nation. Near then sings of various examples of U.S. genocide, including the slaughter of Native Americans and the slaughter of and the expulsion of Chicanos from California. She also mentions that a higher proportion of persons of color have been drafted to serve in Vietnam than live in the U.S. population at large, a point originally made years before by anti-war and Black Power activist Stokely Carmichael. Near claims that U.S. history books lie about all of these atrocities of the past and the present, either outright or by refusing to acknowledge that they ever took place. According to Near, among the few sources of the light of truth are *The Pentagon Papers*, which reveal that the U.S. government has know all along that there was never any democracy in South Vietnam to preserve. While many of Near's points had been covered in other songs of the broadside tradition, making them somewhat old hat in terms of the anti-war movement, her very specific references to the recently published *Pentagon Papers* gives "No More Genocide" its own kind of topicality.

Throughout the album *Hang in There*, Holly Near is supported by a creative instrumentation that mixes orchestral instruments, such as the oboe and violin, with acoustic guitars, drums, and electric bass. Oboe is used especially effectively in "G.I. Movement," a song written for an FTA show at which the singer appeared in 1971 and the use of violin in "Oh America" calls to mind the use of cello in some of the contemporary work of the better-known Harry Chapin, another 1970s musician active in progressive social causes.

Holly Near's "Oh America," published in lead sheet form in *Sing Out!* 22/6 (1974), is a song of hope in which the composer refers to specific individuals and audiences that she had met and seen touched when they learned the truth about what the U.S. military had been doing in Vietnam, presumably through the leaked *Pentagon Papers*. Near mentions that a number of these people have become active in the peace movement, even though they had formerly supported the U.S. role in Southeast Asia. Accompanied by country-style guitar finger picking, Near sings that these new "recruits" to peace activism represent a ray of hope in America: a better, peaceful America may be just around the corner. Near's vocal command allows her to incorporate some text painting into her recorded performance of the song: the subtly faltering voice she uses as she portrays an elderly woman she met on her concert tour effectively mirrors the weariness the woman professes in the song's lyrics.

"One of the cornerstone songs of early 1970s AM radio," according to *All Music Guide* critic Stephen Erlewine (Erlewine 2000), "Billy, Don't Be a Hero" was easily the biggest hit for the pop group Bo Donaldson and The Heywoods, selling more than 3.5 million copies. In terms of the chronology of the war, "Billy, Don't Be a Hero" appeared at a curious time: U.S. forces were basically out of South Vietnam in 1974, but Saigon had not yet fallen and the official end of the war (from the standpoint of the two Vietnams) had not yet occurred. There are several other interestingly curious points about this song: (1) the song was originally a British hit for the group Paper Lace; (2) it was Americanized by record producer Steve Barri, onetime writing partner of P. F. Sloan of "Eve of Destruction" fame; and (3) even cursory study of the lyrics strongly suggests that the song is about a Civil War-era event.

Composed by Peter Callander and Mitch Murray, "Billy, Don't Be a Hero" tells the story of a soldier wearing the blue uniform, presumably of the Union Army, whose fiancée asks him not to be a hero as he prepares to march into war. Billy's company becomes locked in a fierce and desperate battle and a volunteer is needed to get reinforcements. Billy volunteers, but is killed. The anti-war punch line to the song is that Billy's fiancée, upon reading in a letter that her intended died a hero, throws the letter away. Musically, the song is pure top 40 pop, intended to appeal to the widest possible audience. Many found the song to be banal; however, the anti-war slant was potent enough for the Bo Donaldson and The Heywoods recording to be banned by some radio stations, despite its enormous popularity.

Following the end of the U.S. activity in Vietnam, there was a period in which very few songwriters even so much as mentioned the war; it was as though the experience had been so divisive and so painful for the nation that a cooling-off period was needed before issues concerning the aftermath of the war could be addressed. When they eventually began appearing, songs dealing with those issues tended to focus on the plight of Vietnam veterans and thus are detailed in the next chapter.

PRO-GOVERNMENT AND PLIGHT-OF-THE-SOLDIER SONGS

BACKGROUND

Just as the anti-war movement and anti-war musicians revived earlier songs to reflect the movement's views, those supporting American involvement in fighting Communism in Southeast Asia revived earlier patriotic material for performance at rallies and for recordings. Such well-known songs as "The Star-Spangled Banner" and Irving Berlin's "God Bless America" appeared on numerous albums. Since songs such as Berlin's classic are so well known, and since they are so nonspecific to the controversy surrounding the Vietnam Conflict, I will not discuss them in detail. I will focus on newly composed works, many of which both show support for U.S. government policy in Vietnam and comment directly on the anti-war movement. The reader will undoubtedly note that two songs in the public domain, "America the Beautiful" and "The Battle Hymn of the Republic," are quoted frequently, both words and music, in the talking songs supporting U.S. government policy in Southeast Asia. In addition to songs supporting U.S. involvement in the war, I will also deal with songs written in support of the soldiers themselves, as well as with songs describing the plight of the soldier, the returning veteran, and affected family members and loved ones. In many cases there is a close relationship between all of these types of songs: several serve multiple purposes with many songs about the plight of the soldier supporting official U.S. government policy. Some songs written with a focus on the plights of soldiers, however, question government policy; since the focus of these songs was on the soldiers themselves and on their stories, and not on an anti-war statement, I have included them in the present chapter rather than in the Anti-War Songs chapter.

It should be noted that many of the works in the present categories are of the country music genre. In particular, the reader should take note of the large number of country songs studied in this chapter that made the charts between August 1965 and April 1966: Vietnam was a most important topic for songwriters and record buyers in the country genre, particularly in this nine-month period. Country artists also frequently presented benefit concerts supporting the troops, led blood drives, and participated in other similar events. A notable example would be a performance at Vanderbilt University in late 1965 by Chet Atkins, Skeeter Davis, and Eddy Arnold (Artists Support U.S. Servicemen in Vietnam 1966). Since country music played such a prominent role in terms of the output of pro-government material throughout the war, it is important to note the tremendous growth enjoyed by the genre throughout the 1960s, a growth in popularity and distribution well documented by DiMaggio and colleagues (DiMaggio, Peterson, Esco 1972).

It was not just singers who got into the act, by the way. Chet Atkins's 1967 recording of "Battle Hymn of the Republic," which featured the easily identifiable, tasteful piano fills of fellow Nashville legend Floyd Cramer, and an orchestral backing, was not only popular on country radio stations, but the album on which it was featured, *Chet Atkins Picks the Best*, also won the 1967 Grammy Award for Best Instrumental Performance.

Due to the fact that "themes tend to be stated unambiguously" in country music (DiMaggio, Peterson, Esco 1972), especially when compared with other popular genres, the country songs relating to the Vietnam Conflict tend rather bluntly to echo similar themes throughout the period, and frequently incorporate stereotypes of various types of characters, from patriotic, brave soldiers, to obedient, understanding spouses, to those in the anti-war movement, frequently characterized as cowardly, long-haired, poorly dressed, hip-talking students influenced by liberal, atheistic, Communist-leaning college professors. The reader should also keep in mind that because most of the country songs dealing with this particular war do so in such a specific and stereotypical manner, many have seen the same fate as the highly topical, Vietnam-specific anti-war protest songs: they have not faired well outside of their historical context and remain, to a large extent, somewhat dusty documents of their time.

As one considers the predominance of country music in the pro-government category of Vietnam Conflict-related material and the predominance of folk revival protest music in the anti-war category, the reader should keep in mind a musical irony that is, in terms of our study, probably as curious as the irony that Muslims and Jews trace their heritage back to the same person, Abraham. The musical irony is that the two most diametrically opposed styles from a political standpoint, folk revival protest music and country music, both trace their heritage back to Anglo-American folk songs. It is well outside the scope of this study to go into the reasons for the emergence of these widely contrasting political stands in musical genres emerging from the same source, but is certainly worth consideration by the reader.

In contrast with the way in which newly penned patriotic songs led American troops into some of the earliest battles of past wars, rallying songs were relatively slow to come during the early stages of the Vietnam Conflict. Unlike anti-war songs, which started to appear as early as 1961, pro-government songs did not start appearing until U.S. ground troops were introduced in Southeast Asia in 1965. Indeed, throughout the era pro-government songs tended to be written in reaction to activity on the other side of the political spectrum. Because of this the reader will note that many of the songs studied in this chapter are both pro-government and very clearly against those active in the anti-war movement; however, it should be stressed that in no way are the songs studied in this chapter meant to be understood as pro-war statements. The lyrics of many of the songs make it clear that the songwriter or the main character of a story song find war dirty and distasteful; the pro-government songs typically support the U.S. role in Southeast Asia as a necessary evil. The lyrics frequently indicate that not to fight the spread of Communism and for the freedom of the South Vietnamese—the pro-government songwriters clearly place great stock in the domino theory and seem not to acknowledge the dictatorial nature of the South Vietnamese government nor the fact that even a great

American military hero such as Dwight D. Eisenhower knew that a majority of the Vietnamese wanted to be a unified people—would be a greater sin than the sin of warfare.

As the reader might expect, songs written during the conflict in support of the U.S. government's action quickly faded from view at the conclusion of the war. Even more expectedly, no new pro-Vietnam action songs gained any sort of prominence. Songs dealing with the plight of soldiers and their loved ones also became less numerous, at least right at the conclusion of the war. It was as if everyone in the United States of America wanted just to forget about the Vietnam Conflict and the way in which it had nearly torn the nation apart. Tom Paxton's "Born on the Fourth of July," which was based on the true story of Ron Kovic, the subject of an autobiographical book, also entitled *Born on the Fouth of July*, and the subject of the later Oliver Stone film of the same name, was a rare plight-of-the-Vietnam-veteran song of the late 1970s. Curiously, 1982 began a four-year period in which songwriters began to deal with the plight of veterans of the Vietnam Conflict, now largely in the rock genre, with such songs as "Still in Saigon," "Goodnight Saigon," "19," "Front Line," and "Born in the U.S.A." coming into prominence between 1982 and 1985.

THE SONGS

I wish to begin the study of pro-government and plight-of-the-soldier songs with mention of John Dolan's "God, Country and My Baby," although the song clearly tells the story, in first-person form, of a soldier on his way to fight in Europe. I do so because the famous 1961 hit for big-voiced pop singer Johnny Burnette introduced many of the themes common to later Vietnam-specific songs. The basic gist of this pop song, produced with fairly elaborate orchestration, is that the soldier feels he must fight for God, for the United States, and for the woman he leaves behind. Although he expresses a tinge of fear as he prepares to leave, the three-fold reasons for fighting instill in him a drive to successfully complete his task so that he might safely return home.

As we shall see, this "God, Country and My Baby" paradigm became the basis of numerous pro-government and plight-of-the-soldier songs. Perhaps due to nagging questions raised by the repression of Buddhists, the opulent lifestyles of the leaders of South Vietnam, the revolving door of governments in the country, changed on more than one occasion by violent coups, songwriters who followed the Dolan song's lead placed greater emphasis on reaffirming the U.S. government position that democracy was being preserved in South Vietnam: the domino theory stood on shaky ground if the domino that was being propped up were to be acknowledged as a repressive dictatorship.

Another early song not specifically written to deal with the Vietnam Conflict, but which achieved popularity in the early stages of the war, "The Cruel War," also known as "The Cruel War Is Raging," started out life very differently than "God, Country and My Baby." "The Cruel War" is an old Anglo-American folk song in which a young woman expresses her sense of impending loss as her lover, Johnny, prepares to march off to war. In the original folk song, the woman disguises herself as a man so as to fight alongside Johnny: if he is to die, then she will die along with him. Despite the title of the song, "The Cruel War" does not carry an overt anti-war or pro-peace message as much as it deals with the intense feelings of the young woman: so intense are these feelings for her love that she would willingly risk death to be with him. That war is "cruel" is a given—even the most vehement pro-government songs of the Vietnam era accept this as fact—

"The Cruel War" and later, newly composed songs which are not explicitly antiwar in nature either tacitly (in the case of this folk song), implicitly, or explicitly (in the case of Tom T. Hall's several compositions, for example) express the belief that the current war is inevitable and necessary.

"The Cruel War" rose to prominence in 1962 and 1963, while the more than 10,000 U.S. soldiers stationed in South Vietnam were still officially serving as advisors. Peter Yarrow, of the group Peter, Paul & Mary, reworked the traditional folk song, creating the three-voice arrangement recorded by his ensemble for their debut album *Peter, Paul, and Mary*, and issued the following year as a B-side to their single "Stewball." Yarrow also changed the form of the original song a bit, adding a tag phrase at the conclusion of each stanza, and truncating the original number of stanzas. The original tune could be, and probably frequently was, harmonized rather simply back when it was true folk material; Yarrow added some chromaticism to the tenor line giving the Peter, Paul & Mary version more harmonic richness than likely would have been found in, say, a nineteenth-century, spontaneous performance of the song. One other substantive change was made by Yarrow: he altered the melody somewhat by adding step-wise passing tones so as to include more than just the notes of the pentatonic scale used in the original. Readers wishing to study Peter Yarrow's alterations of the traditional folk song may wish to compare the 1962 Peter, Paul & Mary recording with any of the published versions of the original; one notated version is published in *Songs of Peace, Freedom, and Protest* 1970.

Peter, Paul & Mary made the charts several times with "The Cruel War": their 1962 debut album, which included the song, held the #1 spot on *Billboard*'s pop album charts for seven weeks, remaining on the charts for 185 weeks; the 45 rpm single "Stewball," of which "The Cruel War" was the B-side, reached #35 on the *Billboard* pop charts in late 1963; a new version of the song, in which Paul Stookey received cowriter credit, reached #52 on the *Billboard* pop charts in spring 1966 at a crucial point in the war in which U.S. ground troops had been in South Vietnam for more than a year and the sense of loss from combat casualties was hitting home. The Peter, Paul & Mary recordings are beautiful in their three-part arrangements and highly effective in conveying the young woman's sense of devotion to her lover, even in the face of possible death, when they are listened to on their own merit; however, if one knows the original song, with its many additional stanzas, the 1962 version, in particular, can seem a bit thin and sketchy.

Bob Dylan's 1963 composition "John Brown" was another folk revival song to deal with the plight of a soldier. Although Dylan wrote both words and music, the melody is based on the traditional folk tune "900 Miles." The lyrics for "John Brown" were published in *Broadside* #22 (March 1963) and the song was recorded by the composer, using the pseudonym Blind Boy Grunt for contractual reasons, for inclusion on the magazine's album *Broadside Ballads, Vol. 1.* Over the course of twelve stanzas, Dylan tells the story of a mother who proudly sends her son off to war, only to have him return a physically broken man: he is missing his hands, wears a metal brace around his waist, and has had his face shot off. As was the case with "The Cruel War," whatever anti-war subtext that exists can be found in the sheer horror of the soldier's (and his mother's) plight; however, Dylan's focus remains squarely on the story and not on making an *explicitly* anti-war message—hence the song's inclusion in this chapter.

The theme of the effect of war on man-woman relationships was taken up by songwriter Mark Charron in his 1964 "Billy and Sue," recorded by B. J. Thomas and The Triumphs in that year. The Thomas recording was issued twice on small labels in 1964, but with no commercial success. Possibly because the reality of war in Vietnam was beginning to set in—note that Charron's text does not specify that Billy has gone to fight in Vietnam; in fact there is nothing to suggest any particular locale for the war in which he is fighting—the single did make it onto *Billboard's* top 40 pop charts when it was reissued in the summer of 1966. With its echoes of 1950s pop in the background accompaniment, echoes of country music in the low-pitched, reverberation-laden electric guitar part, and western-style harmonica part, the record seems to be aimed at a 1964 audience for young country/pop performers. After the recording made the top 40, it was included on the 1966 album *The Very Best of B. J. Thomas*, a record with a cover photograph showing a soldier and young woman hugging with the implication that he is heading off for war. The photograph of a very clean-cut looking B. J. Thomas on the back cover confirms that this song was not aimed at the heavy-duty rock-and-roll crowd, but at a more middle-of-the-road young audience, with possibly more conservative views.

"Billy and Sue" echoes the familiar themes of the soldier having to go abroad to fight for the preservation of democracy and for the girl left behind, themes found in the songs of war for generations, but heard in a 1960s pop song first in "God, Country and My Baby." The gist of the story of "Billy and Sue" is that Billy has gone off to fight in an unnamed war and the letters he regularly receives from his girlfriend Sue keep pushing him on, helping him survive. Almost predictably, the letters cease for a period of time, causing the soldier to lose his will to fight, his will to survive. Just as Billy begins to lose all hope, he receives one final letter from Sue; however, this missive does not represent a return to Sue's regular schedule of letter writing: it is a "Dear John" letter. Having nothing more for which to live (in the "God, Country and My Baby" paradigm, the third part of the formula apparently significantly overbalances the first two in the Charron song), Billy allows himself to be shot and killed. Considering that the song dates from 1964, while U.S. personnel were still officially acting as "trainers" or "advisors," "Billy and Sue" makes a probably unintentional but surprisingly startling admission of the reality of the pre-1965 role of U.S. personnel in Southeast Asia: Billy was clearly not acting in an advisory role; he was in 1964 directly involved in the combat between South Vietnam and North Vietnam! As I stated earlier, Charron's lyrics do not specify just where Billy was stationed, but I suspect that listeners in 1964 would likely read "Vietnam" into the song. I further suspect that this aspect of the song played a role in the lack of commercial success for B. J. Thomas's first two releases of the record: here we had a single with a contemporary-sounding story line seemingly at odds with official government spin, aimed at a pop or country/pop music audience that most likely accepted the U.S. government's official policy statements. By 1966, after the introduction of U.S. ground troops in South Vietnam, Mark Charron's composition would be believable to B. J. Thomas's audience.

B. J. Thomas recorded another war-related Mark Charron composition, "Viet Nam," which is also found on the singer's *The Very Best of B. J. Thomas* album, despite the title, a collection essentially of pre-fame recordings. "Viet Nam" expresses the belief that the war should not be, but is necessary. The domino theory is espoused and anti-war protesters are said to be counterproductive to ending the war: peace can only come through victory over Communism. Thomas plays the role of a soldier about to be shipped off to Southeast Asia, addressing the song to his girlfriend. Musically, "Viet Nam" is a typical up tempo pop love song with Thomas backed by a rock band, a brass section, and full chorus; in many respects the setting is entirely inappropriate given what Thomas's character is about to experience. With its pomp and pep, though, the song does seem to owe a debt to the Johnny Burnette recording of "God, Country and My Baby."

According to sociologist Jens Lund in his article "Country Music Goes to War," Tom T. Hall's 1965 composition "Hello Vietnam" was the first of the country songs supporting U.S. involvement in Vietnam (Lund 1972a). The song combined the themes of patriotism, the need for immediate action to stem the tide of Communist expansion to secure the future of the United States of America, along with the age-old "girl left behind" motif, as the protagonist of the song says "goodbye" to his home and to his lover and "hello" to Vietnam. In combining these themes, Hall's composition was not only the first great country song supporting the government, but it started a trend: future country songs would commonly combine the same themes. By comparing Hall's song with the earlier "God, Country and My Baby," one can see the extent to which pro-government songwriters addressing the Vietnam Conflict would shift their focus squarely onto the domino theory and the preservation of a perceived democracy in South Vietnam. As a representative composition of a particular time and of a particular genre and political stance, "Hello Vietnam" has endured: it was featured in the 1987 Stanley Kubrick film *Full Metal Jacket*.

As claimed in an advertisement in the January 8, 1966, edition of *Billboard*, the song initially took off in Chicago and Milwaukee. After debuting in August 1965, Johnny Wright's recording was on the *Billboard* country charts for more than twenty weeks, three of them at the #1 position; the song never made it onto the pop charts. With regard to sales and chart activity, "Hello Vietnam" was a bit unusual, as many of the more popular country songs of this type either did relatively well on the pop charts, or at least made some kind of impact. Its vocal, with a pronounced twang, and instrumental style, using pedal steel guitar and Floyd Cramer-style piano fills, probably marked "Hello Vietnam" so much as a country song that audiences not consisting of hard core country fans found little with which they could relate.

While numerous writers and lecturers have dismissed the song as right-wing propaganda, few have actually detailed "Hello Vietnam" or placed it in a historical perspective in terms of how it was influenced by events and how it cast its shadow on later works in the country genre. Whether or not one agrees with the politics of the song, I find it particularly interesting to look at firsts, such as "Hello Vietnam," to try to see them in their historical context.

"Hello Vietnam" made its *Billboard* country chart debut in August 1965. It should be remembered that, while military advisors and some other personnel had been stationed in South Vietnam for some time, U.S. ground troops were first ordered to the nation in March of that year. The first major buildup in the U.S. presence after the initial deployment, however, roughly coincided with the time during which "Hello Vietnam" was on the charts. This very much was a timely record.

Unfortunately, hindsight suggests that the domino theory, so strongly supported by the protagonist of Hall's song, and taken up in Hall's subsequent work and by numerous other country songwriters, may have been the wrong theory for the wrong place at the wrong time: "Hello Vietnam" and similar songs that followed it have not aged particularly well because of this. And the song does not just mention the domino theory: it focuses on it. Unlike the earlier "God, Country and My Baby," which does not detail just how the conflict represents a necessity for preserving the American way of life— recall that the song does not really even specify in what conflict the protagonist is fighting—"Hello Vietnam" finds composer Tom T. Hall detailing the need for preserving democracy in South Vietnam. It is not surprising to me that the first prominent pro-government song of the Vietnam Conflict details the justification for the war: recall that the anti-war movement had been active already for several years before this song was released on vinyl and that one of the major points made by the topical anti-war songwriters was the lack of justification for U.S. involvement in the Southeast Asian country. Naturally, an early songwriter on the other side of the political spectrum would react and counter the points made by the likes of Malvina Reynolds, Tom Parrott, Phil Ochs, and Tom Paxton.

The picture of the soldier singing to his girl in Tom T. Hall's "Hello Vietnam" is that of a loyal young man, ready to do his duty without question. The protagonist is not painted as a warmonger: he acknowledges that war is dirty, should be avoided, but is in this case absolutely necessary. There certainly is nothing to suggest that this young man would be using illicit drugs, raping Vietnamese women, deliberately murdering women and children in order to make the kill statistics look "better," or that he would commit any of the other atrocities that later revelations would suggest that American soldiers had been committing throughout the course of the war. It is interesting to note that, eventually, several years later, some specifics about the darker side of U.S. activity in Southeast Asia and some questions about the advisability of this particular war would find their way even into the pro-government and plight-of-the-soldier repertoire. Questions about the war and revelations of the seamy side of the conflict would remain noticeably absent from the country songs of 1965 and 1966. While we shall see shortly that Hall contributed two other major pro-government country songs a bit later in the period, let us now turn our attention to a decidedly noncountry song, written in reaction to the most notorious anti-war song of 1965.

Fairly lengthy in terms of the rock songs of 1965 at three and one-half minutes, "The Dawn of Correction," written and performed by the vocal trio The Spokesmen (with instrumental accompaniment provided by studio musicians), answers P. F. Sloan's composition "Eve of Destruction." The song features a vocal style, instrumental backing, and form clearly reflecting Barry McGuire's recording of the Sloan song.

From its opening "The Dawn of Correction" exhibits characteristics of its inspiration, being nearly identical in tempo and instrumentation, including the prominent use of electric and acoustic guitars, drums, electric bass, electronic organ, and harmonica. I find the harmonica, in fact, to be better conceived, and more appropriate sounding than the brief harmonica breaks in the McGuire recording, due to their being more fully integrated into The Spokesmen's song. Unfortunately, composers or arrangers felt compelled to include a frankly annoying Jew's harp, which makes its first appearance near the start of the song and then continues throughout. This instrument is completely inexplicable in terms of "Eve of Destruction" and certainly out of character for the new folk-rock style. In fact, it may have been the newness of this sub genre of pop music that prompted the inclusion of this instrument, used in nineteenth- and twentieth-century American folk music, early twentieth-century American "hillbilly" music, and in European folk music for centuries: perhaps it was an attempt to make the recording more obviously "folk sounding." Jew's harp aside, other aspects of "The Dawn of Correction" clearly refer back to Barry McGuire's rendition of "Eve of Destruction," including the lead vocal, which finds the singer using the same kind of harsh, gravel-voiced style of delivery as had McGuire. The rhythmic and basic melodic feel, phrase structure of the song, as well as the insistent rhyme scheme, is also identical to the P. F. Sloan composition. With all of the musical similarities between "Eve of Destruction" and "The Dawn of Correction," and given the fact that the text of The Spokesmen's opus quotes snippets of the Sloan piece as it repudiates each point, the reader may even question how a copyright could have been obtained for "The Dawn of Correction." Musical form, phrase structure, and individual words can not be copyrighted—in fact chord progressions by themselves are not subject to copyright—and composers John Madera, David White, and Ray Gilmore carefully avoid the melody of "Eve of Destruction." Melody, and the way in which it interrelates with the harmonic and rhythmic scheme, is central to defining a song in terms of legal ownership. Even with their melodic avoidances and not-so-obvious melodic inversions found in the chorus sections, however, there is no question what song The Spokesmen are addressing.

While the stanzas of the song mimic "Eve of Destruction" both lyrically and musically, the brief, recurring chorus is worthy of note. Here, The Spokesmen end the first of two phrases with a beautiful deceptive cadence on the minor submediant (vi) in this major-key piece. At this cadence the voices come to rest on an open perfect fifth, creating a harmonic and voicing scheme reminiscent of some of the best of the 1964-period work of Beatles composers and singers John Lennon and Paul McCartney.

"The Dawn of Correction" has long been characterized as a "right-wing reaction" to "Eve of Destruction" (Holdship 1991, for example). Is it truly right wing, and just who were The Spokesmen's intended audience?

The lyrics of "The Dawn of Correction" leave no doubt that the United States must defend South Vietnam: The Spokesmen clearly believe in the validity of the domino theory. The Spokesmen also leave no uncertainty about the fact that they believe America must retain its cache of nuclear weapons to insure negotiations with the Soviets; however, they feel that no one in their right mind would actually push the button. Both of these beliefs might be considered conservative, but were fairly widespread in 1965, although many more Americans likely would have been considerably more uncomfortable with the growing nuclear arsenals of the United States and the Soviet Union had they been aware of some of the post-1965 revelations about just how close the two countries had been to all-out nuclear war during the Cuban Missile Crisis. "The Dawn of Correction" does not stop at championing these conservative causes. The Spokesmen also support the increased voter registration numbers accomplished by civil rights marches; the work of the United Nations, a long-time bane of the political right wing; the fact that some countries were breaking free of the chains of colonialism; and the work of the Peace Corps, designed in large part by Democratic Senator Hubert H. Humphrey, and established by the not-so-very-right-wing President John F. Kennedy. Politically, then, the song exhibits more balance than that with which it is generally credited. The basic gist of the song as I hear it is something like the following: "Look Mr. Sloan and Mr. McGuire, there are some points, Vietnam among them, on which America must not bend, and, while there are some problems in the United States, look at what we've accomplished through evolutionary, rather than revolutionary, means." I also find it most interesting that "The Dawn of Correction" takes P. F. Sloan to task for his tendency to complain without offering concrete suggestions for how to fix the problems he perceives. The tendency for the lyrics of the protest songs of the early and mid-1960s to be overly preachy was noted by a number of critics near the end of the decade and into the 1970s (see Denisoff 1972a and Marcus 1969, for example). The Spokesmen mention this tendency in song at the very same time writers of protest songs were "getting away with" their one-sided approach, in a way beating many popular music critics to the punch.

How was the work of The Spokesmen marketed and to whom? Certainly The Spokesmen's Decca album *The Dawn of Correction* presents the group members as clean cut, with short (by 1965 pop music standards) hair and stylish, but fairly conservative, clothes. The liner notes, which list this recording as being of the genre "Vocal Trio with Instrumental Accompaniment," and the listing of the studio musicians accompanying The Spokesmen are a throw back to late 1950s and pre-Beatles 1960s record jacket presentation techniques. Assuming that Decca's marketing department knew what it was doing, and there is nothing to suggest anything less, then the jacket's advertisement for contemporary albums by the label's other artists Rick Nelson, Brenda Lee, The Kingston Trio, and The Tarriers, acts which had made their first, and most serious sales impact some years before 1965, seems to be aimed not at teens, but rather at those possibly in their early to mid-twenties. Other material on the album, incidentally, includes some folk-inspired work of John Lennon and Paul McCartney, as well as light folk-rock versions of songs (but not explicitly anti-war songs!) by Phil Ochs ("There But for Fortune") and Bob Dylan ("It Ain't Me, Babe"), among others.

Consideration of radio airplay and a comparison of sales chart activity and jukebox activity for an answer song like "The Dawn of Correction" lead to some interesting insights. I have already noted that one method used by disc jockeys to play the very popular "Eve of Destruction" without appearing to take political sides was to "play it safe by allotting equal air time to 'The Dawn of Correction,' an 'answer song' intoned by the Spokesmen" (Music 1965). Some radio stations were even banning the McGuire disc outright, while keeping The Spokesmen's recording on the "okay" list (Battle of Ideologies Set to Music Meets Deejay Resistance Movement 1965). It appears, then, that radio airplay of "The Dawn of Correction" may have been enhanced by the controversy surrounding its near sound-alike, but distinctly anti-war cousin. Although the single reached only #36 on the *Billboard* top 100 pop charts, based on sales, it peaked at #22 in *Cash Box*, the magazine that ranked records based primarily on jukebox play.

The fact that one member of The Spokesmen (David White) had performed with the decidedly nonpolitical Danny & The Juniors of "At the Hop" fame does nothing to suggest that "Dawn of Correction" is anything less than an honest assessment of where the world stood in 1965 from a conservative to centralist viewpoint. Although it does have flaws, such as the ill-advised Jew's harp and the nagging references to the singer of "Eve of Destruction" as "boy," itself a quote from the P. F. Sloan number, this song goes beyond finger pointing, beyond "my country right or wrong" flag waving, and certainly beyond the litany of complaints of "Eve of Destruction," offering suggestions for alleviating some of the problems pointed out, but just ranted about, in Sloan's composition.

Sometimes given as "Tell Them What We're Fighting For," Tom T. Hall's "What We're Fighting For" continued the songwriter's approach begun with "Hello Vietnam": the song is written and sung from the perspective of a soldier communicating with those left back home. The song also combines the soldier's mixed emotions about war with a clear, patriotic resolve that government policy *vis-à-vis* Vietnam is absolutely right. In fact, it may have been the popularity of these two Hall compositions, among the first of the country genre to directly address the war, that prompted other songwriters in the genre to use them as sort of lyrical models.

Dave Dudley, a true country music legend best remembered for his plethora of hit songs about truck driving, recorded the best-known version of "What We're Fighting For." After the record's November 1965 chart debut, it reached #4 in *Billboard*'s country standings. Interestingly, like composer Tom T. Hall's earlier "Hello Vietnam" and his slightly later "Keep the Flag Flying," the Dudley disc made no impact on the pop charts. Unlike the other two songs, "What We're Fighting For" certainly had the potential of being a cross-over hit: Dudley's vocal style does not emphasize the tendencies of many of the hard-core country singers and the instrumental accompaniment makes little reference to hard-core country music, either in instrumentation or performance style.

The text of "What We're Fighting For" takes the form of a letter from a soldier stationed in South Vietnam to his mother. After expressing his love for his mother, the soldier turns his attention to something about which his mother has recently written him:

the fact that people back home are protesting the war and questioning for what the United States is fighting. The bulk of the song finds the soldier asking his mother to tell "them" that the troops, who do not necessarily like the war, are fighting for the freedom of the South Vietnamese people; if these people are allowed to fall under Communist rule, Communism will be creeping ever closer to our own shores. Composer Hall introduces a potentially racist subtext in this song, probably unintentionally. As he has the soldier telling his mother the justification for the war, the only concrete examples of past cases in which it has been important to fight for the freedom of Americans are Pearl Harbor and Korea. In the case of World War II, one might question why only the Japanese are mentioned as an enemy; why not Germany or Italy?

Another question raised by the soldier's communication with his mother in "What We're Fighting For" involves the implication that although his comrades do not necessarily agree with the war, they were all glad to do their patriotic duty and fight Communist aggression. All of the organized anti-war protests seem to come from civilians in the song. Even at this early stage in the war, there were fairly well publicized desertions and refusals to fight (the Fort Hood Three case, for example), and anti-Vietnam Conflict protests by Korean War and World War II veterans: anti-war activity by active or former military personnel is in a sense swept under the rug by Hall. In this way he started another trend in the pro-government songs of the country genre: future songs dealing with the anti-war movement would paint the movement as a "them" (the strictly civilian protesters) versus "us" (the military). In all fairness to Hall, it should be noted that organized anti-war activity by active duty military personnel and by veterans represented a small part of the peace movement in 1965: by 1969 and 1970 veterans would become much better organized and much more vocal in their opposition to the Vietnam Conflict.

One of the tried and true methods for taking advantage of the popularity of a song addressed from one clearly defined character to another used in the 1950s and early 1960s was to quickly write and record a companion song: a second song that would respond to the original hit. Charles Dennis provided lyrics for such a companion to Tom T. Hall's "What We're Fighting For." "I Told Them What You're Fighting For," which uses Hall's music and Dennis's newly written text (actually barely changed from that of the Hall song), finds the mother replying to her soldier son. The legendary Mother Maybelle Carter recorded this answer song, which barely made the country singles charts; by the mid-1960s, rarely did these answer songs that used exactly the same music as the original hit have much sales impact.

Making its country chart debut in mid-December 1965 in *Billboard*, Tom T. Hall's composition "Keep the Flag Flying" eventually reached #31 for singer Johnny Wright; the record was apparently a jukebox favorite, as it reached #9 on the *Cash Box* country charts. In fact, although there was a span of a few months between the debuts of the three Hall compositions, "Keep the Flag Flying," "What We're Fighting For," and "Hello Vietnam" were all on *Billboard*'s country charts at the end of 1965 and in the first several weeks of 1966.

"Keep the Flag Flying" is a moderate-tempo (96 beats per minute) country waltz in which the singer, a soldier, describes how his buddy was killed by a sniper's bullet. As his friend was dying, he made the singer promise to keep the flag of the United States flying not only at home, but also over Vietnam. The song's "punch line" comes at the end of the song when the soldier sings that he will have to write a very sad letter home tonight, telling his parents that one of their sons (his buddy, his brother) is dead. We shall see shortly that Loretta Lynn incorporated a similarly effective surprise ending in her "Dear Uncle Sam," a song that made its chart debut shortly after the run of popularity enjoyed by composer Tom T. Hall. One aspect of "Keep the Flag Flying" that represents a hardening of the political stance taken by Hall in his previous two Vietnam-related song is the insistence that the American flag remain flying over Vietnam. The listener does not get a clear sense that the reason for U.S. involvement is to protect the South Vietnamese: incredibly, they are almost irrelevant in this song—a most questionable move on the part of the composer, but one that would be taken up by other hard-line pro-government policy songwriters later in 1965 and into 1966.

Like Johnny Wright's recording of Hall's "Hello Vietnam," the singer's recording of "Keep the Flag Flying" is country to the core, using Floyd Cramer-inspired piano arpeggios (although they are played with a fairly imprecise rhythm), pedal steel guitar, and finding Wright using the same kind of country phrasing and dialect in his vocal. Although the singer would not make the charts with other Vietnam-related songs, he was to record others, including Harlan Howard's "You're Over There (And I'm Over Here)."

Johnny Wright's recording of the Harlan Howard opus represents just the first of several times that the songwriter would find his war-related music being recorded and sometimes making the country sales charts during the Vietnam era. In "You're Over There (And I'm Over Here)," Howard deals with a soldier who has one more year of service abroad to do. Although the lyrics provide not so much as a hint as to just where the soldier is stationed, the 1965 date of Johnny Wright's recording makes Vietnam seem the most likely place. The soldier is writing back home to his lover, expressing his fear that she will find someone else while he is gone. The focus is so much on this fear that this is one of the few country songs of the Vietnam era to be devoid of pro-government propaganda.

"You're Over There (And I'm Over Here)" is performed on Johnny Wright's album *Country Music Special* in a moderately quick, 120 beats per minute, country-swing style. In fact, aside from its instrumentation, with the use of the pedal steel guitar and electric rhythm guitar, the recording easily could have fit the country-western style of the Korean War era: harmonically, melodically, and lyrically, the song itself could have dated from the World War II era, so firmly is it rooted in the country-western tradition.

Considering the message of Dave McEnery's "It's for God, and Country, and You, Mom (That's Why I'm Fighting in Viet Nam)," evident from the title, and the easygoing country swing of Ernest Tubb's recording, it might seem surprising that the recording did not enjoy the same level of success of songs like "What We're Fighting For" and "Hello Vietnam." Tubb's single made its chart debut on January 1, 1966, right in the middle of the days of chart success for the Tom T. Hall numbers, but found itself on the *Billboard* country charts for a mere two weeks, reaching only #48. The problem may have been in the Decca Records artists and repertoire department's choice of long-time country star Ernest Tubb for the song: the 50-plus-year-old baritone simply does not sound believable as a young soldier writing home to his mother. Incidentally, Ernest Tubb and Redd Stewart's earlier "The Soldier's Last Letter" also saw a resurgence of popularity in the mid-1960s.

While a fairly large number of the songs studied in this book were by only moderately well-known or even obscure composers and performers, "Dear Uncle Sam" finds one of the best-known country performers of the 1960s and 1970s, Loretta Lynn, writing and singing a true, and very believable, masterpiece describing the plight of the woman left behind by her recently drafted man.

Following quickly on the heels of the three Tom T. Hall compositions, all of which were on *Billboard*'s country charts in January 1966, and Ernest Tubb's brief touch of the charts with "It's for God and Country and You, Mom," Lynn's "Dear Uncle Sam" made its debut on the *Billboard* country charts on February 5, 1966. The record enjoyed substantial success, remaining on the charts for fourteen weeks and reaching a high point of #4.

Lynn's first-person character is writing a letter to Uncle Sam saying that she needs her man far more than does the U.S. military. She goes on to indicate that she understands that her man must serve, but that she still misses him terribly. At that point a trumpet enters playing "Taps" within the chordal structure of the song. To the astute listener, the opening phrases of "Taps" are most remarkable as they make it clear that the harmonic structure of the entire song has been based on a harmonization of the usually unaccompanied bugle call. After the entrance of the trumpet, there is a delayed entrance of Loretta Lynn's spoken voice, which begins in the middle of a musical phrase and acknowledges her receipt of a telegram that begins with those dreaded words: "I regret to inform you." At that point, when it becomes clear that her man has died, the music suddenly breaks off. After the abrupt cutoff a mixed chorus enters singing a plagal cadence, the famous "Amen" cadence of Protestant hymnody, on the syllable "ah."

Lynn's "Dear Uncle Sam" effectively manipulates the listener's mood. By beginning with some predictable, almost banal lines with predictable pairings of rhyming words, she sets up the expectation that this will be a typical "oh, how I miss my man"-type song, and nothing more than that. Her use of the trumpet in what is otherwise a typically stringed-instrument-based country texture at first seems to be for the purpose of simply sounding "military." Lynn's deliberate delay in speaking what turns out to be the "punch line" of the song, the part that tugs on the listener's heart strings, heightens the impact of her words while also giving the listener time to develop some questions about the purpose of the trumpet and then to realize that the trumpet has been playing a bugle call associated with military funerals. In its move from banality to meaningfulness, through the use of contrasting instrumental and vocal texture, "Dear Uncle Sam" represents a higher level of sophistication than that previously heard in the pro-government and plight-of-the-soldier repertoire. The most commercially successful song of the type was shortly to follow.

SSgt. Barry Sadler's recording of "Ballad of the Green Berets" was the biggest-selling single and was included on one of the fastest-selling albums of all of the recordings made that overtly address the Vietnam Conflict. In fact, the single, which made its chart debut in February 1966 when nearly 200,000 U.S. soldiers were stationed in Southeast Asia, sold more than two million copies over the course of two months and Sadler's album *Ballads of the Green Berets* sold approximately one million copies in less than five weeks. The single held on to the top slot in the *Billboard* pop singles charts for five consecutive weeks and reached #2 on the magazine's country charts. For seven weeks the Sadler record was at #3 or higher on the *Cash Box* pop charts. The song's success on the country charts in particular is strong testimony to its general popularity: Sadler's recording contains no overt references to country-western style. As Denisoff 1990 chronicles, in terms of its chart activity and sales statistics, "Ballad of the Green Berets" was the most successful topical song of any type and related to any subject during the decade of the 1960s. Making these results even more remarkable is the fact that the pro-government and plight-of-the-soldier songs tended to be more popular with older audiences than the anti-war recordings of the same period; older audiences were significantly less likely to purchase 45 rpm singles than were the young. How was it that this song managed to achieve the commercial appeal that it did?

Written by the injured former Green Beret SSgt. Barry Sadler in 1965, "Ballad of the Green Berets" glorifies the sacrifices of the members of that elite U.S. fighting force, expressing a pride in service to the nation. What it does not do is glorify war or try to justify the Vietnam Conflict: the fight for freedom is briefly mentioned, but the pro-government slant of the song is considerably muted, especially compared with some of its contemporaries from the country genre. In fact, my casual conversations with a regional folk revival performer active in the mid-1960s indicate that it was not unheard of for a musician to sing "Ballad of the Green Berets" at the same performance as "Blowin' in the Wind" or "Where Have All the Flowers Gone?" The way in which Sadler crafted his tribute in part is responsible for the song's popularity: the text begins by looking at the characteristics, the achievements, and the sacrifices of the unnamed men of the force, moving into the sacrifice and final request of one Green Beret. By moving from the general to the specific, Sadler gives flesh to the soldier, allowing his audience better to identify not only with the individual character, but also with these troops as a whole.

Apparently the RCA Victor label recognized the huge potential of Sadler's song, as the composer's recording of "Ballad of the Green Berets" benefited from a sensitive orchestration by noted arranger Sid Bass and the backing of some of the label's talented session musicians. Bass's arrangement begins with a march-like snare drum and rhythm guitar, adding a sousaphone-like bass guitar providing primarily chord roots and fifths for the second stanza. The rest of the song continues the pattern of adding one new element, including male chorus, organ, and a brass and saxophone section, for each new stanza. Unlike some of the earlier pro-government and plight-of-the-soldier recordings from the country genre, some of which were marred by such things as out-of-tune backing vocals and occasionally indifferent orchestrations, the Sid Bass arrangement of "Ballad of the Green Berets" manages to support SSgt. Sadler's vocal coherently and in a way that artfully counterpoints Sadler's plain, folksy vocal style. The build to a climax as the tale turns its focus to one fallen Green Beret's mailed request to his wife that their young son someday wear the coveted head covering symbolizing the rare military achievement heightens the emotional impact of the record.

I mentioned earlier that SSgt. Sadler's recording of "Ballad of the Green Berets" achieved great commercial success on the country charts, despite the generic pop nature of the recording. The recording also received heavy rotation on country radio stations. A standard practice, probably more common in the country genre than elsewhere in the pop music of the 1960s, was for record labels to try to cash in on the success of a rival's release by issuing a recording on their own label by one of their contracted artists. Given its success on the country charts, it is probably no surprise that "Ballad of the Green Berets" was covered by a fair number of country artists; it almost seemed to become a mandatory album track for a time. Among the more notable covers is Autry Inman's, which is more easily identifiable as country music, from the singer's twangy vocal style to his freer (less military) treatment of rhythm. The inclusion of Chet Atkins-inspired electric guitar figures also defines the Inman recording as one aimed more closely at a country music audience.

The history of former Green Beret SSgt. Barry Sadler's military career, his writing of "Ballad of the Green Berets," and his attempts to have the song recorded are detailed by Denisoff 1990. Denisoff also details the way in which Robin Moore's name came to be attached to the song and the media blitz created by RCA Victor to help turn Sadler's recording into the major hit that it was. I highly recommend the article for readers looking for additional details on the song, its genesis, and its place in American society in 1966.

After the success of "Ballad of the Green Berets," RCA Victor issued an album by SSgt. Barry Sadler, *Ballads of the Green Berets*. Containing eleven other Sadler-composed numbers, including "Letter from Vietnam," "Saigon," and "The Soldier Has Come Home," the album largely continues the single's theme of illuminating the courage and sacrifices of the U.S. troops serving in Vietnam. The lyrics exude a kind of melancholy throughout the album as Sadler details the hell that the still-young war was. Perhaps recognizing that a country audience might be the most likely group of consumers willing to purchase an entire album of Vietnam-specific, plight-of-the-soldier material, the collection finds Sadler backed in a western swing style on several numbers and with more overt instrumental references to country guitar style throughout than had been found on the song "Ballad of the Green Berets."

Given the huge commercial success of "Ballad of the Green Berets," and given the fact that the end of the song found a fallen member of that group of soldiers asking his wife to make sure that their young son someday wore the green beret, perhaps it was inevitable that songwriters would craft a response from the wife to the fallen soldier. Peggy Barsella and Frank Catana did just that, writing "He Wore the Green Beret." The song, recorded by Nancy Ames, barely made it onto the *Billboard* pop charts, reaching a zenith of #89 shortly after the Sadler song had created its sensation.

In "He Wore the Green Beret," Barsella and Catana address the courage of the fallen Green Beret and acknowledge the terrible conditions faced by the U.S. troops fighting in Southeast Asia and the questions surrounding our nation's involvement in the conflict. In the end they conclude that freedom must be won for the Vietnamese. The conclusion of the song finds the widow of Barry Sadler's soldier giving assurances that, indeed, some day their boy will become a Green Beret.

Unfortunately, "He Wore the Green Beret" and the Nancy Ames recording of the song come off as too much of a crass cash-in attempt. The recording reverts to an irrelevant early-1950s pop style, while stealing Sid Bass's brass and reed fanfares from Barry Sadler's recording of "Ballad of the Green Berets." The song very liberally mirrors the melody and harmonic progression of Woody Guthrie's "This Land Is Your Land," while giving no credit to folk legend. As if that were not enough, the unnamed arranger uses the clichéd technique of modulation to build up the intensity from stanza to stanza to excess, to the extent that five different key areas are used. To top it all off, Ames's sobbing through the lyrics and her full-throated delivery tend to come off not as a believable expression of loss and then fortitude, but rather as cheap sensationalism. If part of the charm of the Sadler record was due to the singer's everyman type of voice and the vocal restraint he showed, then a large part of the problem with "He Wore the Green Beret" is that Ames pulls out all the stops in an attempt to sell the song, nearly reaching the level of excess found in some vaudeville performers of the early twentieth century; it is very nearly a self parody. The record's brief flirtation with the charts suggests that perhaps the public too felt that the protagonist of SSgt. Barry Sadler's song deserved a more sensitive response.

While most of the talking blues-form pieces relating to the Vietnam Conflict were written in opposition to the war, some composers who supported the U.S. presence in Southeast Asia also turned to the form. Kris Kristofferson's "Vietnam Blues" is such a work. The best-known recording of the song, that of Dave Dudley, reached #12 on the *Billboard* country singles charts, after making a March 12, 1966, debut. The piece was covered by a number of other country artists, most notably Autry Inman.

Kristofferson's "Vietnam Blues" finds the singer taking the role of a serviceman on leave in Washington, D.C. The character encounters strange-looking anti-war protesters (sporting long hair, beards, and weird clothing) who raise his ire by attempting to get him to sign a petition supporting Ho Chi Minh. The soldier expresses his anger that these civilians, who are so willing to let a soldier die for them, are also so quick to condemn that same soldier. The soldier states that he too does not relish the prospect of dying, but affirms that he will not crawl away from his responsibilities to keep American safe from Communism like these protesters are all too quick to do. The rap has a feeling of authenticity: one could easily imagine a soldier who strongly believed in the domino theory and who was about to be sent to Southeast Asia sharing the feelings of Kristofferson's character. Incidentally, the left-wing writer Irwin Silber attempted to debunk Kristofferson's stereotypical portrayal of those in the peace movement in his *Sing Out!* article "A Study in Illusion and Reality" (Silber 1967c).

Both the Dave Dudley and the Autry Inman recordings of "Vietnam Blues" feature bouncy, fairly quick accompaniments of acoustic and electric guitars and drums. Dudley takes a slightly freer rhythmic approach in his rap than does Inman; Dudley's freedom is more typical of the genre. Dudley's vocal timbre, phrasing, and the aforementioned rhythmic rubato combine to enhance the authenticity of Kristofferson's text, while Inman's suffers from an overwrought attempt to sound nasty.

Following his highly successful "Ballad of the Green Berets" by a couple of months, SSgt. Barry Sadler's recording of "The 'A' Team" made it to #28 on the *Billboard* pop charts and #46 during a brief stay on the magazine's country charts in spring 1966. The song was cowritten by Sadler, Leonard Whitcup, and Phyllis Fairbanks and finds the singer again detailing the courage of the Green Berets. Unlike Sadler's earlier mega-hit, "The 'A' Team" does not tug on the listener's emotions: it is a more ordinary song, like most of those on the singer/songwriter's earlier album *Ballads of the Green Berets* (the album appeared between the two singles and does not include the present song). Probably most notable about the song is its pleasant western swing style and its timeliness: about a month before the record's April 1966 chart debut, the Green Berets had been very much in the news when Communist forces captured a U.S. Special Forces (Green Beret) camp in the A Shau Valley. The success of what is essential a country-styled number in the pop charts was probably due in part to the public's response to the tragedy of the loss of those American Green Berets killed and captured in the March raid and Sadler's name recognition based on his earlier "Ballad of the Green Berets."

Had Cindy Walker's song "Distant Drums" been released on vinyl at the time of its recording by Jim Reeves in 1963 or 1964, the resulting single certainly would have been considered prophetic by the time of the late 1964 Gulf of Tonkin Resolution or at least when U.S. ground troops were introduced in Vietnam in spring 1965. As it happened Reeves's producer, Nashville legend Chet Atkins, decided that the song "was not particularly relevant to the American public's experiences of the moment" (Liner notes to *Distant Drums* 1966). Atkins left the song in the can and Reeves died in a tragic plane crash in July 1964. Chet Atkins' decision can be called into question, given the benefit of hindsight; however, the reader should keep in mind that U.S. Secretary of Defense Robert McNamara had predicted in November 1963 that troop levels soon would be dropping with 1,000 of the then 15,000 military advisors due to be sent home within a matter of months. Apparently Atkins believed the official U.S. government line on the conflict, which deprived Cindy Walker the chance to be seen as the musical prophet she was.

The delay did no harm to sales; when "Distant Drums" finally was released in April 1966, it went to the top of *Billboard's* country charts, remaining at #1 for four weeks. *Cash Box* listed the single at #1 in its country charts for three consecutive weeks; it remained on the *Cash Box* country charts for an unusually long nineteen weeks. Although the record did not mirror the extent of its country chart success in the pop genre, it was one of Jim Reeves's relatively rare forays onto the pop charts, hitting #45 in *Billboard*.

Walker's lyrics indicate that there are hints of war in the air. Musically, this is played out in the Reeves recording by the use of a military side drum to introduce the first stanza and the use of bugles in the second. Rare among the country songs released in 1965 and 1966, "Distant Drums" entirely deals with the relationship between a man and a woman at a time in which war is on the horizon; there are no pro-government statements in the song, probably due to the fact that it had been written several years before. The singer, taking the role of a young man apparently of draft age or recently drafted, suggests that he may have to go to war soon, and asks the woman to whom the song is addressed to marry him so that they might share as much time as possible. Singer Reeves and producer Atkins use a moderate tempo of approximately 98 beats per minute, appropriate for the understated ballad. Reeves's baritone voice is quiet and reassuring sounding, probably more appropriate for the nation's mood in 1964 than at the time of the record's release when some 200,000 U.S. troops were in the heat of battle in Vietnam. In spite of this apparent contradiction, however, the record generally was more successful on the country charts than nearly all of the plethora of records that made a point of expressing support for U.S. military action in Southeast Asia; the song has a more universal, nonpolitically motivated appeal.

Not only is "Distant Drums" a classic song of love during wartime, and not only was Jim Reeves's performance perfectly fitted to the material, several details in the instrumental arrangement also help make the record a true classic. The use of a quarter-note, two eighth-note side drum ostinato throughout the recording provides for a thematic coherence, mirroring the song's title, and the use of vibraphone, while unusual in a country song, is inspired. The strings play in a mariachi-style harmony, typical of some of the early western swing of Texas, Reeves's home state. Roy Orbison's 1965 recording of the song was also quite effective, but enjoyed none of the commercial success enjoyed posthumously by Jim Reeves.

Labeled by its composer Harlan Howard "the greatest song I have ever written" (Law Grooves Patriotic Disk 1966, 50), "The Minute Men (Are Turning in Their Graves)" continued the trend in country music of reiterating the domino theory and equating protest of the war with cowardice and even treason; Howard makes a significantly stronger statement here than he did in "You're Over There (And I'm Over Here)." In this song the composer unequivocally states that the peace protesters wish to live as slaves to Communism and are treasonous in their refusal to defend the United States. No longer is the Vietnam Conflict a war to help the South Vietnamese defend themselves as in the 1965 pro-government country songs; now the North Vietnamese seem to be on North America's shores. While the lyrics of the chorus were clearly meant to stir up patriotic emotions in the listener by painting George Washington and Thomas Jefferson as potential supporters of the Vietnam Conflict, one must question whether Washington and Jefferson truly would have supported U.S. intervention in a small, poor country in southeastern Asia; in order for Howard's text to have any validity, these leaders would have had to have seen America's international role as a nation builder through the use of military might.

Stonewall Jackson's recording of "The Minute Men (Are Turning in Their Graves)" reached #24 on the *Billboard* country singles charts after its April 30, 1966, debut. The recording includes the by-then fairly standard technique of using military-style snare drum rudiments in the chorus and features a heavily "country" style in terms of instrumentation (featuring the banjo), rhythmic feel, and vocal inflection. The song's structure also owes much to folk and traditional country music. After a four-measure banjo-based introduction, the song basically alternates stanza and chorus, with each stanza having an *aa'ab* phrase structure, while the choruses have a *cdcd* structure. Curiously, the *a'* and *b* phrases of each stanza are five measures long (four measures of vocal plus one measure of instrumental fill); all of the other phrases are of a more standard four-measure length. Another country composer, Mel Tillis, would take up Harlan Howard's use of musical phrases with an unusual, odd number of measures, asymmetrically balancing vocal and instrumental fill a year later in his "Ruby, Don't Take Your Love to Town."

Harlan Howard's use of phrases of varying lengths must cause us to re-examine right-wing writer Gary Allen's musical expert Dr. Crow, quoted earlier (Allen 1969). In musical theory it is customary to speak of rhythm on various levels of structure, from the lengths of individual pitches and silences, to those involving larger-scale relationships between measures, phrases, and sections of compositions. It seems curious that Dr. Crow limited his criticism of mixed meters to measure-by-measure relationships, which he claims to find in unidentified left-wing rock songs, but apparently found nothing untoward in the present, *documented* use of hyper-metrical mixture of quadruple and quintuple units in ultra-right-wing material.

While it was more common during the course of the Vietnam Conflict for left-wing writers to parody pro-government songs by substituting leftist lyrics for the original, the reverse sometimes took place. *Sing Out!* 16/2 (April-May 1966) contained PFC Robert Hall's lyrics for "The Universal Pacifist," a reaction to Buffy Sainte-Marie's anti-war song "The Universal Soldier." Private Hall's lyrics tell the other side of the story, blaming those who do not wholly support all-out war efforts for making more frequent wars necessary.

Categorizing songs as I have done in this book makes for some interesting, and possibly jarring, juxtapositions. Such is the case with obscure Chicago blues musician Johnny Shines's "So Cold in Vietnam," a mid-1966 song that deals strictly with the plight of a soldier, from the soldier's perspective, but seems neither to support the war effort nor provide any commentary against it. Due to Shines's obscurity as a recording artist—he released only a couple of handfuls of single records during his career—and the fact that "So Cold in Vietnam" sold few copies, the song probably impacted the lives of few people. The song does provide us with an example, however, of how a composer could use the setting of a soldier stationed in Vietnam in order to create topical-sounding music totally divorced from the politics of Vietnam as an issue.

Accompanied by himself on guitar and by an electric bassist and drummer, Shines sings a twelve-bar blues-form lament about how much he misses his woman back home. His main concern, stated at the beginning and taken up in one of the later stanzas, is the lack of communication he is experiencing: he seems not to receive any mail from his loved one. Since I have only been able to hear the song on a Testament Records album compiling some of Johnny Shines's earlier blues sides, and not the original release, it is problematic to have to comment on the recording quality. The quality of the reissue is fairly poor, sounding like a low-budget recording done in an inadequate studio: it is not up to the standards of even 1966 technology. Assuming that this is representative of the original release, the producer did not seem to have placed a great deal of emphasis on the understandability of the text, or perhaps was working in a situation in which Shines could not be given the kind of audio treatment a big-name recording artist would have received. It is almost as if the *timbre* of the voice is more important than the literal meaning of the text. This stands in sharp contrast to the J. B. Lenoir blues discussed in the previous chapter. Although the Lenoir piece also suffers from less-than-stellar recording, Lenoir's producer made certain to bring the singer's voice forward enough in the mix to make his stinging remarks easy to hear and to understand: the importance of his message, as compared with Shines's more innocuous lament about the temperature in South Vietnam and the lack of communication with his loved one, dictated as much. It's not that "So Cold in Vietnam" is a bad song, or a terrible recording, it just suffers from the same audio problems so many of the obscure blues sides exhibit, and it dwells on so little related to the war that the singer could have been practically anywhere and in any situation away from his woman, and the song would require only a few modest text changes. We shall see a slightly later example of a work in the blues genre even further removed from the reality of the war in the form of Big Amos Patton's "Going to Vietnam."

Allen Peltier's "Day for Decision," recorded by country disc jockey Johnny Seay (given as Johnny Sea on the original release) in mid-1966, is one of the more unusual pro-government works of the Vietnam era, particularly in its use of a wide spectrum of musical material in support of its message. The song was a *Billboard* top 40 pop hit, and reached #14 on the *Billboard* country singles charts and #8 in the *Cash Box* country charts.

The gist of the text of "Day for Decision" is that a cancer of lack of confidence and lack of pride in country is causing a lack of patriotism in America and is playing into the hands of America's enemies and the enemies of a democratic way of life. Ernie Freeman's musical arrangement is what sets "Day for Decision" apart from the plethora of other talking songs supporting the U.S. role in Vietnam. Freeman includes ominous minor key music behind Seay's talk about patriotism, underscoring the importance for regaining a sense of patriotic pride to help insure the health of democracy. Freeman also none too subtly incorporates pentatonic, generically oriental-sounding music behind the text concerning how America's enemies are exploiting the current lack of patriotism in our land. Overlooking that the "oriental" music sounds as though it is played on the Japanese koto (!), the reference is clearly to the North Vietnamese and Viet Cong. "Day for Decision" quotes the music of "Onward Christian Soldiers" and finishes with a huge choral finale on "America, the Beautiful," backed by strings, percussion, and a small brass section. The use of "Onward Christian Soldiers" brings to mind the questions raised in 1967 by Tom Paxton in "The Cardinal": if the Vietnam Conflict is a holy war of Christianity, what is the American Jewish soldier to do, and what of the Christian Viet Cong soldier? Presumably, Seay's predominantly White, Christian, country audience did not raise such questions. Johnny Seay's *Day for Decision* album also contained "God Bless America," "When Johnny Comes Marching Home," "The Star Spangled Banner," and other patriotic and inspirational songs; the title track is the only song fully to benefit from the arranger's text painting. Throughout "Day for Decision," speaker Seay modulates his voice with sensitivity to the meaning of the text.

The traditional country, bluegrass duo of Charlie Moore and Bill Napier released a thoroughly Vietnam-related album, *Country Music Goes to Viet Nam*, in 1966. The collection was one of the most obviously patriotically packaged of all the albums supporting the U.S. presence in Southeast Asia. The red, white, and blue bedecked album cover includes prominently displayed logos of the U.S. Army, Navy, Air Force, and Marines, along with the captions "Moore and Napier Sing Red Blooded Songs" and "War Songs for the True American." While a few of the songs are retreads of earlier, non-Vietnam specific material, four of the new songs stand out: Jimmie Osborne's "God Please Protect America," and the Moore and Napier compositions "Is This War a Useless War," "I'll be Home," and "Have I Come Home to Die?"

Jimmie Osborne's "God Please Protect America" finds Moore and Napier accompanied by guitars, fiddle, mandolin, drums played by brushes, and acoustic bass in a Bill Monroe-influenced, bright country/bluegrass swing. The song is a plea to God to protect the United States in this time of trouble and a reminder to the citizens that only through prayer can our troops march on to victory. Osborne does not attempt to justify the war; since the Vietnam Conflict is a fact, he is most concerned with bringing the troops safely home through victory with the help of the Almighty.

In a fascinating combination of perhaps coincidental melodic and harmonic references, Moore and Napier's "Is This War a Useless War?" bears resemblance to both Woody Guthrie's "This Land Is Your Land" and Felice and Boudleaux Bryant's "Bye, Bye Love," as popularized by the Everly Brothers. The lyrics of the song justify the Vietnam Conflict as a battle for freedom and for liberty; however, the freedom and liberty of the Vietnamese, or even the South Vietnamese, is never mentioned. According to Moore and Napier, we are fighting in Vietnam entirely for the sake of our children here in America. All in all the song, like Harlan Howard's earlier "The Minute Men (Are Turning in Their Graves)," tends to sound very self-serving for this very reason. In terms of its instrumentation and vocal harmony, "Is This War a Useless War?" fits the mold of the Moore and Napier performance of "God Please Protect America."

"I'll Be Home," another Bill Monroe-influenced bluegrass number written by Moore and Napier, concerns a letter written by a soldier serving in Vietnam to his sweetheart back home. The soldier writes his assurances that he will return home someday, once the war has ended; however, because the letter is unfinished and unsigned, the woman knows he is dead.

The theme of a woman's betrayal of her fiancé while he is serving in Vietnam, and the disastrous results upon the soldier's return, defines Charlie Moore and Bill Napier's bluegrass song "Have I Come Home To Die?" The song, in a gentle waltz time, is written from the standpoint of the soldier. In the first several stanzas, he tells of the hardships he has been through in Vietnam and then asks the title question in the choruses. The final stanza finds the soldier returning and having his beloved's new man finding the soldier and the woman holding each other. A single bullet ends the soldier's life. Several other songwriters were to take up the very general theme of the returning veteran finding that a relationship has soured after his return, as we shall see.

In four songs, all specifically written around the theme of the Vietnam Conflict, Charlie Moore and Bill Napier cover quite a bit of ground, in fact covering all of the topics on which Vietnam-oriented country songwriters placed their focus for a decade, from a prayer for victory, to a somewhat self-serving justification for the war, to a story of a woman who discovers via an unfinished letter that her sweetheart has died, to a story of betrayal, reconciliation, and murder. Despite the familiar themes and despite the patriotic packaging, Moore and Napier's Vietnam-focused bluegrass album seems to have made little commercial impact; perhaps the bluegrass style was a bit too "old school" to generate sales. Two individual songs by pop singers, Pat Boone's "Wish You Were Here, Buddy" and Bobby Vinton's "Coming Home Soldier," fared somewhat better with the general public in late 1966.

After making an October 1966 debut, Pat Boone's "Wish You Were Here, Buddy," eventually made it to #49 on the *Billboard* pop singles chart and #51 on the *Cash Box* pop singles charts. The song was also contained on Boone's album *Wish You Were Here, Buddy*, a package dedicated to the U.S. soldiers fighting in Vietnam; however, the album enjoyed none of the single's modest commercial success: it failed to enter *Billboard*'s top 100 pop album chart. *All Music Guide* critic Arthur Rowe sums up the song perhaps better than any of the numerous commentators who have dealt with "Wish You Were Here, Buddy," when he writes that the song's "flippant sarcasm, directed at those very 'buddies' who inspired the song, is stingingly effective and makes its points better than a well-crafted oratory every could" (Rowe 2000). According to Rowe the song "was not a warmonger's anthem, as some chose to interpret it, but rather an expression of [Boone's] moral support for those Americans who were doing their country's bidding and yet endured the double-distilled disregard, even the contempt, of a number of protesters and demonstrators back home" (Rowe 2000). As Arthur Rowe suggests, a number of other critics, such as DiMaggio and colleagues 1972, and Lund 1972a, focused on the more negative, militaristic aspects of the song.

Pat Boone takes the role of a soldier writing home to his longhaired, draft protesting high school buddy. He pokes fun at his buddy's lack of bravery and appearance, sarcastically telling his friend that he wishes he were with him in Vietnam. Buoyed by a brisk tempo and the smirk in Boone's voice, the sarcasm of the song is tempered by a touch of humor. One of the best examples is found in Boone's comparison of his buddy's bravery with that of famed boxer Cassius Clay, later known as Muhammad Ali, who sought conscientious objector status, despite his success at obliterating opponents in the ring. Even when the Boone character indicates that he will come looking for his buddy when he returns, presumably to throw a punch or two, or three, the delight, the nasty little laugh in the singer's voice helps the listener better to understand the soldier's feelings, and perhaps suggests that he may be content to cut his buddy verbally; however, if I were Boone's buddy, I don't know that I would wait around to find out. Although "Wish You Were Here, Buddy" enjoyed somewhat disappointing sales, compared with Pat Boone's hits of the late 1950s and early 1960s, the song is significant because of the singer/songwriter's use of this sarcastic humor; humor of any sort was a rarity in pro-government and plight-of-the-soldier songs: most were, like some of the anti-war songs, preachy. The humor, biting and politically one sided though it may be, opens the song up to listeners who may not agree with the support for U.S. involvement in Vietnam but who can appreciate a well-constructed verbal putdown, much as the humor of Phil Ochs's "Draft Dodger Rag" can be appreciated on its own level, apart from the political leanings of the song. It is not just the humor that allows Boone to effectively score points. The fact that the soldier's anger is expressed on a first-person level and is well reflected in the singer's use of his voice contribute, making "Wish You Were Here, Buddy" part of a continuum of first-person songs of barely controllable, nearly physically manifested outbursts of anger; Dave Dudley's reading of Kris Kristofferson's "Vietnam Blues" was the earliest such song and Merle Haggard's "The Fightin' Side of Me" was to score a knockout on the country charts in 1970.

Gene Allen and pop singer Bobby Vinton coauthored Vinton's hit "Coming Home Soldier." The Vinton single reached #11 on the *Billboard* pop charts after debuting in November 1966. Taking the form of a slow, 12/8 meter, late-1950s-style ballad with elaborate and overly pompous orchestration by record producer Robert Mersey, the song finds Vinton taking the role of a common, undecorated foot soldier who is on his way home. While Vinton pays a passing nod to his work overseas (the locale in which he has been serving is not disclosed) to keep America free, any political message is muted; the focus is on the happiness the soldier feels to be returning to his beloved. While the single may have sold well, the unbridled optimism of Vinton's returning veteran is marred somewhat by being set to a tune that sounds suspiciously like a remake of Vinton's 1964 hit "Mr. Lonely"; however, Vinton includes a nice piece of text painting is his use of the unexpected bIII (C major) chord on the words "Purple Heart" in this A major song.

Backed by a military snare drum cadence throughout and by a chorus, lush-sounding string arrangement, and majestic horns, Illinois Senator Everett McKinley Dirksen read the text of Charles O. Wood (a pseudonym for well-known news broadcaster Charles Osgood) and John Cacavas's "Gallant Men." While Vietnam is not mentioned, the intent of the record, which won the 1967 Grammy Award as Best Spoken Word Recording, is to pay tribute not just to the gallant soldiers of America's past, but also to those serving in the then-current war. That this is probably the most artfully orchestrated song studied in this book should come as no surprise as John Cacavas was one of the top television and film composer/arrangers active in the 1960s and 1970s. The record is largely successful in delivering a message of support for America's troops past and present, although Sen. Dirksen allows a touch of a singsong quality to invade his reading of an entirely solemn text.

"Gallant Men" enjoyed some sales success, reaching #29 on the *Billboard* pop charts, #58 on the same magazine's country charts (despite the fact that musically there is absolutely nothing resembling country music about this record), and the patriotic Dirksen album *Gallant Men* hit #16 on the *Billboard* pop album charts. As one might reasonably expect, based on the types of establishments in which the machines tended to be located, the single seemed to be a record that one would buy, rather than listen to on a jukebox: it only went to #43 during its short stay on the *Cash Box* pop charts.

Although he became more widely known as a country singer in the 1970s, Mel Tillis was in 1967 one of the better-known, well-respected songwriters in the genre. His great contribution to the Vietnam-related repertoire was "Ruby, Don't Take Your Love to Town." Of all of the songs detailing the plight of returning veterans of the war, the Tillis song undoubtedly enjoyed the most interesting recording history, a history of evolution from a hit country song to a top 40-oriented hybrid of country, folk, and pop.

The text of "Ruby, Don't Take Your Love to Town" is written from the viewpoint of a Vietnam veteran. We learn from his pleas to his wife that he was paralyzed in the war, and realizes that he is unable to satisfy Ruby's sexual needs. The veteran pleads with Ruby to love him despite his infirmity and to refrain from looking for sexual satisfaction from another man. When we learn that Ruby has left him to go out on the town, the paralyzed man expresses his anger by suggesting that he would kill Ruby if he were able.

A number of commentators have focused on one particular and very minor part of Tillis's text as an indication that by 1967 the war in Vietnam no longer was so overwhelmingly supported by country music audiences as it once had been. At one point the veteran asks that his wife not blame him for his paralysis, since it was not he that started the war in Southeast Asia. In referring to the war as "crazy," the veteran hints that perhaps he had been paralyzed in a war in which he served out of a sense of patriotic duty, but which he did not support. Ray Pratt, in his article "'There Must Be Some Way Outta Here!': The Vietnam War in American Popular Music," makes one of the strongest assertions concerning the subtext of Tillis's lyrics, writing that song indicates that "the war was now a big mistake in the minds of those called on to fight it." Pratt takes this subtext to a more general level by stating that the popularity of "Ruby, Don't Take Your Love to Town" among country music fans suggests "one could see that the social base of support [for the war] was collapsing among the very groups listening to it, who constituted both an important sector of pro-administration support and also a substantial source of troops for the war" (Pratt 1998, 172). While Pratt's assertion may seem a bit hyperbolical, the implication of a veteran's description of the war does seem to represent at least a chink in the armor of unquestioned pro-government support in country songs; by 1971, Garman, Hoffman, and Barr's country song "Congratulations" would turn the war's effect on one veteran into a fully anti-war statement. Despite the apparent break with the "party line," Tillis's focus remains squarely on the plight of the veteran and not on the political questions surrounding the war itself.

Making its *Billboard* country chart debut on April 1, 1967, Johnny Darrell's recording of "Ruby, Don't Take Your Love to Town" hit #7 on the *Cash Box* country charts during its fourteen week run. The record was on the *Billboard* country singles charts for fifteen weeks, topping out at #9. The Darrell recording features a fairly simple arrangement with the singer backed by acoustic guitars, acoustic bass, and lightly played drums. In contrast to Mel Tillis's own 1967 recording, which includes additional instrumentalists, a chorus, and an overbearing soprano obbligato, the accompaniment never overwhelms the singer. Darrell delivers a straightforward country-styled vocal performance, with level dynamics and a near steady state inflection: he seems to be intent on allowing the Tillis text tell the story without his own interpretation influencing the listener.

As I have mentioned previously, it was quite common in the 1960s, especially in the country genre, for commercial success to breed cover versions of songs. The legendary country singer George Jones also recorded "Ruby, Don't Take Your Love to Town." Jones's rendition, at a fairly quick tempo of 164 beats per minute (a bit faster than the Johnny Darrell recording), stays closely in line with the style of Darrell's hit version. The singer's tone and accent, as well as the prominent use of pedal steel guitar in the accompaniment texture, hold to the country tradition. And Jones, like Darrell, allows the song itself to tell the story; there is very little change in the texture from stanza to stanza and very little in the way of vocal inflection to set off particular lines of the text. Waylon Jennings's recording, also of 1967, similarly retains Darrell's straightforward approach.

Bobby Goldsboro's 1967 recording of "Ruby, Don't Take Your Love to Town," included on his colorfully titled album *The Romantic, Wacky, Soulful, Rockin', Country, Bobby Goldsboro*, represents the first significant interpretive shift for the song. As implied by his album's title, Goldsboro's rendition combines folk, country, and pop influences. Instrumentally, this can be seen in the slightly greater emphasis on the drums, the use of an electronic organ with a Leslie speaker system, and the retention of acoustic rhythm guitar. His tempo is a bit brisker than that of the country performers who tackled the song, clocking in at 184 beats per minute; however, like Johnny Darrell and George Jones, Goldsboro keeps a four-beat feel. Goldsboro's arranger throws in a couple of tricks not found in the strictly country performances: the song modulates upward in key for the third stanza and the instrumentalists incorporate rhythmic breaks to accompany Goldsboro singing about Ruby slamming the door as she goes out on the town. Rockabilly legend Carl Perkins would cover the song near the end of the war, in 1973.

The best-known recording of Tillis's "Ruby, Don't Take Your Love to Town," however, was by The First Edition, featuring lead singer Kenny Rogers. The First Edition single reached #6 on the *Billboard* pop charts and #39 on *Billboard*'s country charts following a June 1969 debut. On the *Cash Box* pop singles charts it reached a high of #7 during its fourteen-week run. The group's *First Edition '69* album art—"Ruby, Don't Take Your Love to Town" was included on the package—presents them as a twenty-something, hip, popish ensemble. For all appearances the album seems to be aimed at an audience that had grown up several years before with the folk revival. At the time artists such as The Byrds, Michael Nesmith of The Monkees, Rick Nelson with his Stone Canyon Band, and others were successfully combining pop, rock, and country music into a sort of hybrid style. The First Edition's rendition of "Ruby, Don't Take

Your Love to Town" combines these styles, with a healthy dose of folk revival thrown into the mix.

The first distinctive feature of The First Edition recording is the drum introduction; the earlier country versions had all included acoustic guitar-based introductions to set the tonality. The first pitched instrument the listener hears is Kenny Rogers's unaccompanied lead vocal on the first phrase, inflected with the throaty, under-supported (with air) crackle that would become one of his most distinctive trademarks at the height of his popularity in the late 1970s. Although some would later see this as an easily parodied affectation, Rogers was still so unrecognized in 1969 that the sound seems to be specifically tailored to his character in "Ruby, Don't Take Your Love to Town." As such, it conveys a sense of frustration, resignation, and physical weakness perfect for the role, but exhibited by none of the song's earlier interpreters.

It is not just Rogers's vocal styling that sets The First Edition's recording of the Tillis song apart. Unlike each of the earlier versions, the current performance puts the song into a two-beat feel. Although the perceived tempo is 106 beats per minute, each of those beats contains twice the information found in the four-beat versions of the song, making The First Edition's performance over 10 percent faster than Bobby Goldsboro's. The First Edition's use of space, too, contrasts with the earlier versions of the song.

The phrase structure of "Ruby, Don't Take Your Love to Town" was altered not only by The First Edition, but also by the earlier country performers. In Mel Tillis's own recording of his song, the first, third, and fourth stanzas all begin with four seven-measure phrases, each consisting of four measures of vocal material followed by a three-measure instrumental fill. The second stanza, which features a melodic variant, begins with a five-measure phrase: four measures of vocal material plus one instrumental measure; the next three phrases in the second stanza are each seven measures in length. (The variant in the second stanza gives the song an unusual *abaa* form.) The subsequent 1967 and 1968 versions by Johnny Darrell, George Jones, Bobby Goldsboro, and Waylon Jennings standardize the phrase structure in each stanza to four measures of voice followed by a one-measure instrumental fill. In doing so these performers negate the sense of space apparently intended by composer Tillis; however, Tillis's use of space tends to be distracting, primarily due to the meandering harmonies during the instrumental fills. The First Edition expands these standardized units, unusual as they are, to nine-measure phrases: a four-measure vocal line followed by five instrumental measures. (Incidentally, Carl Perkins, in his 1973 rockabilly influenced recording, reverts back to Tillis's original phrase structure, although Perkins reverses the order of the second and third stanzas giving the song a more conventional *aaba* form.) The additional time allotted to the instrumental break by The First Edition might have been necessitated by the break-neck tempo, but it works structurally in full support of Tillis's text. The space between the first vocal phrase, in which the singer notices that Ruby is dressed up and made up, and the second, in which he asks Ruby if she is planning on going out, gives the impression that the protagonist briefly contemplates the situation, concludes that perhaps Ruby is planning an infidelity, and then asks her about it. Throughout the song, other pairings of vocal phrases (but certainly not all) similarly enjoy the benefit of this space. While Tillis did not convincingly pull this off, The First Edition do—despite the fact that its instrumental breaks are proportionally longer—by minimizing emphasis on Tillis's original, floating harmonic scheme.

The First Edition's version of the song also features some country-style finger picking in the acoustic guitar parts and generally more variety in the instrumental fills, probably out of necessity created by the expansion of the fills discussed above. Another notable feature, probably borrowed from Bobby Goldsboro's approach, is the emphasis on percussion as Rogers sings that he knows that Ruby has indeed stepped out on him because he has heard the door slam; however, The First Edition greatly expand the percussive emphasis to incorporate auxiliary percussion instruments such as shakers and guiro. (Carl Perkins retains this heavy emphasis on percussion in this section of his later recording.) The First Edition's changes to the song extend right up to the last vocal line, here a spoken plea invoking the name of The Almighty—it is sung in the earlier recorded versions—in one final attempt to get Ruby to turn around. In the hands of The First Edition, Mel Tillis's "Ruby, Don't Take Your Love to Town" becomes one of the best-constructed documents of the plight of a one particular Vietnam veteran, and a catchy record that still manages to sound both fresh and relevant.

Big Amos Patton's 1967 blues "Going to Vietnam" came out of the Memphis, Tennessee, "downhome blues" scene that virtually guaranteed a radio boycott in key northern urban centers, according to Colin Escot's liner notes for the compilation album *Hi Records: The Blues Sessions* (Escot 1988).   The regionally based airplay discrimination described by Escot is curious given that Patton's style is so closely aligned with that of electric Chicago-style blues. Although the song probably affected very few people, I briefly wish to discuss the text and setting as it provides some insight into one of the problems with some of the Vietnam-related material I encountered when studying some of the songs covered in this book. Patton takes on the persona of a man who has just been called up for service. Addressing his lover, he tells her to stay in touch and expresses concern that she will remain true to him while he is gone; however, the text is so general that he could be going anywhere. There is nothing about the music to suggest Vietnam, no overt text painting, no musical portrayals of machine guns, and so forth. And the moderately fast shuffle feel to the song does not seem to support the degree of concern Patton expresses in his text. In the case of "Going to Vietnam," the site of the war seems just to be a convenient, perhaps topical-sounding place for a fairly general blues in which the lyrical focus is on the singer's concern that his woman might soon be stepping out.

The text of a letter to his son, a pipe rack complete with pipes, a can for tobacco, an expensive-looking desk pen, and a barometer (which reads "fair") with a small globe on top all adorn a desk on the cover of Victor Lundberg's album *An Open Letter*. The 1967 album features Robert Thompson's spoken composition "An Open Letter to My Teenage Son." Lundberg also released the piece as a single with commercial success: the record reached #10 on the *Billboard* pop charts and #6 on the *Cash Box* pop charts. The commercial success enjoyed by the single release of the song is all the more impressive when one considers that the probable audience for the piece (parents of teenagers) generally was more prone to purchase albums than singles.

As suggested by its title, the text of "An Open Letter to My Teenage Son" takes the form of a letter. The Victor Lundberg recording finds the speaker, a resonant baritone, backed by a well-produced orchestral and choral arrangement of "The Battle Hymn of the Republic." The music is very much in the background of the recording's mix: the focus is clearly on Lundberg. Treated with a bit of artificial-sounding reverberation, Lundberg tells his son his feelings on such subjects as the wearing of long hair and beards, the existence of God, the immorality of war, and the necessity for serving one's country in the military.

"An Open Letter to My Teenage Son" has been dismissed by a number of writers with virtually no serious discussion of the text. I wish to mention at least a couple of points as food for thought. At times the father's letter sounds reasonable: he often explains why he feels a particular way on an issue. He does, however, place much of the onus on his son, to the extent that the son must be willing to fight for his rights in order to earn them. This raises some serious questions with regards to the Bill of Rights and the father's understanding of the concept of grace (he claims to be deeply religious). That the Bill of Rights guarantees some basic rights for citizens no matter what their political views seems to be at odds with the father's expressed beliefs. The father's ultimate statement, that his son will be disowned if he burns his draft card, seems also to be contradictory to the penultimate statement that, no matter what the son does, the father will continue to love him. In my view the issues raised by the father's feelings, beliefs, and how he would act on them are much more interesting to consider and debate than the texts of some of the more "cut and dried" songs of the era. Yes, it could be dismissed as right-wing propaganda, but it is a well-constructed recording with few flaws pertaining to how it tries to rally people—parents, most likely as I imagine that few teenagers of the time were much taken by the record—to a particular viewpoint.

Thompson's text includes an interesting dig at attempts to legislate morality. While no explanation is given, the statement could refer to anti-discriminatory legislation that was being passed at the time of the piece's recording, or, for that matter, any of a number of pieces of progressive legislation. The text also includes some rather uncomfortable sexism near the piece's conclusion, and the crescendo into the line in which the father tells his son that he should burn his birth certificate if the young man chooses to burn his draft card is almost menacing in tone.

Incidentally, that globe pictured on the front of Victor Lundberg's album is turned so as to simultaneously show North America and southeastern Asia, including the two Vietnams. The reader might recall that Pete Seeger's *Young vs. Old* album pictured a similar globe. Based on the political view espoused by Lundberg throughout the collection, it appears that the globe is meant to show just how close the United States and Vietnam are, in support of the domino theory (recall that the implication of the photo on *Young vs. Old* was the connectedness of the two lands).

Another spoken piece by Robert Thompson, "My Buddy Carl," found its way onto the B-side of "An Open Letter to My Teenage Son." Here, Lundberg takes on the persona of a White U.S. Army officer serving in Vietnam. He tells the listener that recently enemy snipers killed two of his men and that he found that one of the soldiers had a letter to his congressman on his person. The officer proceeds to read the letter. The young soldier tells his congressman about the heroism of his buddy Carl who died the day before. He goes on to question congressional attempts to legislate morality, mentioning that he is against anti-discrimination legislation. The young man asks the congressman, though, to introduce a bill to integrate heaven so that when he dies, he might be with his buddy Carl, who was White. While the text, again backed by an orchestral and choral quotation of "The Battle Hymn of the Republic," might tug at the emotions, the clear implication that laws against racial discrimination must be bad because this young soldier, clearly African American, says so, seems to be deeply flawed: the soldier's beliefs about the appropriateness of anti-discriminatory legislation was undoubtedly a minority view among Blacks at the time.

Victor Lundberg's *An Open Letter* album contains one other notable Vietnam-related work, this cowritten by Robert Thompson and Sid Feller. "In the Slime of Vietnam" finds Thompson's text backed by original music by Feller. Speaker Lundberg, this time taking the role of the universal soldier sending a letter home, tells of all the faces he has and roles that are played by those serving in the military. In many respects this is a pro-soldier, pro-government-action version of Buffy Sainte-Marie's "The Universal Soldier."

Sid Feller's music and orchestral arrangement give strong support and rival the writing of John Cacavas ("Gallant Men") for quality among the works studied in this book. The works of Robert Thompson would not be the last musical pieces to use the form of a letter to express a pro-government message.

Taking the form of four letters, the first from Bud, a soldier, to his parent; the second from Tommy, an anti-war activist hippie, to his parents; the third from Bud's sergeant to Bud's parents; and the fourth from Tommy to his parents, "The Ballad of Two Brothers" highlights the contrast between young people involved in the anti-war movement and those serving in Vietnam, and culminates in the transformation of Tommy, the hippie, into Tommy the army private. Bob Braddock, Curly Putnam, and Bill Killen wrote the song, which was recorded by Autry Inman in 1968.

Autry Inman's three-and-one-half-minute reading of this talking song features an evolving musical setting that paints the picture of the four letters in vivid, although stereotypical detail. Military snare drums and a sparse acoustic rhythm guitar accompany the first letter, in which the soldier, Bud, expresses his resolve in fighting for the freedom of the South Vietnamese. He feels compelled to fight to help insure that the next battle for freedom over tyranny is not closer to home. Bud obviously believes in the domino theory: the theory that if one Asian nation fell to Communism, others would surely follow. This theory had, of course, been used to support American involvement in Southeast Asia in the first place and became one of the justifications for the expansion of the conflict into Laos and Cambodia in 1968 and 1969, around the time of "The Ballad of Two Brothers." The songwriters carefully have Bud stressing what he can give throughout his narrative: the last line of his letter, in fact, expresses his selfless concern with brother Tommy.

While the listener might feel sympathetic toward Bud, the use of an overabundance of ultra-hip expressions by Tommy, such as "groovy," "out of sight," and "my bag," in the second letter paints him as nothing more than a caricature, with whom probably no one hearing the song in 1968 could *seriously* relate. The musical setting, featuring appropriately heavy rock drumming, electric bass guitar, and electric lead guitar, supports the view of Tommy as a hippie. Among the more interesting parts of Tommy's letter is his claim that his college economics professor convinced him that the Vietnamese would be just as well off under Communism as under a democratic capitalistic system. As college campuses became prime focal points for pro-peace activity from 1967 and 1968 on, a typical tactic of the right wing was to claim that liberal professors were transforming formerly patriotic American youth into pawns of the Communists. Clearly, the right wing could hold up as evidence the early and ongoing activism of high-profile professors like Noam Chomsky, Staughton Lynd, Franz Schurmann, and Howard Zinn. Although evidence concerning the development of political belief systems overwhelmingly suggests that college professors could not possibly be brainwashing students as right-wing writers (and songwriters) suggested—many other factors would have to have been at work for much longer periods of time—this accusation against intellectuals would become commonplace in right-wing articles and editorials, and would be the entire focus of one later right-wing song, "Mister Professor." Tommy also questions how his parents can support Bud's murdering of the North Vietnamese and Viet Cong and ends his letter with a not-so-subtle request for an extra $50. This request clearly paints Tommy as a person concerned solely with self, in sharp contrast with Bud. I find it unfortunate that the songwriters give the listener virtually nothing to flesh out Tommy as a young man whose ideas might be debated seriously. The impact of his later conversion from hippie Tommy Smith to Private Tommy Smith suffers as a result of his having been initially presented as a caricature.

The brief third letter, written by Bud's sergeant to inform the young man's parents of their son's bravery in meeting death in combat, features the entrance of a chorus, wordlessly vocalizing "The Battle Hymn of the Republic." As "The Ballad of Two Brothers" moves into a new letter from Tommy, we learn that the death of his brother has greatly affected the former hippie, anti-war protester: his musical theme begins to slow, the choral vocalizing now replaces the electric guitar, and the drums segue from a rock beat into a military cadence. All of this takes place as he signs his last letter as Private Tommy Smith.

While brother Tommy seems to have been easily impressionable to the point of not being believable as a character—having been quickly and easily converted to Communism and the hippie lifestyle by his economics professor and just as quickly and easily having been converted to a soldier serving in Vietnam—"The Ballad of Two Brothers" was sufficiently potent in its emotional appeal to make the charts. The Autry Inman recording reached #48 during its seven weeks on *Billboard*'s pop charts, #51 in the final week of its five-week run on the *Cash Box* pop singles charts, and #14 during its fifteen-week appearance on the *Billboard* country charts.

Perhaps the most popular song among servicemen at the zenith of the Vietnam Conflict (Greenway 1970, 853), Jimmy Webb's composition "Galveston" reached #4 on the *Billboard* pop singles charts, was #1 on *Billboard*'s country charts for three weeks and #1 on *Cash Box's* country charts for two weeks for Glen Campbell in spring 1969. Campbell, who was frequently to collaborate with Webb following the success of "Galveston," recorded the definitive version of the song. Given its great commercial success, and given the fact that it was so popular pop song among servicemen stationed in South Vietnam, it is curious that the recording, with its full orchestration, country pop style, and fairly upbeat tempo, finds musical setting and text somewhat at odds.

Campbell sings of a young woman he left behind in his hometown of Galveston, Texas and of the fact that he misses both her and the city a great deal. While much of the text describes the aspects of Galveston missed by the singer, he does make two references to the war: (1) setting the stage for his reason for leaving Galveston by mentioning that he is cleaning his gun and (2) referring to his fear of dying. The references are so fleeting that they simply serve to set the stage for the song: the main focus is on the city and the woman left behind. In fact, the singer could have been forced to leave for some other reason and the record probably still could have been successful, such a strong melodic hook and top 40 production does it have. That having been said, it should be noted that the cover art for the album Galveston also places the singer in the military: Campbell appears to be in uniform and we see his beloved in silhouette with the ocean in the background.

Perhaps the full orchestration by Al De Lory, the moderately fast tempo (120 beats per minute), heavy use of syncopation in the melodic line, the major tonality, and the fact that the singer is placed in Vietnam without much dwelling on Southeast Asia all serve to deliver an unspoken sense of optimism. If so, and I do believe that the song can be understood that way, perhaps we have the explanation for its immense popularity among the soldiers serving overseas.

As was the case with numerous Jimmy Webb compositions in the late 1960s and early 1970s, the catchy rhythms and easy-to-remember melodic hooks made them popular material for middle-of-road and easy listening acts, including purely instrumental ensembles; "Galveston" was also recorded by such musical acts as The Ventures, Lawrence Welk, and Roger Williams.

The B-side of his #7 hit single "Atlantis," Donovan's 1969 "To Susan on the West Coast Waiting" reached #35 on the *Billboard* pop charts. The song takes the form of a sung letter by an American soldier stationed in Vietnam, Rudy, to his lover, Susan, waiting for him back home. The song features Donovan singing in a weepy, child-like style, supported by a chirpy female chorus and minimal instrumentation. This, combined with a singsong, simplistic rhyme scheme clearly finds Donovan attempting to paint Rudy as a child in a man's body, unable to cope with his situation in Vietnam. If the song were placed in a cinematic context, perhaps supporting the portrayal of a young soldier unable to cope with the emotions associated with war, the song could have a chilling effect. As it is, devoid of any extra-musical support, the convergence of all of the above features causes the song to teeter on the edge of pretentiousness.

As drug use among young people became more and more widespread, as the war in Southeast Asia continued to expand beyond the borders of the Vietnams, and as clashes between protesters and police at home became increasingly violent in 1969, Merle Haggard recorded his classic "Okie from Muskogee." The record immediately struck a chord among country music audiences tired of the drug abuse and tired of seeing their nation put down and ripped apart from within. After making its *Billboard* country chart debut in October 1969, the song went to the #1 position, holding onto it for four of its sixteen weeks on the charts. In their 1972 study of country music, DiMaggio and colleagues. find that super-patriotic country songs tend to be remembered far longer than "equally popular love songs of the same year" (DiMaggio, Peterson, and Esco 1972, 44). Such is the case with the Haggard number as it remains widely known thirty years after its introduction.

Haggard's magnum opus features a folk-like tune and middle-of-the-road country stylings that can appeal to a wide segment of the audience for country music. While the composer deals with a number of issues, the simple, unquestioned pride he expresses for his country and the fact that residents of Muskogee, Oklahoma, do not burn their draft cards are the two most relevant themes insofar as this study goes. While the veracity of Haggard's assertion about the state of the draft resistance movement in Oklahoma might be open to question, many commentators seemed to give Merle Haggard a wider berth than some of the other pro-government country singer/songwriters. As John Grissim wrote of the sentiments Haggard expresses in "Okie from Muskogee," "OK, he's doing his thing and, anyway, he's only saying what all those people believe" (Grissim 1970).

Merle Haggard's "The Fightin' Side of Me," an only slightly later song, expresses a similar patriotism, in many respects echoing the sentiments (and some of the same phrases) of the 1965-66 pro-government songs of Harlan Howard, Tom T. Hall, and others. There are important but subtle differences between the approaches of the professional songwriters of 1965 and the singer/songwriter of 1969-70. After somewhat offhandedly acknowledging the right of anti-war protesters to rally for their cause, Haggard makes a strong point that it is *specifically* the protesters' running down of the nation that brings out his fighting side. By expressing his patriotism in this way, Haggard displays a bit more of an even-handed approach than some of his predecessors who failed even to acknowledge the activists' right of dissent. Haggard also increases the appeal of his song by bringing what was frequently more of an abstract expression of patriotism and anger at the protest movement in the earlier days of the conflict, to a personal level: America's detractors rile him personally. Taking the emotions to this personal level potentially allows those who agree with Merle Haggard's assessment of the peace movement to find a strong, appealing affirmation in "The Fightin' Side of Me," and allow those who may not agree with him totally to appreciate the song as Haggard's personal testament to his emotions, as suggested by the earlier quote from Grissim. The commercial appeal of the song eclipsed most of the earlier, more emotionally abstract songs of patriotism: "The Fightin' Side of Me" spent three weeks at #1 on *Billboard*'s country singles charts during its fourteen-week run. Haggard achieved a positive response even from some of the established old guard of country music: Ernest Tubb was quoted as saying that "The Fightin' Side of Me" expresses "the way all of us really feel" (Lund 1972b, 89). Haggard's performances of his songs received hugely positive response from his concert audiences, as evidenced by his live recordings of both "Okie from Muskogee" and "The Fightin' Side of Me."

The popularity of Merle Haggard's songs of "my country, right or wrong" may have been a result in part of his down-to-earth, "Bakersfield Sound" performance style, which combined the least dated aspects of traditional country and western music with the instrumental and vocal influences of rock and roll. (The rock influence is most easily detected in "The Fightin' Side of Me.") Another part of the equation was probably the simple fact that the war, and the protest movement against it, had been going on for such a long time, and the wounds felt across the country had by 1970 been opened so deeply that the more right-wing country fans had become more staunch in their support of the government position on Vietnam. Certainly Haggard's more personal expression of his emotions played a role too. That Merle Haggard represented a voice with a deeply personal, folk-like sincerity at the end of the 1960s finds support in the fact that he was profiled by Alice Foster 1970 in the normally left-leaning magazine *Sing Out!* at the time of his chart triumphs with "Okie from Muskogee" and "The Fightin' Side of Me."

While not achieving the degree of chart success or having the lasting impact of the contemporary songs of Merle Haggard, Bill Anderson's recording of his collaboration with Bob Talbert, "Where Have All Our Heroes Gone," did well enough to make it to #6 in *Billboard*'s country charts and #8 in the *Cash Box* country charts. Anderson blasts draft card burners, Communist folk singers who refuse to pay taxes—obviously aimed at Joan Baez, who is, however, not mentioned by name—and agitators who start riots. He claims that what America needs more than anything else are heroes for young people to emulate. Among the heroes he mentions are Charles Lindberg, John Wayne, Dwight D. Eisenhower, John F. Kennedy, the astronauts, Joe DiMaggio, Winston Churchill, Jesse Owens, and Martin Luther King, Jr. It was Anderson's inclusion of the last two, in particular, that caused some radio censorship of the single: a report in *Billboard* indicated that some country radio stations bleeped out parts of the song (presumably the names of the Black heroes and possibly former President Kennedy) (Hero-Hitting Tune Stirring Rhubarb 1970). Presumably only the male children of Bill Anderson's 1970 needed heroes, as the likes of Amelia Earhart, Wilma Rudolph, Eleanor Roosevelt, Babe Zaharias, and other women are noticeably missing.

While "Where Have All Our Heroes Gone?" is certainly upbeat, with a tempo of just over 120 beats per minute, and features a catchy melodic hook in which a mixed chorus asks the title question, it represents more the old wave of country music than the works of Merle Haggard. Bill Anderson's anti-anti-war song uses pedal steel guitar and is less rock-and-roll oriented, with a lighter rhythmic feel than Haggard's works.

Ray Stevens's 1970 composition "America, Communicate with Me" finds the singer/songwriter/producer walking the middle ground between the anti-war demonstrators of the left and the "America, Love It or Leave It" conservatives of the right. In fact, the recording begins with two very brief snippets of highly polarized person-in-the-street interviews. When the interview subjects are asked what they think of all the demonstrations sweeping America—recall that this was the year of perhaps the most violent campus demonstrations against the war, with the killing of four students at Kent State University taking place in May 1970—a female respondent states that the demonstrators should either love America or leave it, while a male subject replies that perhaps the demonstrators have a valid point and that America needs to change direction in order to survive.

A dramatic chord following the interview segments introduces the song proper. Stevens sings that he is sick of demonstrations declaring the war in Vietnam to be wrong, but that he is also sick of the pro-war rhetoric and the lies and half-truths of the nation's politicians. The singer indicates that no situation is as cut and dried, or black and white as what the opposing sides in the Vietnam controversy would have one believe. Stevens believes that communication is what is missing in the country. He sings that only through open communication can Americans work through these troubling times. Stevens refers to three bullets that fell leaders who are very much needed today, presumably referring to John F. Kennedy, Robert Kennedy, and Rev. Martin Luther King, Jr., although Stevens does not name the leaders.

Perhaps one of the more under-appreciated popular musicians of the 1960s and 1970s, Ray Stevens not only wrote and sang the song, but also produced the recording and wrote the arrangements. He utilizes a full orchestra and chorus, in addition to the standard instruments of a rock band in this purely top-40-oriented pop song. The arrangement includes a number of creative touches that provide support for Stevens's text. The musician incorporates a few gospel-style references, from the use of a heavy vibrato in the Hammond organ, to some of the singer's improvisatory phrase endings. "America, Communicate with Me" contains several tempo changes throughout and a quote of "Auld Lang Syne" in the chorus sections. Stevens also has a solo trombone quote a phrase from "The Star-Spangled Banner" in the song's chorus sections, immediately following his plea for Americans to start communicating.

"America, Communicate with Me" was released by Ray Stevens as a single and enjoyed very modest success, reaching #45 on the *Billboard* pop charts, but making it all the way to #38 on the jukebox-heavy *Cash Box* charts. The album *Ray Stevens...Unreal!!!*, which included the song, did not make it onto *Billboard*'s or *Cash Box*'s charts.

Although sometimes cited as a famous example of ultra right-wing propaganda from the Vietnam Conflict era, Harlan Howard's "Mister Professor" enjoyed relatively little sales success, reaching only #71 on the *Billboard* country charts and disappearing after a scant two weeks, and little jukebox success, never even appearing on *Cash Box*'s country charts, making the Leroy Van Dyke recording more of an obscurity than what one might commonly be led to believe.

Composer Harlan Howard blames liberal college professors for leading students into atheism, draft avoidance, arson, and protest marches, and he asks "Mister Professor" to stick with teaching the facts and to keep his liberal thoughts and his attempts to turn students into pacifistic cowards out of the classroom. I would suggest that Harlan Howard's apparent mistrust of the well educated comes directly from the facts of the demography of audiences for his style of music. According to DiMaggio and colleagues, "analysis of data from the Pulse survey of ten cities...shows quite clearly that country music fans are less well-educated than the average radio listener" (DiMaggio, Peterson, Esco 1972, 49). Howard's character, in fact, mentions that the professor is more educated than he; he seems to feel that what the professor has in terms of greater education, he lacks in patriotism, courage, and common sense. The title character in "Mister Professor" seems to have been inspired by well-publicized anti-war activity of some influential intellectuals. In his book *The Politics of Protest*, Jerome Skolnick writes, "professors like Noam Chomsky, Staughton Lynd, Franz Schurmann, and Howard Zinn not only disseminated information but also helped define the movement's consciousness." He further acknowledges the "centrality of college students to the growth of anti-war sentiment" (Skolnick 1969, 59-60). The potential problem with putting these two facts together, as mentioned in the discussion of "The Ballad of Two Brothers," is that studies of learning and the development of belief systems suggest that it would be very difficult for a college professor to brainwash a student in the manner suggested by "Mister Professor." While progressive college educators may have had some influence over the willingness of students to participate in political rallies against the Vietnam Conflict, the seeds of college students' pro-peace activism had to have been planted and nurtured much earlier in their lives. In some respects then, "Mister Professor" adds two plus two and comes up with a sum of twenty-two.

In addition to Leroy Van Dyke's rendition of "Mister Professor," the composer, Harlan Howard, issued the song on his 1971 *To the Silent Majority with Love* album. The composer's performance is in a quick waltz tempo in a traditional country style that features tasty fiddle answers to the vocal phrases. Both recordings, in fact, are pleasant enough traditional country performances; however, the extremism and incongruence of the text and the musically dated style of the song apparently was too much for all but the most hard-nosed hard-core country fans: the Leroy Van Dyke single was one of the least commercially successful anti-protester records of the Vietnam era, infamous though it may be.

According to one jukebox programmer, Pat Swartz of Modern Specialty in Madison, Wisconsin, "if we programmed this record in jukebox locations along State Street near the campus here our windows would probably be busted" (Paige 1971, 36). Indeed, "The Battle Hymn of Lt. Calley" caused fights in bars in the mid-western United States, was played only sporadically on the radio due to extreme levels of controversy it aroused, was banned from armed forces radio, and sold more than a quarter-million copies in a week. There were reports from across the country that stores could not keep up with the demand for the record and that customers were going to record stores specifically for this song. The recording by Terry Nelson and C Company reached #49 on *Billboard*'s country charts, #37 on the magazine's pop charts, and #26 on the *Cash Box* country charts, while another recording, by John Deer Co., reached #47 on the *Cash Box* country charts, failing to make the *Billboard* charts; all of this despite the fact that both recordings were issued practically simultaneously on relatively small, independent labels lacking the distribution capabilities of the majors. A third single version, by country legend Tex Ritter, was scheduled to be released, but remained unissued by Capitol Records because the legal case against Lieutenant William Calley was ongoing (Cap Nixes Disk: Seeks Not to "Glorify" Calley 1971). Julian Wilson and James M. Smith's song was a topical, broadside-like phenomenon from April to June 1971, yet by July 1971, it had virtually disappeared. Jens Lund, in his *Popular Music and Society* article "Country Music Goes to War" (Lund 1972a), deals with the broadside-like nature of the song.

The song uses the tune of "The Battle Hymn of the Republic," with lyrics that tell a romanticized version of the life of William Calley through the time of the My Lai massacre. Among the themes covered in the lyrics are the following: (1) the Viet Cong were impossible to distinguish from ordinary civilians, with the implication being that the Viet Cong were responsible for the massacre because they did not play war fairly; (2)

Calley and his comrades were just following orders; (3) while "we" brave soldiers were over in Vietnam fighting to defend freedom, "they" were protesting in the streets of America working to defeat U.S. soldiers; and (4) the military command has been responsible for making tactically questionable decisions while the ordinary soldiers bravely and obediently did what was asked of them. This fourth point, by the way, refers directly to the Hamburger Hill incident mentioned in the Background chapter. The Calley character makes no apologies in this song for killing the more than 100 civilians murdered at the village of My Lai.

Some of Lt. Calley's claims at his trial, and some of the claims made by his character in this song, are frankly disturbing, chief among them the claim that he should not be held responsible for following orders. Nazi war criminals made the same claim at the Nuremberg Trials following World War II to justify the atrocities they committed. Another of the song's claims, that those in the anti-war movement were working for the defeat of U.S. troops, also seems to be questionable: those in the peace movement would argue that they in fact were working in support of the soldiers, working for their safe return. In fairness to the anti-war movement, it also should be noted that left-wing songwriters had been pointing out the unwinnable nature of a war in Vietnam since before U.S. ground troops were committed in 1965, as were Kennedy administration advisors at the very start of the 1960s. What unquestionably struck a chord with audiences was the way in which songwriters Julian Wilson and James M. Smith allude to the follies of the military command, a command that had come under intense fire for making scapegoats of junior officers like Lt. Calley. Due in large part to the song's criticism of the U.S. military command, and to the fact that the Calley case was still under review when the recordings were released, the Armed Forces Network, as well as some commercial radio stations, banned the discs.

The C Company recording of "The Battle Hymn of Lt. Calley" finds singer Terry Nelson backed by banjo, military snare drum, acoustic guitar, and a choir. Nelson sings with attention to the meaning of the text, which he enhances through his inflection. In comparison, the less commercially successful John Deer Co. recording is somewhat quicker in tempo with the vocalist racing through the lyrics in an even-toned, less expressive manner. "The Battle Hymn of Lt. Calley" was not the only topical song supportive of the junior officer and critical of the military command and critical of the perceived lack of fairness with which the Viet Cong conducted their part of the war: an artist named Nelson Trueheart reportedly recorded a truly obscure song, "Morning in My Lai," which failed to make any of the singles charts.

Taking the stand that people today are not brave enough to "be men," C. Cooper and Blaine Smith's "Must We Fight Two Wars" deals with the belief that America is at war on two fronts, in Vietnam and at home against the anti-war protesters. On Autry Inman's recording, included on his album *The Ballad of Two Brothers*, the narration is backed by "Battle Hymn of the Republic" and "Onward Christian Soldiers." The narration quotes John F. Kennedy, Benjamin Franklin, Abraham Lincoln, and Nathan Hale and suggests that unless America changes course and fully supports the war effort, the Communists will take over not only in Vietnam but potentially closer to home.

Written and recorded by bluesman Big Joe Williams, "Army Man in Vietnam" finds a father expressing his regret that two of his six sons are serving on the front lines in Vietnam. The song is in a conventional twelve-bar blues form, recalling early twentieth-century rural blues in its sparse electric guitar and harmonica accompaniment, played by Williams and Charlie Musselwhite, respectively. After introducing the listener to the protagonist and the dilemma faced by his two sons, Williams reflects on his feeling that it is too bad that eighteen-year-old boys have to become men in Vietnam. As he continues from chorus to chorus, Williams's voice gradually builds in anger: indeed the text also gradually changes mood, from lamentation to true anger at the war. One curious aspect of the text is Williams's assertion that an atomic bomb should be dropped on North Vietnam to end the war. It is clearly a piece of hyperbola meant to express the extent of his frustration at having two young sons fighting in the war. The reader might recall that a number of anti-war protest songs of the early and mid-1960s focused on the possibility that the Vietnam Conflict would bring the United States into a direct confrontation with the Soviet Union or China and trigger a worldwide nuclear holocaust. That Big Joe Williams was able to use the image of ending the war in the manner in which World War II had been ended as a rhetorical device reflects the extent to which the serious threat of a worldwide nuclear holocaust developing out of the Vietnam Conflict had calmed by the early 1970s; the war fully had developed a life of its own. It should also be noted that by this time, fears among protest musicians that the war in Vietnam would lead to thermonuclear war also seem to have been assuaged; virtually all of the anti-war songs from this period too were Vietnam specific. I have included discussion of the Williams blues here as the primary focus is on the father's feelings about having his boys on the front lines; any anti-war feeling that Williams expresses seems to be of a personal nature, specifically related to the plight of his sons.

Junior Wells's curiously titled "Vietcong Blues"—Wells makes no reference to the South Vietnamese rebels in the lyrics—from the same period, represents the urban, Chicago, electric side of the blues genre. The Wells opus is a slow 12/8 meter twelve-bar blues and features the electric guitar work of Buddy Guy. The song begins with Wells singing that he is feeling blue because he just received a letter from his brother who is stationed in Vietnam. He goes on to tell of the pain he feels, and the pain that is felt by the mothers, fathers, and wives who have loved ones fighting in the war. Possibly because the text seems to be improvised – unlike most twelve-bar blues for pieces the rhyme schemes differ substantially from stanza to stanza and some stanzas are absent rhymes altogether – Wells is a bit ambiguous in terms of whom he is addressing. One part of the song does seem to be directed toward anti-war protesters, asking how they would feel if it were their brothers stationed in Vietnam, and suggesting that they try to understand his feelings, even though they show no respect for their country. The musician does not really say that he agrees with government policy, but indicates that as long as the troops are abroad, they must fight, if for nothing else but their own survival. Wells sings with passion and incredible dynamic contrast throughout and guitarist Buddy Guy and bassist Jack Meyers add some interesting sequential fills, which, while not reaching the level of atonality, certainly are not constrained to the customary blues scale.

Representing a different stylistic approach than any of the previous recordings dealing with the fate of the soldiers fighting in Southeast Asia discussed in this chapter, Jimmy Cliff's reggae composition "Vietnam" was first issued in 1969 on a minor, independent record label. The song was more widely available from 1970 on. "Vietnam" is fairly quick for the reggae genre, clocking in at 108 beats per minute. The perky rhythms, major key, and relatively quick tempo seem to work against Cliff's story, which finds him first receiving a letter from a friend stationed in Vietnam telling Cliff that he will be returning soon and asking Cliff to give his regards to the soldier's lover, Mary. The second stanza finds the soldier's mother receiving a telegram the next day informing her that her son is dead. After a stanza-long electronic organ solo, the second stanza is repeated. Cliff makes no direct comment on the war and, surprisingly, does not detail the soldier's mother's reaction; apparently it is up to the listener to decide how to read the ambiguous, conflicting moods of the song.

The cover of the Wilburn Brothers' album *Little Johnny from Down the Street* features a foreground photograph of a freckle-faced, "Dennis the Menace"-looking boy. This boy is the personification of the title character of the Larry G. Whitehead song "Little Johnny from Down the Street." Lyrically, the song begins like a country version of the old Jerry Leiber and Mike Stoller song "Charlie Brown" (popularized by The Coasters), as the singers recount the youthful misadventures of Johnny. A serious note enters Whitehead's text, though, when Johnny falls in love, is drafted, and sent to Vietnam. The song concludes with the acknowledgment that Johnny died in combat before he was able to return and marry the girl whose pigtails he used to pull. With its start on the third scale step and its motion around scale-step three in the opening phrase, the tune bears more than a passing resemblance to the Buddy Holly, Bob Montgomery composition "Love's Made a Fool of You," popularized by the Bobby Fuller Four in 1966. Significantly, composer Larry Whitehead does not seek to justify the Vietnam Conflict in his song, even though it is part of the generally pro-government country genre; the composer's focus is squarely on Johnny's story.

The Wilburn Brothers' recording of "Little Johnny from Down the Street" is quick, clocking in at 164 beats per minute in a solid, four-beat feel. The group incorporates a bit of text painting, going into a half-time rhythmic feel in the instrumental parts when they reach the line about the sacrifice that Johnny made. The bouncy, light style perfectly fits the initial image of little Johnny; however, the relatively small musical nod given to the major mood shift of the text is only partially effective. The Wilburn Brothers' single reached #36 on the *Cash Box* country charts and #37 on the *Billboard* country charts, while the album, the last to make the charts for the group, hit #31 on *Billboard*'s country album charts.

The postcard motif in the design of the album cover for Bruce Springsteen's 1973 *Greetings from Asbury Park, N.J.* suggests to the listener that the album will present a snapshot of a slice of New Jersey life. The song "Lost in the Flood" presents not so much a snapshot as a movie-like documentary of a scene centered in part on one aimless, alienated Vietnam veteran. Springsteen's lyrics, like those of the *Highway 61 Revisited* Bob Dylan, pan impressionistically around the veteran and other lost souls on the New Jersey cityscape to the extent that the listener is able to feel the general sense of malaise, even though (or perhaps because) this is no straightforward narrative. Springsteen was to revisit the theme of the disenfranchised-feeling Vietnam veteran, but in a considerably more pointedly direct (though misunderstood) way in his 1984 "Born in the U.S.A."

As American involvement in the painful Vietnam Conflict came to a close and as the violent anti-war protests subsided, Canadian radio broadcaster Gordon Sinclair wrote and read an editorial about his U.S. neighbors on Ontario radio station CFRB on June 5, 1973. Both Canadian Byron MacGregor and American country music star Tex Ritter recorded versions of the editorial, backed by patriotic music in the form of the tune "America." Both records made their chart debuts on January 26, 1974. MacGregor's single reached #4 on the *Billboard* pop charts and #59 on the magazine's country charts, while Ritter's topped out at #90 on the pop charts, faring significantly better on the *Billboard* country charts, where it hit #35, probably based on Ritter's stature within the country music field.

In "The Americans" Sinclair details examples of how the United States of America had been quick to help bail out other countries from debt and in times of natural and human disasters in the past and in the present. He also details some of America's recent problems in which no other country so much as offered to help, including flooding of the Mississippi River and the economic disaster faced by U.S. railroad companies in the early 1970s. The editorial acknowledges the problems of the controversial Vietnam Conflict but concludes that America will come together as a nation again and will again take its rightful place as the leader of the free world. Sinclair's statement of faith in his neighbors to the south came at a crucial time: the success of the recorded versions of the text rightfully suggest that this editorial was taken to heart by a nation seriously in need of mending some deep wounds.

The wounds opened by the Vietnam Conflict were slow to heal. That Americans needed to have a cooling-off period, a time in which to forget about the war and its problems, probably helped in part to fuel the popularity of disco music, which coincidentally emerged right as American troops were fully withdrawn from Vietnam. Little by little musicians began to deal with the plight of the veterans, many of whom were shattered physically and/or emotionally, in their songs. The first of these post-war songs to gain prominence was Tom Paxton's "Born on the Fourth of July," based on Vietnam veteran Ron Kovic's 1976 autobiographical book of the same name. Kovic's story would also become widely known through his emotionally charged speech at the 1976 Democratic National Convention and from the much later Oliver Stone film based on the veteran's autobiography. Paxton's 1977 song finds the musician telling the story of Kovic, who, during his second tour of duty in Southeast Asia, was shot and paralyzed. Although Paxton was well known for his anti-war songs in the 1960s, "Born on the Fourth of July" demonstrates his range as a songwriter. The focus here is entirely on Kovic's story, his plight, as it were, and on Kovic's range of emotions; never does Paxton take advantage of Kovic's situation to make a political statement. In a sense Paxton's song demonstrates the transformation that had come over many involved in the anti-war movement: now that the war was over and the soldiers were home, many formerly involved in the anti-war cause rallied around the broken veterans, the still-living victims of the war.

Five years after Tom Paxton's "Born on the Fourth of July," musicians seemed suddenly to take interest in the plight of the Vietnam veterans. Stevie Wonder's "Front Line," a six-minute track found on his 1982 album *Stevie Wonder's Original Musiquarium I*, chronicles the life of such a veteran, portrayed in the first person by Wonder.

Wonder's character felt that he had to commit to something after high school, so he enlisted in the army and was sent to Vietnam. He contrasts what he learned in church as a child, the commandment "Thou Shall Not Kill," with the reality of life in the jungles of Vietnam; however, the veteran's questioning of the war is such a minor part of the story as not to constitute a significant anti-war statement. The protagonist of "Front Line" found himself on the front lines of battle, had his legs blown off, and now finds himself at the rear of the line when it comes to making a go at life back home.

Stevie Wonder's "Front Line" is quick in tempo, features a solid dance beat, and shares much stylistically with some of the composer's better-known funk numbers, such as "Living for the City." This funkiness, incidentally, is largely due to Wonder's use of significant amounts of sixteenth-note syncopation in the instrumental parts. The instrumentation is thick, with multiple electric guitar and multiple electronic keyboard parts. Unlike some of the other fast, danceable songs studied in this book, I find Wonder's "Front Line" completely believable. Perhaps it is because of the songwriter's history of dealing with social issues in a funky, dance style, and his indefinable ability as a vocalist to "sell" a song no matter what its subject matter.

Stevie Wonder's "Front Line" dealt primarily with the physical damage suffered by a veteran and the societal and economic hardships he suffers as a result of the loss of his legs. Aside from the obvious physical damage done to veterans of the Vietnam Conflict, the psychological damage, defined as post-traumatic stress syndrome, became widespread public knowledge. Dan Daley's "Still in Saigon," recorded by the southern rock group The Charlie Daniels Band for their 1982 album *Windows*, deals with a veteran suffering from the ailment.

"Still in Saigon" is recorded in the archetypical southern rock style, featuring twin lead electric guitars, and tells the story of a soldier, from a first-person standpoint, who was so deeply affected by his experiences in the jungles of Vietnam that he is still plagued by flashbacks. To my ears "Still in Saigon" is somewhat less successful as a stand-alone song than Stevie Wonder's "Front Line"; however, in the context of The Charlie Daniels Band's album, which, as the title suggests, provides a window on part of American life, the song plays a significant role. "Still in Saigon" segues directly into a song lamenting the lack of a spirit of wandering and adventure in contemporary America; when we hear the two songs juxtaposed, we know why the Vietnam veteran is not infected with wanderlust and we feel even more empathy for him.

Billy Joel's 1982 "Goodnight Saigon" continued the early 1980s pop music focus on Vietnam veterans. Joel's contribution to the literature begins as a gentle rock ballad, with the singer backed by piano and guitar. Joel incorporates the *musique concrète* sounds of crickets in the night and helicopters. Eventually drums, strings, and a male chorus enter as the song builds in intensity. The text deals with the bond of brotherhood that existed among the soldiers fighting in Vietnam. Joel makes the point that when one is out on the field of battle, it does not matter whether the war is right or wrong: the soldier's survival and the survival of his comrades is the only issue. The composer also alludes to the soldiers listening to tapes of The Doors and smoking hashish in order to make it psychologically through the horrors of war in the jungles of Southeast Asia. "Goodnight Saigon" was included on Joel's #7 album *The Nylon Curtain*. The single release of the song, which followed the album by several months, made it only to #56 on the *Billboard* pop charts.

Written, recorded, and making the pop music charts in 1984, approximately ten years after the end of the war, Bruce Springsteen's "Born in the U.S.A." made a huge commercial impact; the single, which reached #9 on the *Billboard* charts, spent seventeen weeks on the charts and remains a frequently played song on radio stations programming material from the 1980s. The album *Born in the U.S.A.* was also a hit for Springsteen, holding onto the #1 position in *Billboard*'s pop album charts for seven weeks; it remains his best-known and best-selling collection to date. The song shows what one representative veteran, the protagonist of the song, had experienced in the decade since returning from active duty. In the context of the album from which it came, the song also paints a picture, in a small way, of America's coming to grips with the controversial war and a generation's coming of age.

Despite, or perhaps because of its popularity, "Born in the U.S.A." remains one the most misunderstood and frequently misinterpreted songs of the 1980s. Noted rock critic Greil Marcus writes: "Springsteen begins 'Born in the U.S.A.' with a great scream. Not only does he maintain it throughout the performance, he somehow modulates it, makes it talk." Marcus describes the song as being "about the debt the country owes to those who suffered the violation of the principles on which the country was founded, and by which it has justified itself ever since" (Marcus 1984, 95). Did listeners understand the song as a call for veterans' rights, a statement of the futility of the war, and a subtle acknowledgment of the racist overtones of the war? According to Ray Pratt, a minority of listeners correctly heard the message (Pratt 1994, 181). Most heard the repetitive title phrase as a statement of blind patriotism and virtually ignored the all-important text of the stanzas.

Springsteen's "Born in the U.S.A." features electric guitars, electronic keyboards, the composer's passionate vocals, and heavily played drums: it is in many respects a prototypical 1980s rock performance. The title line's two-measure melodic motive runs throughout the song in the keyboard and is the basis of virtually all of the vocal line's melodic material: this is a rare monothematic song. The structure of the song and the hard rock performance style convincingly portray the veteran who, due to some misdeeds in his youth, was sent to Vietnam, saw his brother die in combat, returned to the United States, and now has to fight to get a job, feeling rejected by the country of his birth.

The early 1980s focus on Vietnam veterans on pop singles and album charts was wrapped up with Englishman Paul Hardcastle's "19." After making its chart debut on June 1, 1985, the single rose to #15 on the *Billboard* pop charts; the 12-inch extended mix held onto the #1 spot on the *Cash Box* 12-inch single chart for three weeks and Hardcastle's music video for the song was #26 on the *Cash Box* music video chart in the first week of its two-week run.

The piece is basically a disco dance instrumental track, synthesizer based, with snippets of historical facts about the U.S. soldiers and the Vietnam Conflict inserted. Hardcastle also incorporates snippets of interviews with soldiers and a section sung by a female chorus reinforcing the fact that the average age of the U.S. soldiers stationed in Vietnam was nineteen. The spoken text contrasts the Vietnam Conflict and World II: the average age of World War II soldiers was 26, in Vietnam it was 19; in World War II the average tour of duty was longer, but in Vietnam soldiers were subjected to hostile enemy fire nearly every single day. Hardcastle's "19" is highly effective in reminding us of the plight of U.S. soldiers in Vietnam and chillingly dramatizes the continuing legacy of the war in the form of post-traumatic stress syndrome.

The cover art for Hardcastle's 12-inch single shows the title "19" in large red letters against a black background. There is a collage of grainy, colorized black-and-white photographs of combat scenes. The only photograph showing soldiers' faces has their eyes blocked out with thick black bands giving them a faceless quality, suggesting that they are just numbers or pawns in a game. Incidentally, Johann Hozel, known professionally as Falco, used Hardcastle's approach of overlaying a text with a focus on historical facts over what is essentially an instrumental dance track for his 1986 #1 hit "Rock Me Amadeus."

Probably one of the most fitting wrap-ups to the songs of the veteran is the 1998 album *Where Have All the Flowers Gone: A Vietnam Veterans Memorial Album* by George Grove (Timber Grove Records, 1998). Grove's compact disc includes a special appearance by The Kingston Trio, of which Grove is one of the current members. In addition to new songs of the veteran's experience by composers such as J. A. Elliot, David Maloney, and David Buskin, stanzas of Pete Seeger's "Where Have All the Flowers Gone?" are interspersed, as are Grove's readings of Steve Mason's poems, born of the Vietnam veteran's experience.

SELECTED DISCOGRAPHY

"'2+2=?'" (Bob Seger)

The Bob Seger System. 45 rpm phonodisc. Capitol 2143, 1968.

Ramblin' Gamblin' Man. The Bob Seger System. 33-1/3 rpm phonodisc. Capitol ST-172, 1968.

"19" (Paul Hardcastle)

Paul Hardcastle. 45 rpm phonodisc. Chrysalis 42860, 1985. Also issued in 12-inch, 45 rpm extended "Destruction" mix version, Chrysalis 4-V9-42875, 1985.

"'A' Team, The" (Leonard Whitcup, Phyllis Fairbanks, Barry Sadler)

SSgt. Barry Sadler. 45 rpm phonodisc. RCA Victor 8804, 1966.

Ballads of the Green Berets. SSgt. Barry Sadler. Reissued on compact disc. Collector's Choice Music CCM037-2, 1997. (Note: "The 'A' Team" is available only on the compact disc reissue of *Ballads of the Green Berets.*)

"Alice's Restaurant Massacree" (Arlo Guthrie)

Alice's Restaurant. Arlo Guthrie. 33-1/3 rpm phonodisc. Reprise RS-6267, 1967. Reissued on compact disc, Reprise RS-6267.

"Alice's Rock & Roll Restaurant." Arlo Guthrie. 45 rpm phonodisc. Reprise 0877, 1969. (Note: This single is a shortened version of the original 1967 song.)

"America, Communicate with Me" (Ray Stevens)

Ray Stevens. 45 rpm phonodisc. Barnaby 2016, 1970.

Ray Stevens...Unreal!!! Ray Stevens. 33-1/3 rpm phonodisc. Barnaby Z-30092, 1970.

Ray Stevens' Greatest Hits. Ray Stevens. 33-1/3 rpm phonodisc. Barnaby 30770, 1971. Reissued on compact disc, Rhino 72867, 1997.

"American Eagle Tragedy" (Peter Rowan)

American Eagle Tragedy. Earth Opera. 33-1/3 rpm phonodisc. Elektra EKS 74038, 1969.

Bosstown Sound – 1968: The Music & The Time. Various artists. "American Eagle Tragedy" performed by Earth Opera. Two compact discs. Big Beat CDWIK2 167, 1996.

"American Woman" (Randall Bachman, Burton Cummings, Michael James Kale, Garry Peterson)

American Woman. The Guess Who. 33-1/3 rpm phonodisc. RCA Victor LSP-4266, 1970. (Note: This album contains the extended version of "American Woman.")

The Guess Who. 45 rpm phonodisc. RCA Victor 0325, 1970.

The Best of The Guess Who. The Guess Who. 33-1/3 rpm phonodisc. RCA Victor 1004, 1971. Reissued on compact disc, RCA 3662-2-R. (Note: This album contains the extended version of "American Woman.")

Live at the Paramount. The Guess Who. 33-1/3 rpm phonodisc. RCA Victor LSP-4779, 1972. Reissued on compact disc, Buddha 99753, 2000. (Note: This live album contains a sixteen-minute version of "American Woman," featuring a lengthy blues jam.)

Sounds of the Seventies: 1970. Various artists. "American Woman" performed by The Guess Who. Compact disc. Time-Life SOD-01, 1989. (Note: This compilation contains the shorter, single version of "American Woman.")

Rock On 1970. Various artists. "American Woman" performed by The Guess Who. Compact disc. Madacy 1970, 1996. (Note: This compilation contains the shorter, single version of "American Woman.")

"Americans (A Canadian's Opinion), The" (Gordon Sinclair)

Byron MacGregor. 45 rpm phonodisc. Westbound 222, 1974.

The Americans. Byron MacGregor. 33-1/3 rpm phonodisc. Westbound WB-1000, 1974.

Tex Ritter. 45 rpm phonodisc. Capitol 3814, 1974.

"Army Man in Vietnam" (Joe Lee Williams)

> *Thinking of What They Did to Me.* Big Joe Williams. 33-1/3 rpm phonodisc. Arhoolie 1053, 1970.

"Ball of Confusion (That's What the World Is Today)" (Norman Whitfield, Barrett Strong)

> The Temptations. 45 rpm phonodisc. Gordy 7099, 1970.

> *Involved.* Edwin Starr. 33-1/3 rpm phonodisc. Gordy GS 956, 1971.

> *Rhythm & Blues: 1970.* Various artists. "Ball of Confusion" performed by The Temptations. Compact disc. Time-Life RHD-18, 1989.

> *Songs of Protest.* Various artists. "Ball of Confusion" performed by The Temptations. Simultaneously issued on 1-7/8 ips audio cassette and compact disc, Rhino 70734, 1991.

> *Hitsville USA: The Motown Singles Collection, 1959-1971.* Various artists. "Ball of Confusion" performed by The Temptations. Simultaneously issued on 1-7/8 ips audio cassette and compact disc, Motown 6312, 1992.

> *Motown Year by Year: The Sound of Young America, 1970.* Various artists. "Ball of Confusion" performed by The Temptations. Simultaneously issued on 1-7/8 ips audio cassette and compact disc, Motown 530528, 1995.

> *Rock On 1970.* Various artists. "Ball of Confusion" performed by The Temptations. Compact disc. Madacy 1970, 1996.

"Ballad of the Fort Hood Three, The" (Pete Seeger)

> *Young vs. Old.* Pete Seeger. 33-1/3 rpm phonodisc. Columbia CS-9873, 1969.

"Ballad of the Green Berets, The" (SSgt. Barry Sadler, Robin Moore)

> SSgt. Barry Sadler. 45 rpm phonodisc. RCA Victor 8739, 1966.

> *Ballads of the Green Berets.* SSgt. Barry Sadler. 33-1/3 rpm phonodisc. RCA Victor LPM-3547, 1966. Reissued on compact disc. Collector's Choice Music CCM037-2, 1997.

> *The Ballad of Two Brothers.* Autry Inman. 33-1/3 rpm phonodisc. Epic 26428, 1968.

> *I Didn't Raise My Boy to Be a Soldier.* Eli Radish. 33-1/3 rpm phonodisc. Capitol ST-244, 1969. (Note: This album contains songs of wartime composed throughout the twentieth century.)

More American Graffiti. Various artists. "The Ballad of the Green Berets" performed by SSgt. Barry Sadler. Two 33-1/3 rpm phonodiscs. MCA 2-11006, 1979.

Nipper's Greatest Hits: The '60s, Vol. 2. Various artists. "The Ballad of the Green Berets" performed by SSgt. Barry Sadler. Simultaneously issued on 1-7/8 ips audio cassette, RCA 8475-4-R and compact disc, RCA 8475-2-R, 1988.

Super Hits of the '60s. Various artists. "The Ballad of the Green Berets" performed by SSgt. Barry Sadler. Simultaneously issued on 1-7/8 ips audio cassette and compact disc, Hollywood 283, 1992.

Super Hits, Vol. 3. Various artists. "The Ballad of the Green Berets" performed by SSgt. Barry Sadler. Simultaneously issued on 1-7/8 ips audio cassette and compact disc, Hollywood 167, 1994.

Billboard Top Pop Hits 1966. Various artists. "The Ballad of the Green Berets" performed by SSgt. Barry Sadler. Simultaneously issued on 1-7/8 ips audio cassette and compact disc, Rhino 71936, 1995.

Super Box of Rock, Vol. 3. Various artists. "The Ballad of the Green Berets" performed by SSgt. Barry Sadler. Simultaneously issued on compact disc as K-Tel 3519 and Dominion 3519, 1995.

#1 Hits: The '60s Decade. Various artists. "The Ballad of the Green Berets" performed by SSgt. Barry Sadler. Simultaneously issued on 1-7/8 ips audio cassette and compact disc, Number 1 Hits 5515, 1998.

'60s Decade #1 Hits. Various artists. "The Ballad of the Green Berets" performed by SSgt. Barry Sadler. Compact disc. Boxsets 9220, 1999.

Decade of the '60s. Various artists. "The Ballad of the Green Berets" performed by SSgt. Barry Sadler. 33-1/3 rpm phonodisc. RCA 6061, n.d.

"Ballad of Two Brothers, The" (Bob Braddock, Curly Putnam, Bill Killen)

Autry Inman. 45 rpm phonodisc. Epic EP S-10389, 1968.

The Ballad of Two Brothers. Autry Inman. 33-1/3 rpm phonodisc. Epic 26428, 1968.

Country Shots: God Bless America. Various artists. "Ballad of Two Brothers" performed by Autry Inman. Simultaneously issued on 1-7/8 ips audio cassette and compact disc, Rhino 71645, 1994.

"Battle Hymn of Lt. Calley, The" (Julian Wilson, James M. Smith)

Wake up America. C Company featuring Terry Nelson. 33-1/3 rpm phonodisc. Plantation PLP 15, 1971.

C Company featuring Terry Nelson. 45 rpm phonodisc. Plantation 73, 1971.

The John Deer Co. 45 rpm phonodisc. Royal American 34, 1971.

"The Battle Hymn of Lt. Calley" and Other Hits. Various artists. "The Battle Hymn of Lt. Calley" performed by The John Deer Co. 33-1/3 rpm phonodisc. Royal American 1006, 1971.

"Battle Hymn of the Republic, The" (traditional tune)

Chet Atkins Picks the Best. Chet Atkins. 33-1/3 rpm phonodisc. RCA, 1967.

"Big Draft Medley, The" (various)

The Four Preps. 45 rpm phonodisc. Capitol 4716, 1962.

Campus Encores with The Four Preps. The Four Preps. 33-1/3 rpm phonodisc. Capitol T-1647, 1962.

"Billy and Sue" (Mark Charron)

B. J. Thomas and The Triumphs. 45 rpm phonodisc. Bragg 103, 1964. Reissued as Warner Brothers 5491, 1964 and Hickory 1395, 1966.

The Very Best of B. J. Thomas. B. J. Thomas. 33-1/3 rpm phonodisc. Hickory Records LPS-133, 1966.

Greatest Hits. B. J. Thomas. Simultaneously issued on 1-7/8 ips audio cassette, Rhino R4-70752 and compact disc, Rhino R2-70752, 1990.

"Billy, Don't Be a Hero" (Mitch Murray, Peter Callander)

Bo Donaldson and The Heywoods. 45 rpm phonodisc. ABC 11435, 1974.

Bo Donaldson and The Heywoods. Bo Donaldson and The Heywoods. 33-1/3 rpm phonodisc. ABC Records ABCD-824, 1974.

The Best of Bo Donaldson and The Heywoods. Bo Donaldson and The Heywoods. Compact disc. Varese Sarabande 5724, 1996.

"Blowin' in the Wind" (Bob Dylan)

The Freewheelin' Bob Dylan. Bob Dylan. 33-1/3 rpm phonodisc. Columbia CK-8786, 1963. Reissued on compact disc, Columbia CK-8786.

In the Wind. Peter, Paul & Mary. 33-1/3 rpm phonodisc. Warner Brothers WS-1507, 1963. Reissued on compact disc, Warner Brothers 2-26224.

Peter, Paul & Mary. 45 rpm phonodisc. Warner 5368, 1963.

The Evening Concerts: Newport Folk Festival 1963. Various artists. "Blowin' in the Wind" performed by Bob Dylan and Peter Yarrow. Available on 1-

7/8 ips audio cassette, Vanguard CV-77002 and compact disc, Vanguard VCD-77002.

Broadside Ballads, Vol. 1. Various artists. "Blowin' in the Wind" performed by The New World Singers. 33-1/3 rpm phonodisc. Broadside B-301; Folkways 05301, 1964.

Come My Way. Marianne Faithfull. 33-1/3 rpm phonodisc. Decca 4688, 1965.

Live at Ciro's. Dick Dale & The Del-Tones. 33-1/3 rpm phonodisc. Capitol 2293, 1965.

You've Got to Hide Your Love Away. Silkie. 33-1/3 rpm phonodisc. Fontana 67548, 1965. Reissued on compact disc, One Way 31441, 1996.

Stevie Wonder. 45 rpm phonodisc. Tamla 54136, 1966.

Uptight. Stevie Wonder. 33-1/3 rpm phonodisc. Tamla 268, 1966.

Bob Dylan's Greatest Hits. Bob Dylan. 33-1/3 rpm phonodisc. Columbia KCL-2663, 1967. Reissued on compact disc, Columbia CK-9463.

Greatest Hits. Stevie Wonder. 33-1/3 rpm phonodisc. Motown 282, 1968. Reissued as Motown 11075.

"Forrest Gump" Original Soundtrack. Various artists. Simultaneously issued on 1-7/8 ips audio cassette and compact disc, Sony 66329, 1994.

Live at Newport. Judy Collins. Simultaneously issued on 1-7/8 ips audio cassette and compact disc. Vanguard 77013, 1994. (Note: The recordings on this release were made at the Newport Folk Festival, 1959-66.)

The Best of "Broadside," 1962-1988. Various artists. "Blowin' in the Wind" performed by The New World Singers. Five compact discs. Smithsonian/Folkways 40130, 2000.

"Born in the U.S.A." (Bruce Springsteen)

Born in the U.S.A. Bruce Springsteen. 33-1/3 rpm phonodisc. Columbia QC-38653, 1984. Reissued on compact disc.

Bruce Springsteen. 45 rpm phonodisc. Columbia 04680, 1984.

"Born on the Fourth of July" (Tom Paxton)

New Songs from the Briarpatch. Tom Paxton. 33-1/3 rpm phonodisc. Vanguard 79395, 1977. Reissued on compact disc, Vanguard VMD-79395.

The Best of the Vanguard Years. Tom Paxton. Compact disc. Vanguard 79561, 2000.

"Bring the Boys Home" (Gregory Perry, Angelo Bond, General Johnson)

Freda Payne. 45 rpm phonodisc. Invictus 9092, 1971.

"Bring Them Home" (Pete Seeger)

Young vs. Old. Pete Seeger. 33-1/3 rpm phonodisc. Columbia CS 9873, 1969.

"Buy a Gun for Your Son" (Tom Paxton)

Ain't That News! Tom Paxton. 33-1/3 rpm phonodisc. Elektra EKL-298/EKS-7298, 1965.

"Coming Home Soldier" (Gene Allen, Bobby Vinton)

Bobby Vinton. 45 rpm phonodisc. Epic 10090, 1966.

Bobby Vinton Sings the Newest Hits. Bobby Vinton. 33-1/3 rpm phonodisc. Epic LN-24245, 1967.

16 Most Requested Songs. Bobby Vinton. Compact disc. Columbia 47855, 1991.

"Congratulations (You Sure Made a Man Out of Him)" (I. Garman, C. Hoffman, J. Barr)

Arlene Harden. 45 rpm phonodisc. Columbia 45420, 1971.

"Cruel War, The" (Peter Yarrow, Paul Stookey)

Peter, Paul, and Mary. Peter, Paul & Mary. 33-1/3 rpm phonodisc. Warner Brothers WS-1449, 1962. Reissued as Warner Brothers 1449, 1990. Reissued on 1-7/8 ips audio cassette, Warner Brothers M5-1449 and compact disc, Warner Brothers 2-1449, 1988.

Peter, Paul & Mary. B-side to "Stewball." 45 rpm phonodisc. Warner Brothers 5399, 1963.

Peter, Paul & Mary. 45 rpm phonodisc. Warner Brothers 5809, 1966.

The Cowsills in Concert. The Cowsills. 33-1/3 rpm phonodisc. MGM SE-4619, 1969. Reissued on 1-7/8 ips audio cassette, Razor & Tie 2038, 1994 and compact disc, Razor & Tie 2038, 1996.

"Dawn of Correction, The" (John Madera, David White, Ray Gilmore)

The Spokesmen. 45 rpm phonodisc. Decca 31844, 1965.

The Dawn of Correction. The Spokesmen. 33-1/3 rpm phonodisc. Decca DL 4712, 1965.

"Positively 4th Street" and Other Message Folk Songs. The Living Voices; Anita Kerr, arranger. 33-1/3 rpm phonodisc. RCA Camden CAL-947, 1966.

Sixties Rule!: Chapter One. Various artists. "The Dawn of Correction" performed by The Spokesmen. Compact disc. One Way 22034, 1991.

Vintage Collectibles, Vol. 2: 1963-1969. Various artists. "The Dawn of Correction" performed by The Spokesmen. Compact disc. MCA Special Products 22131, 1995.

"Day for Decision" (Allen N. Peltier)

Johnny Sea. 45 rpm phonodisc. Warner Brothers 5820, 1966.

Day for Decision. Johnny Sea. 33-1/3 rpm phonodisc. Warner Brothers 1659, 1966. Reissued as *American Reflections* by Johnny Seay on compact disc, Lost Gold Records LGR-4339, 1999.

"Dear Uncle Sam" (Loretta Lynn)

Loretta Lynn. 45 rpm phonodisc. Decca 31893, 1966.

1966 Country and Western Award Winners. Various artists. "Dear Uncle Sam" performed by Loretta Lynn. Decca DL-4837, 1966.

Loretta Lynn's Greatest Hits. Loretta Lynn. 33-1/3 rpm phonodisc. Decca DL-75000, 1968. Reissued as MCA MCA-1. Reissued on compact disc, MCA MCAD-31234.

Country's Greatest Hits of the '60s, Vol. 1. Various artists. "Dear Uncle Sam" performed by Loretta Lynn. Simultaneously issued on 1-7/8 ips audio cassette and compact disc, MCA Special Products 20435, 1994.

Honky Tonk Girl: The Loretta Lynn Collection. Loretta Lynn. Multiple compact discs. MCA 11070, 1994.

"Distant Drums" (Cindy Walker)

Roy Orbison. 45 rpm phonodisc. Monument 906, 1965. (Note: The song was the B-side of "Let the Good Times Roll.")

Jim Reeves. 45 rpm phonodisc. RCA Victor 8789, 1966.

The Best of Jim Reeves, Vol. 2. Jim Reeves. 33-1/3 rpm phonodisc. RCA Victor LSP-3482, 1966. Reissued on compact disc.

Distant Drums. Jim Reeves. 33-1/3 rpm phonodisc. RCA Victor LPM-3542/LSP-3542, 1966. Reissued on compact disc, DCC 156, 1998.

Country Charley Pride. Charley Pride. 33-1/3 rpm phonodisc. RCA Victor LSP-3645, 1966.

Monumental Hits. Roy Orbison. 33-1/3 rpm phonodisc. Monument 69147, 1975.

The Legendary Roy Orbison. Roy Orbison. Four compact discs. Columbia 46809, 1990. Also issued as Sony A4K-46809.

Country Music Classics, Vol. 18 (1965-70). Various artists. "Distant Drums" performed by Jim Reeves. Compact disc. K-Tel 3110, 1993.

Billboard Top Country Hits: 1966. Various artists. "Distant Drums" performed by Jim Reeves. Simultaneously issued on 1-7/8 ips cassette, Rhino R4-70687 and compact disc, Rhino R4-70687, n.d.

"Dove, The" (Ewan MacColl)

Broadsides, Songs and Ballads. Pete Seeger. 33-1/3 rpm phonodisc. Folkways Records FA-2456, 1964.

"Down by the Riverside" (traditional)

Waist Deep in the Big Muddy. Pete Seeger. 33-1/3 rpm phonodisc. Columbia CS 9505, 1967. Reissued on 1-7/8 ips audio cassette and compact disc, Sony 57311, 1994.

"Draft Dodger Rag" (Phil Ochs)

I Ain't Marching Anymore. Phil Ochs. 33-1/3 rpm phonodisc. Carthage 4422, 1965. Reissued as Elektra 7287. Reissued on compact disc, Hannibal 4422, 1995.

Live at Newport. Phil Ochs. Compact disc. Vanguard 77017-2, 1996.

Farewells & Fantasies. Phil Ochs. Three compact discs. Elektra R2-73518, 1997.

Generations of Folk, Vol. 2: Protest & Politics. Various artists. "Draft Dodger Rag" performed by Phil Ochs. Compact disc. Vanguard 78001-2, 1998.

"Draft Morning" (David Crosby, Chris Hillman, Roger McGuinn)

The Notorious Byrd Brothers. The Byrds. 33-1/3 rpm phonodisc. Columbia CL 2775/CS 9575, 1968. Reissued on compact disc, Columbia CK-9575. Also issued on compact disc, Sony 65151, 1997.

"Draft Resister" (John Kay, Goldy McJohn, Larry Byrom)

Monster. Steppenwolf. 33-1/3 rpm phonodisc. Dunhill DS 56066, 1969. Reissued on compact disc, MCA 31328, 1990.

Steppenwolf "Live." Steppenwolf. Two 33-1/3 rpm phonodiscs. Dunhill 50075, 1970. Reissued on compact disc, MCA 6013, 1989.

"Eve of Destruction" (P. F. Sloan)

Barry McGuire. 45 rpm phonodisc. ABC Dunhill 4009, 1965.

Eve of Destruction. Barry McGuire. 33-1/3 rpm phonodisc. Dunhill D-50003, 1965.

It Ain't Me Babe. The Turtles. 33-1/3 rpm phonodisc. White Whale WW-111, 1965. Also issued as White Whale 7111. Reissued on 1-7/8 ips audio cassette and compact disc, Rhino 151.

"Positively 4th Street" and Other Message Folk Songs. The Living Voices; Anita Kerr, arranger. 33-1/3 rpm phonodisc. RCA Camden CAL-947, 1966.

Songs of Protest. Various artists. "Eve of Destruction" performed by Barry McGuire. Simultaneously issued on 1-7/8 ips audio cassette and compact disc, Rhino 70734, 1991.

Best of the '60s and '70s: Protest Rock. Various artists. "Eve of Destruction" performed by Barry McGuire. Simultaneously issued on 1-7/8 ips audio cassette and compact disc. Priority 53701, 1992.

The Best of Folk Rock. Various artists. "Eve of Destruction" performed by Barry McGuire. Simultaneously issued on 1-7/8 ips audio cassette and compact disc, K-Tel 3438, 1995.

Vintage Collectibles, Vol. 2: 1963-1969. Various artists. "Eve of Destruction" performed by Barry McGuire. Compact disc. MCA Special Products 22131, 1995.

Classic Rock: 1965—The Beat Goes On. Various artists. "Eve of Destruction" performed by Barry McGuire. Compact disc. Time-Life 2CLR-08, n.d.

Time-Life's Treasury of Folk, Vol. 4: Folk Rock. Various artists. "Eve of Destruction" performed by Barry McGuire. Compact disc. Time-Life Music 21, n.d.

"Fightin' Side of Me, The" (Merle Haggard)

Merle Haggard. 45 rpm phonodisc. Capitol 2719, 1970.

The Fightin' Side of Me. Merle Haggard. 33-1/3 rpm phonodisc. Capitol ST 451, 1970.

Merle Haggard Takes Philadelphia—Live! Merle Haggard. 33-1/3 rpm phonodisc. Capitol ST-451, 1970.

A&E Biography. Merle Haggard. Simultaneously issued on 1-7/8 ips audio cassette and compact disc, Capitol 30204, 1999. (Note: This collection was released to coincide with the Haggard profile on the A&E cable television network's *Biography* program.)

"Flowers of Peace, The" (Pete Seeger)

Broadsides, Songs and Ballads. Pete Seeger. 33-1/3 rpm phonodisc. Folkways Records FA-2456, 1964.

I've Lost My Yo Yo. The Brandywine Singers. Compact disc. Folk Era 1452, 1999.

"Fortunate Son" (John C. Fogerty)

Willy & the Poor Boys. Creedence Clearwater Revival. 33-1/3 rpm phonodisc. Fantasy F-8397, 1969. Reissued on compact disc, Fantasy FCD-4515-2.

Creedence Clearwater Revival. 45 rpm phonodisc. Fantasy 634, 1969. (Note: The song was the B-side of "Down on the Corner.")

More Creedence Gold. Creedence Clearwater Revival. 33-1/3 rpm phonodisc. Fantasy F-9430, 1973. Reissued on compact disc, Fantasy FCD-9430-2.

Chronicle. Creedence Clearwater Revival. 33-1/3 rpm phonodisc. Fantasy CCR-2, 1976. Reissued on compact disc, Fantasy FCD-623-CCR2, 1990.

Best of Creedence Clearwater Revival, Vol. 2. Creedence Clearwater Revival. 33-1/3 rpm phonodisc. Fantasy 510, 1988.

"Forrest Gump" Original Soundtrack. Various artists. "Fortunate Son" performed by Creedence Clearwater Revival. Simultaneously issued on 1-7/8 ips audio cassette and compact disc, Sony 66329, 1994.

John Fogerty: Wrote a Song for Everyone. Various artists. "Fortunate Son" performed by Al Perry and The Cattle. Compact disc. Rubber Rabbit 5 196, 1996.

"Prefontaine" Original Soundtrack. Various artists. "Fortunate Son" performed by Creedence Clearwater Revival. Compact disc. Hollywood 162104, 1997.

"Front Line" (Stevie Wonder)

Stevie Wonder's Original Musiquarium I. Stevie Wonder. Two 33-1/3 rpm phonodiscs. Tamla 6002, 1982. Also issued on two compact discs, Motown 374636022, 1982.

"G.I. Movement" (Holly Near)

Hang in There. Holly Near. 33-1/3 rpm phonodisc. Redwood Records RRS-3800, 1973.

"Gallant Men" (Charles O. Wood [Charles Osgood], John Cacavas)

Senator Everett McKinley Dirksen. 45 rpm phonodisc. Capitol 5805, 1966.

Gallant Men. Senator Everett McKinley Dirksen. 33-1/3 rpm phonodisc. Capitol 2643, 1969.

"Galveston" (Jimmy Webb)

Glen Campbell. 45 rpm phonodisc. Capitol 2428, 1969.

Galveston. Glen Campbell. 33-1/3 rpm phonodisc. Capitol ST-210, 1969.

All-Time Favorites. Glen Campbell. Simultaneously issued on 1-7/8 ips audio cassette and compact disc, Capitol 35780, 1995.

Country Music Classics, Vol. 18 (1965-70). Various artists. "Galveston" performed by Glen Campbell. Compact disc. K-Tel 3110, 1993.

The Glen Campbell Collection (1962-1989). Glen Campbell. Two compact discs. Razor & Tie 2129, 1997.

"Give Peace a Chance" (John Lennon, Paul McCartney)

The Plastic Ono Band. 45 rpm phonodisc. Apple 1809, 1969.

Live Peace in Toronto 1969. The Plastic Ono Band. 33-1/3 rpm phonodisc. Apple SW-3362, 1969.

Shaved Fish. John Lennon and The Plastic Ono Band. 33-1/3 rpm phonodisc. Apple SW-3421, 1975.

The John Lennon Collection. John Lennon. Compact disc. Capitol/Parlophone CDP591516, 1989.

"God, Country and My Baby" (John Dolan)

Johnny Burnette. 45 rpm phonodisc. Liberty 55379, 1961.

Johnny Burnette's Hits and Other Favorites. Johnny Burnette. 33-1/3 rpm phonodisc. Liberty LST-7206, 1963.

Death, Glory and Retribution. Various artists. "God, Country and My Baby" performed by Johnny Burnette. 33-1/3 rpm phonodisc. EMI 17187, 1985.

The Best of Johnny Burnette. Johnny Burnette. Issued on 1-7/8 ips audio cassette and compact disc. Capitol/Alliance 99997, 1992.

"God Please Protect America" (Jimmie Osborne)

Country Music Goes to Viet Nam. Charlie Moore and Bill Napier. 33-1/3 rpm phonodisc. King 982, 1966.

"Going to Vietnam" (Amos Patton)

Big Amos Patton. 45 rpm phonodisc. MOC 665, 1967.

Hi Records: The Blues Sessions. Various artists. "Going to Vietnam" performed by Big Amos Patton. Two 33-1/3 rpm phonodiscs. Hi Records D-HIUKLP 427, 1988.

"Goodnight Saigon" (Billy Joel)

The Nylon Curtain. Billy Joel. 33-1/3 rpm phonodisc. Columbia BL-38200, 1982. Also issued on compact disc.

Billy Joel. 45 rpm phonodisc. Columbia 03780, 1983.

Greatest Hits, Volume I and Volume II. Billy Joel. Two compact discs. Columbia G2K-40121, 1985.

"Handsome Johnny" (Louis Gossett, Jr., Richie Havens)

Mixed Bag. Richie Havens. 33-1/3 rpm phonodisc. Verve FT/FTS-3006, 1966. Reissued on compact disc, Verve 835210.

Woodstock: Three Days of Peace & Music. Various artists. "Handsome Johnny" performed by Richie Havens. Simultaneously issued on multiple 1-7/8 ips audio cassettes and compact discs, Atlantic 82634/82636, 1994.

"Hang in There" (Holly Near)

Hang in There. Holly Near. 33-1/3 rpm phonodisc. Redwood Records RRS-3800, 1973.

"Happy Xmas (War Is Over)" (Yoko Ono, John Lennon)

John Lennon, Yoko Ono, The Plastic Ono Band, and The Harlem Community Choir. 45 rpm phonodisc. Apple 1842, 1971.

Shaved Fish. John Lennon and The Plastic Ono Band. 33-1/3 rpm phonodisc. Apple SW-3421, 1975.

The John Lennon Collection. John Lennon. Compact disc. Capitol/Parlophone CDP591516, 1989.

"Have I Come Home to Die?" (Charlie Moore, Bill Napier)

Country Music Goes to Viet Nam. Charlie Moore and Bill Napier. 33-1/3 rpm phonodisc. King 982, 1966.

"He Wore the Green Beret" (Peggy Barsella, Frank Catana)

Nancy Ames. 45 rpm phonodisc. Epic 10003, 1966.

As Time Goes By. Nancy Ames. 33-1/3 rpm phonodisc. Epic LN 24197, 1966.

"Hello Vietnam" (Tom T. Hall)

Kitty Hawkins. Capa 130, 1965.

Johnny Wright. 45 rpm phonodisc. Decca 31821, 1966.

Hello Vietnam. Johnny Wright. 33-1/3 rpm phonodisc. Decca DL-4698, 1966.

1966 Country and Western Award Winners. Various artists. "Hello Vietnam" performed by Johnny Wright. Decca DL-4837, 1966.

There's a Star-Spangled Banner Waving Somewhere. Dave Dudley. 33-1/3 rpm phonodisc. Mercury MG-21057/SR-61057, 1966.

Stanley Kubrick's "Full Metal Jacket"—Original Soundtrack. Various artists. "Hello Vietnam" performed by Johnny Wright. Compact disc. Warner Brothers 925613-2, 1987.

"Hole in the Ground" (Tom Parrott)

The Best of "Broadside," 1962-1988. Various artists. "Hole in the Ground" performed by Tom Parrott. Five compact discs. Smithsonian/Folkways 40130, 2000.

"I Ain't Marching Anymore" (Phil Ochs)

I Ain't Marching Anymore. Phil Ochs. 33-1/3 rpm phonodisc. Carthage 4422, 1965. Reissued as Elektra 7287. Reissued on compact disc, Hannibal 4422, 1995.

Songs of Protest. Various artists. "I Ain't Marching Anymore" performed by Phil Ochs. Compact disc. Simultaneously issued on 1-7/8 ips audio cassette and compact disc, Rhino 70734, 1991. (Note: This is the "electric" version of the song, previously available only as a 45 rpm single in the United Kingdom.)

Live at Newport. Phil Ochs. Simultaneously issued on 1-7/8 ips audio cassette and compact disc, Vanguard 77017, 1996. (Note: The recordings on this disc were made at Ochs's appearances at the 1963, 1965, and 1966 Newport Folk Festivals.)

Farewells & Fantasies. Phil Ochs. Three compact discs. Elektra R2-73518, 1997. (Note: This is the definitive Phil Ochs collection, and includes both the original and the "electric" versions of "I Ain't Marching Anymore.")

Generations of Folk, Vol. 2: Protest & Politics. Various artists. "I Ain't Marching Anymore" performed by Phil Ochs. Compact disc. Vanguard 78001, 1998.

"I-Feel-Like-I'm-Fixin'-to-Die Rag" (Joe McDonald)

Country Joe and The Fish. 45 rpm extended play phonodisc. 1965.

I Feel Like I'm Fixin' to Die. Country Joe and The Fish. 33-1/3 rpm phonodisc. Vanguard VSD-79266, 1967.

Woodstock. Various artists. "I-Feel-Like-I'm-Fixin'-to-Die Rag" performed by Country Joe and The Fish. Two 33-1/3 rpm phonodiscs. Atlantic, 1970. Reissued on compact discs, Atlantic A2 500.

More American Graffiti. Various artists. "I-Feel-Like-I'm-Fixin'-to-Die Rag" performed by Country Joe and The Fish. Two 33-1/3 rpm phonodiscs. MCA 2-11006, 1979.

Songs of Protest. Various artists. "I-Feel-Like-I'm-Fixin'-to-Die Rag" performed by Country Joe and The Fish. Simultaneously issued on 1-7/8 ips audio cassette and compact disc, Rhino 70734, 1991.

The First Three EPs. Country Joe and The Fish. Compact disc. One Way 30990, 1994.

Vietnam Experience. Country Joe McDonald. Compact disc. One Way 30991, 1995.

"I Told Them What You're Fighting For" (Charles Dennis, Tom T. Hall)

A Living Legend. Mother Maybelle Carter. 33-1/3 rpm phonodisc. Columbia CL 2475/CS 9275, 1966.

"I'll Be Home" (Charlie Moore, Bill Napier)

Country Music Goes to Viet Nam. Charlie Moore and Bill Napier. 33-1/3 rpm phonodisc. King 982, 1966.

"Imagine" (John Lennon)

Imagine. John Lennon. 33-1/3 rpm phonodisc. Apple SW-3379, 1971. Reissued on compact disc.

John Lennon. 45 rpm phonodisc. Apple 1840, 1971.

Shaved Fish. John Lennon. 33-1/3 rpm phonodisc. Apple SW-3421, 1975.

The John Lennon Collection. John Lennon. Compact disc. Capitol/Parlophone CDP591516, 1989.

"In the Slime of Vietnam" (Robert Thompson, Sid Feller)

An Open Letter. Victor Lundberg. 33-1/3 rpm phonodisc. Liberty LST-7547, 1967.

"Is There Anybody Here?" (Phil Ochs)

Phil Ochs in Concert. Phil Ochs. 33-1/3 rpm phonodisc. Elektra EKS-7310, 1966.

Farewells & Fantasies. Phil Ochs. Three compact discs. Elektra R2-73518, 1997.

"Is This War a Useless War?" (Charlie Moore, Bill Napier)

Country Music Goes to Viet Nam. Charlie Moore and Bill Napier. 33-1/3 rpm phonodisc. King 982, 1966.

"It Ain't Me, Babe" (Bob Dylan)

Another Side of Bob Dylan. Bob Dylan. 33-1/3 rpm phonodisc. Columbia CL-2193, 1964. Reissued on compact disc, Columbia CK-08993. Reissued on compact disc, Sony 8993, 1990.

Five. Joan Baez. 33-1/3 rpm phonodisc. Vanguard VRS-9160, 1964. Reissued on 1-7/8 ips audio cassette and compact disc, Vanguard 79160, 1993.

Johnny Cash. 45 rpm phonodisc. Columbia 43145, 1964.

The Turtles. 45 rpm phonodisc. White Whale 222, 1965.

It Ain't Me Babe. The Turtles. 33-1/3 rpm phonodisc. White Whale WW-111, 1965. Also issued as White Whale 7111. Reissued on 1-7/8 ips audio cassette and compact disc, Rhino 151.

The Dawn of Correction. The Spokesmen. 33-1/3 rpm phonodisc. Decca DL-74712, 1965.

You've Got to Hide Your Love Away. Silkie. 33-1/3 rpm phonodisc. Fontana 67548, 1965. Reissued on compact disc, One Way 31441, 1996.

Bob Dylan's Greatest Hits. Bob Dylan. 33-1/3 rpm phonodisc. Columbia KCL-2663, 1967. Reissued on compact disc, Columbia CK-9463.

Best of The Turtles. The Turtles. Simultaneously issued on 1-7/8 ips audio cassette, Rhino R4-70177 and 33-1/3 rpm phonodisc, Rhino RNLP-70177, 1987. Reissued on compact disc, Rhino 71027, 1995.

The Best of Folk Rock. Various artists. "It Ain't Me Babe" performed by The Turtles. Simultaneously issued on 1-7/8 ips audio cassette, K-Tel 3438; and compact disc, K-Tel 3438, 1995.

Rock & Roll Reunion: Class of '65. Various artists. "It Ain't Me, Babe" performed by The Turtles. Compact disc. Madacy 2941, 1997.

Classic Rock: 1965 – The Beat Goes On. Various artists. "It Ain't Me, Babe" performed by The Turtles. Compact disc. Time-Life 2CLR-08, n.d.

"It Better End Soon" (Robert Lamm, Walter Parazaider, Terry Kath)

Chicago II. Chicago. Two 33-1/3 rpm phonodiscs. Columbia PG-24/KGP-24, 1970. Reissued on compact disc, Columbia CGK-24.

"It's for God, and Country, and You Mom (That's Why I'm Fighting in Viet Nam)" (Dave McEnery)

Ernest Tubb and His Texas Troubadours. 45 rpm phonodisc. Decca 31861, 1966.

"John Brown" (Bob Dylan)

Broadside Ballads, Vol. 1. Various artists. "John Brown" performed by Blind Boy Grunt [Bob Dylan]. 33-1/3 rpm phonodisc. Broadside B-301; Folkways 05301, 1964.

The Best of "Broadside," 1962-1988. Various artists. "John Brown" performed by Blind Boy Grunt [Bob Dylan]. Five compact discs. Smithsonian/Folkways 40130, 2000.

"Keep the Flag Flying" (Tom T. Hall)

Johnny Wright. 45 rpm phonodisc. Decca 31875, 1966.

Country Music Special. Johnny Wright. 33-1/3 rpm phonodisc. Decca DL-4770, 1966.

"Kill for Peace" (Tuli Kupferberg)

The Fugs. The Fugs. 33-1/3 rpm phonodisc. ESP-Disk 1028, 1966.

The Best of "Broadside," 1962-1988. Various artists. "Kill for Peace" performed by The Fugs. Five compact discs. Smithsonian/Folkways 40130, 2000.

"Last Night I Had the Strangest Dream" (Ed McCurdy)

Waist Deep in the Big Muddy. Pete Seeger. 33-1/3 rpm phonodisc. Columbia CS 9505. Reissued on 1-7/8 ips audio cassette and compact disc, Sony 57311, 1994.

Collected Works. Simon and Garfunkel. Three compact discs. Columbia C3K-45322, 1981. Also issued as Sony 45322.

"Lay Down (Candles in the Rain)" (Melanie Safka)

Melanie. 45 rpm phonodisc. Buddah 167, 1970.

Candles in the Rain. Melanie. 33-1/3 rpm phonodisc. Buddah BDS-5060, 1970. Simultaneously reissued on 1-7/8 ips audio cassette and compact disc,

Kama Sutra 5060, 1994. (Note: The title of this album is sometimes given as *Lay Down (Candles in the Rain)*.)

"Letter from Vietnam" (Barry Sadler)

Ballads of the Green Berets. SSgt. Barry Sadler. 33-1/3 rpm phonodisc. RCA Victor LPM-3547, 1966. Reissued on compact disc. Collector's Choice Music CCM037-2, 1997.

"Letter to Dad, A" (Bill Dean, Ron Marshall)

Every Father's Teenage Son. 45 rpm phonodisc. Buddah BDA-25, 1967.

"Little Johnny from Down the Street" (Larry G. Whitehead)

The Wilburn Brothers. 45 rpm phonodisc. Decca 32608, 1970.

Little Johnny from Down the Street. The Wilburn Brothers. 33-1/3 rpm phonodisc. Decca DL 75173, 1970.

"Lost in the Flood" (Bruce Springsteen)

Greetings from Asbury Park, N.J. Bruce Springsteen. 33-1/3 rpm phonodisc. Columbia KC-31903, 1973. Reissued on compact disc.

"Lyndon Johnson Told the Nation" (Tom Paxton)

Ain't That News! Tom Paxton. 33-1/3 rpm phonodisc. Elektra EKL-298/EKS-7298, 1965.

I Can't Help Wonder Where I'm Bound: The Elektra Years. Tom Paxton. Compact disc. Rhino 73515, 1999.

The Best of the Vanguard Years. Tom Paxton. Compact disc. Vanguard 79561, 2000. (Note: Paxton's performance of "Lyndon Johnson Told the Nation" on this disc was recorded at the 1964 Newport Folk Festival and was previously unreleased.)

"Machine Gun" (Jimi Hendrix)

Band of Gypsys. Band of Gypsys. 33-1/3 rpm phonodisc. Capitol STAO-472; Polydor 2406002, 1970. Reissued on compact disc, Classic Compact Disc 472, 2000.

Midnight Lightning. Jimi Hendrix. 33-1/3 rpm phonodisc. Reprise MS-2229, 1975.

The Essential Jimi Hendrix, Volume 2. Jimi Hendrix. 33-1/3 rpm phonodisc. Reprise HS-2293, 1979.

"Marblehead Messenger" (Andy Kulberg, Jim Roberts)

The Marblehead Messenger. Seatrain. 33-1/3 rpm phonodisc. Capitol SMAS-829, 1971.

"Masters of War" (Bob Dylan)

The Freewheelin' Bob Dylan. Bob Dylan. 33-1/3 rpm phonodisc. Columbia CK-8786, 1963. Reissued on compact disc, Columbia CK-8786.

"Military Madness" (Graham Nash)

Graham Nash. 45 rpm phonodisc. Atlantic 2827, 1971.

Songs for Beginners. Graham Nash. 33-1/3 rpm phonodisc. Atlantic SD-7204, 1971. Reissued on compact disc.

"Minute Men (Are Turning in Their Graves), The" (Harlan Howard)

Stonewall Jackson. 45 rpm phonodisc. Columbia 43552, 1966.

All's Fair in Love and War. Stonewall Jackson. 33-1/3 rpm phonodisc. Columbia CL-2509/CS-9309, 1966.

Country Shots: God Bless America. Various artists. "The Minute Men (Are Turning in Their Graves)" performed by Stonewall Jackson. Simultaneously issued on 1-7/8 ips audio cassette and compact disc, Rhino 71645, 1994.

"Mister Professor" (Harlan Howard)

Leroy Van Dyke. 45 rpm phonodisc. Decca 32756, 1970.

To the Silent Majority, With Love. Harlan Howard. 33-1/3 rpm phonodisc. Nugget Records MRLP-105, 1971.

"Moratorium" (Buffy Sainte-Marie)

She Used to Wanna Be a Ballerina. Buffy Sainte-Marie. 33-1/3 rpm phonodisc. Vanguard VSD-79311, 1971.

"Must We Fight Two Wars?" (C. Cooper, Blaine Smith)

The Ballad of Two Brothers. Autry Inman. 33-1/3 rpm phonodisc. Epic 26428, 1968.

"My Buddy Carl" (Robert Thompson)

An Open Letter. Victor Lundberg. 33-1/3 rpm phonodisc. Liberty LST-7547, 1967.

"No More Genocide" (Holly Near)

> *Hang in There*. Holly Near. 33-1/3 rpm phonodisc. Redwood Records RRS-3800, 1973.

"Oh America" (Holly Near)

> *Hang in There*. Holly Near. 33-1/3 rpm phonodisc. Redwood Records RRS-3800, 1973.

"Ohio" (Neil Young)

> Crosby, Stills, Nash & Young. 45 rpm phonodisc. Atlantic 2740, 1970.

> *4 Way Street*. Crosby, Stills, Nash & Young. Two 33-1/3 rpm phonodiscs. Atlantic 902, 1971. Reissued on compact disc, Atlantic 82408-2.

> *Journey Through the Past*. Neil Young. Two 33-1/3 rpm phonodiscs. Warner Brothers 6480, 1972.

> *So Far*. Crosby, Stills, Nash & Young. 33-1/3 rpm phonodisc. Atlantic 18100, 1974. Reissued on compact disc, Atlantic 82648-2.

> *CSN*. Crosby, Stills, Nash (& Young). Four compact discs. Atlantic 82319-2, 1992.

"Okie from Muskogee" (Merle Haggard, Eddie Burris)

> Merle Haggard. 45 rpm phonodisc. Capitol 2626, 1969.

> *Okie from Muskogee*. Merle Haggard. 33-1/3 rpm phonodisc. Capitol ST-384, 1969. Reissued on compact disc, Cema Special Products, 57246, 1992.

> *The Fightin' Side of Me*. Merle Haggard. 33-1/3 rpm phonodisc. Capitol ST-451, 1970. Reissued on compact disc, King 1460, 1996.

> *Jim Kweskin's America*. Jim Kweskin. 33-1/3 rpm phonodisc. Reprise 6464, 1971.

> *The Best of the Best of Merle Haggard*. Merle Haggard. 33-1/3 rpm phonodisc. Capitol 11082, 1972. Reissued on compact disc, Liberty 91254, 1991.

> *"Platoon."* Various artists. "Okie from Muskogee" performed by Merle Haggard. Simultaneously issued on 1-7/8 ips audio cassette, Atlantic 81742-4 and compact disc, Atlantic 81742-2, 1986.

> *A&E Biography*. Merle Haggard. Simultaneously issued on 1-7/8 ips audio cassette and compact disc, Capitol 30204, 1999. (Note: This collection was released to coincide with the Haggard profile on the A&E cable television network's *Biography* program.)

Country U.S.A.: 1969. Various artists. "Okie from Muskogee" performed by Merle Haggard. Compact disc. Time-Life 08, n.d.

"One More Parade" (Bob Gibson, Phil Ochs)

All the News That's Fit to Sing. Phil Ochs. 33-1/3 rpm phonodisc. Elektra EKL-269/EKS-7269, 1964.

Farewells & Fantasies. Phil Ochs. Three compact discs. Elektra R2-73518, 1997.

"Open Letter to My Teenage Son, An" (Robert Thompson)

Victor Lundberg. 45 rpm phonodisc. Liberty 55996, 1967.

An Open Letter. Victor Lundberg. 33-1/3 rpm phonodisc. Liberty LST-7547, 1967.

Twelve Top Hits. Various artists. "An Open Letter to My Teenage Son" performed by Bobby Sims. 33-1/3 rpm phonodisc. Modern Sound MS 1050, 1968.

"Peace Train" (Cat Stevens)

Teaser and the Firecat. Cat Stevens. 33-1/3 rpm phonodisc. A&M SP-4313, 1971. Reissued on compact disc, A&M 75021-4313-2.

Cat Stevens. 45 rpm phonodisc. A&M 191, 1971.

Greatest Hits. Cat Stevens. 33-1/3 rpm phonodisc. A&M SP-4519, 1975.

The Roots of Rock: Soft Rock. Various artists. "Peace Train" performed by Cat Stevens. Simultaneously issued on 1-7/8 ips audio cassette and compact disc, Rebound 520372, 1995.

The Very Best of Cat Stevens. Cat Stevens. Compact disc. Polygram 541387, 2000.

"Peace Will Come (According to Plan)" (Melanie Safka)

Melanie. 45 rpm phonodisc. Buddah 186, 1970.

Leftover Wine. Melanie. 33-1/3 rpm phonodisc. Buddah BDS 5066, 1970.

"Question" (Justin Hayward)

The Moody Blues. 45 rpm phonodisc. Threshold 67004, 1970.

A Question of Balance. The Moody Blues. 33-1/3 rpm phonodisc. Threshold , 1970.

This Is The Moody Blues. The Moody Blues. Two 33-1/3 rpm phonodiscs. Threshold 2 THS 12/13, 1974.

Rock On 1970. Various artists. "Question" performed by The Moody Blues. Compact disc. Madacy 1970, 1996.

The Moody Blues Anthology. The Moody Blues. Two compact discs. Polygram 31456-5430-2, 1998.

"Requiem for the Masses" (Terry Kirkman)

The Association. B-side of "Never My Love." 45 rpm phonodisc. Warner Brothers 7074, 1967.

Inside Out. The Association. 33-1/3 rpm phonodisc. Warner Brothers WS-1696, 1967.

Greatest Hits! The Association. 33-1/3 rpm phonodisc. Warner Brothers WS1767, 1968. Reissued on compact disc, Warner Brothers 1767.

"Revolution" (John Lennon, Paul McCartney)

The Beatles. The Beatles. Two 33-1/3 rpm phonodiscs. Apple SWBO 101, 1968. Reissued on compact disc, Capitol 46443. (Note: The song is called "Revolution No. 1" on this release.)

The Beatles. 45 rpm phonodisc. Apple 2276, 1968. (Note: The song was the B-side of "Hey Jude.")

Hey Jude. The Beatles. 33-1/3 rpm phonodisc. Apple SW 385, 1970.

Past Masters, Volume Two. The Beatles. Compact disc. Capitol C2-90044, 1988.

"Ruby, Don't Take Your Love to Town" (Mel Tillis)

Life Turned Her That Way. Mel Tillis. 33-1/3 rpm phonodisc. Kapp KL-1514, 1967.

Johnny Darrell. 45 rpm phonodisc. United Artists 50126, 1967.

Ruby, Don't Take Your Love to Town. Johnny Darrell. 33-1/3 rpm phonodisc. United Artists UAL 3594/UAS 6594, 1967.

The Romantic, Wacky, Soulful, Rockin', Country, Bobby Goldsboro. Bobby Goldsboro. 33-1/3 rpm phonodisc. United Artists UAL 3599, 1967.

Love of the Common People. Waylon Jennings. 33-1/3 rpm phonodisc. RCA Victor 3825, 1967. Reissued on compact disc, Buddha 99620, 1999.

The George Jones Story. George Jones. 33-1/3 rpm phonodisc. Musicor M2S-3159, 1968.

The First Edition '69. The First Edition. 33-1/3 rpm phonodisc. Reprise RS 6328, 1969.

Kenny Rogers and The First Edition. 45 rpm phonodisc. Reprise 0829, 1969.

The Best of Waylon Jennings. Waylon Jennings. 33-1/3 rpm phonodisc. RCA Victor LSP-4341, 1970.

My Kind of Country. Carl Perkins. 33-1/3 rpm phonodisc. Mercury SRM-1-691, 1973. Reissued on compact disc, Rebound 520523.

All Time Greatest Hits, Vol. 2. Kenny Rogers and The First Edition. Compact disc. MCA Special Products MCAD-22056, 1989.

Country Stars of Branson, Missouri. Various artists. "Ruby, Don't Take Your Love to Town" performed by Kenny Rogers and The First Edition. Simultaneously issued on 1-7/8 ips audio cassette and compact disc, MCA Special Products 20878, 1995.

Country Heartbreakers. Various artists. "Ruby, Don't Take Your Love to Town" performed by Kenny Rogers and The First Edition. Compact disc. Fine Tune 1124, 1999.

Through the Years: A Retrospective. Kenny Rogers. Four compact discs. Capitol 33183, 1999.

Country Hall of Fame. Various artists. "Ruby, Don't Take Your Love to Town" performed by Kenny Rogers and The First Edition. Compact disc. Columbia River Entertainment Group 1141, n.d.

Country U.S.A.: 1969. Various artists. "Ruby, Don't Take Your Love to Town" performed by Kenny Rogers and The First Edition. Compact disc. Time-Life 08, n.d.

Time-Life's Treasury of Folk, Vol. 4: Folk Rock. Various artists. "Ruby, Don't Take Your Love to Town" performed by Kenny Rogers and The First Edition. Compact disc. Time-Life Music 21, n.d.

"Run Through the Jungle" (John C. Fogerty)

Creedence Clearwater Revival. 45 rpm phonodisc. Fantasy 641, 1970.

Cosmo's Factory. Creedence Clearwater Revival. 33-1/3 rpm phonodisc. Fantasy 8402, 1970. Reissued on compact disc, Fantasy 8402, 2000.

Chronicle. Creedence Clearwater Revival. Fantasy , CCR2, 1976. Reissued on compact disc, Fantasy FCD-623-CCR2, 1990.

"Saigon" (Barry Sadler)

> *Ballads of the Green Berets.* SSgt. Barry Sadler. 33-1/3 rpm phonodisc. RCA Victor LPM-3547, 1966. Reissued on compact disc. Collector's Choice Music CCM037-2, 1997.

"Saigon Bride" (Nina Dusheck, Joan Baez)

> *Joan.* Joan Baez. 33-1/3 rpm phonodisc. Vanguard VRS-9240, 1967. Reissued on compact disc, Vanguard 79240, 1993.

"Save the Country"(Laura Nyro)

> The 5th Dimension. 45 rpm phonodisc. Bell 895, 1970.

> *Portrait.* The 5th Dimension. 33-1/3 rpm phonodisc. Bell 6045, 1970.

> *Greatest Hits on Earth.* The 5th Dimension. Simultaneously issued on 1-7/8 ips audio cassette and compact disc, Arista 8335.

> *Up-Up and Away: The Definitive Collection.* The 5th Dimension. Two compact discs. Arista 18961, 1997.

"Scarborough Fair/Canticle" (Paul Simon, Arthur Garfunkel)

> *Parsley, Sage, Rosemary and Thyme.* Simon and Garfunkel. 33-1/3 rpm phonodisc. Columbia 9363, 1966. Reissued on 1-7/8 ips audio cassette, Columbia PCT-132, and compact disc, Columbia CK-9363.

> Simon and Garfunkel. 45 rpm phonodisc. Columbia 44456, 1968.

> *Mrs. Robinson.* Simon and Garfunkel. 45 rpm extended play phonodisc. CBS 6400, 1968.

> *The Graduate.* Simon and Garfunkel. 33-1/3 rpm phonodisc. Columbia 3180, 1968. Reissued on compact disc, Columbia CK-3180.

> *Simon and Garfunkel's Greatest Hits.* Simon and Garfunkel. 33-1/3 rpm phonodisc. Columbia KC-31350, 1972. Reissued on compact disc, Columbia JCT-31350.

> *Collected Works.* Simon and Garfunkel. Three compact discs. Columbia C3K-45322, 1981. Also issued as Sony 45322.

"Seven O'Clock News/Silent Night" (Paul Simon)

> *Parsley, Sage, Rosemary and Thyme.* Simon and Garfunkel. 33-1/3 rpm phonodisc. Columbia 9363, 1966. Reissued on 1-7/8 ips audio cassette, Columbia PCT-132; and compact disc, Columbia CK-9363.

Collected Works. Simon and Garfunkel. Three compact discs. Columbia C3K-45322, 1981. Also issued as Sony 45322.

"Side of a Hill, The" (Paul Kane [Paul Simon])

The Paul Simon Songbook. Paul Simon. 33-1/3 rpm phonodisc. CBS 62579, 1965.

"Simple Desultory Philippic (Or How I Was Robert McNamara'd Into Submission), A" (Paul Simon)

The Paul Simon Songbook. Paul Simon. 33-1/3 rpm phonodisc. CBS 62579, 1965.

Parsley, Sage, Rosemary and Thyme. Simon and Garfunkel. 33-1/3 rpm phonodisc. Columbia 9363, 1966. Reissued on 1-7/8 ips audio cassette, Columbia PCT-132; and compact disc, Columbia CK-9363.

Collected Works. Simon and Garfunkel. Three compact discs. Columbia C3K-45322, 1981. Also issued as Sony 45322.

"Singin' in Viet Nam Talkin' Blues" (Johnny Cash)

Johnny Cash. 45 rpm phonodisc. Columbia 45393, 1971.

Man in Black. Johnny Cash. 33-1/3 rpm phonodisc. Columbia 30550, 1971.

"Sky Pilot" (Eric Burdon, Vic Briggs, John Weider, Barry Jenkins, Daniel McCulloch)

Eric Burdon and The Animals. 45 rpm phonodisc. MGM 13939, 1968.

The Twain Shall Meet. Eric Burdon and The Animals. 33-1/3 rpm phonodisc. MGM SE-4537, 1968.

Songs of Protest. Various artists. "Sky Pilot" performed by Eric Burdon and The Animals. Simultaneously issued on 1-7/8 ips audio cassette and compact disc, Rhino 70734, 1991.

"So Cold in Vietnam" (Johnny Shines)

Masters of Modern Blues, Volume 1: The Johnny Shines Band. The Johnny Shines Band. Testament Records T-2212, n.d. (Note: The liner notes give the recording date as June 1966, but it is not clear when this track was initially released.)

"Soldier Has Come Home, The" (Barry Sadler)

Ballads of the Green Berets. SSgt. Barry Sadler. 33-1/3 rpm phonodisc. RCA Victor LPM-3547, 1966. Reissued on compact disc. Collector's Choice Music CCM037-2, 1997.

"Soldier's Last Letter, The" (Ernest Tubb, Redd Stewart)

> *Hello Vietnam.* Johnny Wright. 33-1/3 rpm phonodisc. Decca DL-4698, 1966.

> *There's a Star-Spangled Banner Waving Somewhere.* Dave Dudley. 33-1/3 rpm phonodisc. Mercury MG-21057/SR-61057, 1966.

> *Branded Man/I Threw away the Rose.* Merle Haggard. 33-1/3 rpm phonodisc. Capitol ST-2789, 1967.

> Merle Haggard. 45 rpm phonodisc. Capitol 3024, 1971.

"Something in the Air" (Speedy Keen)

> Thunderclap Newman. 45 rpm phonodisc. Track 2656, 1969.

> *"The Magic Christian"—Original Soundtrack.* Various artists. "Something in the Air" performed by Thunderclap Newman. 33-1/3 rpm phonodisc. Commonwealth United Records CU-6004, 1970.

> *Hollywood Dream.* Thunderclap Newman. 33-1/3 rpm phonodisc. Track SD-8264, 1970.

> *The Summer of Love Album.* Various artists. "Something in the Air" performed by Thunderclap Newman. Compact disc. Crimson 542, 1998.

"Still in Saigon" (Dan Daley)

> *Windows.* The Charlie Daniels Band. 33-1/3 rpm phonodisc. Epic FE-37694, 1982. Reissued on compact disc, Sony 65228, 1997.

"Stop the War Now" (Norman Whitfield, Barrett Strong)

> Edwin Starr. 45 rpm phonodisc. Gordy 7104, 1970.

> *Involved.* Edwin Starr. 33-1/3 rpm phonodisc. Gordy GS 956, 1971.

"Sweet Cherry Wine" (Tommy James, Richard Grasso)

> Tommy James and The Shondells. 45 rpm phonodisc. Roulette 7039, 1969.

> *The Very Best of Tommy James and The Shondells.* Tommy James and The Shondells. Compact disc. Rhino R2-71214, 1993.

"Talkin' Vietnam Blues" (Phil Ochs)

> *Live at Newport.* Phil Ochs. Compact disc. Vanguard 77017-2, 1996.

"Talking Vietnam Pot Luck Blues" (Tom Paxton)

> *Morning Again.* Tom Paxton. 33-1/3 rpm phonodisc. Elektra EKS-74019, 1968.

The Compleat Tom Paxton Recorded Live. Tom Paxton. Two 33-1/3 rpm phonodiscs. Elektra 7E-2003, 1970.

I Can't Help Wonder Where I'm Bound: The Elektra Years. Tom Paxton. Compact disc. Rhino 73515, 1999.

"To Susan on the West Coast Waiting" (Donovan Leitch)

Barabajagal. Donovan. 33-1/3 rpm phonodisc. Epic BN-26481, 1969.

Donovan. 45 rpm phonodisc. Epic 10434, 1969.

Donovan's Greatest Hits. Donovan. Compact disc. Epic EK-65730, 1999. (Note: "To Susan on the West Coast Waiting" is included only on the compact disc reissue of *Donovan's Greatest Hits.*)

"Turn! Turn! Turn! (To Everything There Is a Season)" (Pete Seeger)

The Bitter and the Sweet. Pete Seeger. 33-1/3 rpm phonodisc. Columbia CL-1916, 1962.

The Byrds. 45 rpm phonodisc. Columbia 43424, 1965.

What's New Harmonicats? The Harmonicats. 33-1/3 rpm phonodisc. Columbia CS-9225, 1966. (Note: This album contains an arrangement of the song orchestrated for harmonica trio with instrumental ensemble.)

The Byrds' Greatest Hits. The Byrds. 33-1/3 rpm phonodisc. Columbia 9516, 1967. Reissued on compact disc, Columbia CK-9516. Also issued on compact disc as Sony 9516.

Judy Collins. 45 rpm phonodisc. Elektra 45680, 1969.

Recollections: The Best of Judy Collins. Judy Collins. 33-1/3 rpm phonodisc. Elektra 74055, 1969. Reissued on compact disc.

Rock's Greatest Hits. Various artists. "Turn! Turn! Turn!" performed by The Byrds. Four 33-1/3 rpm phonodiscs. Columbia P4S-5914, 1972.

Best of the '60s and '70s: Protest Rock. Various artists. "Turn! Turn! Turn!" performed by The Byrds. Simultaneously issued on 1-7/8 ips audio cassette and compact disc. Priority 53701, 1992.

Rock Classics. Various artists. "Turn! Turn! Turn!" performed by The Byrds. Compact disc. Sony Special Products 13867, 1993.

Live at Newport. Judy Collins. Simultaneously issued on 1-7/8 ips audio cassette and compact disc. Vanguard 77013, 1994. (Note: The recordings on this release were made at the Newport Folk Festival, 1959-1966.)

"Forrest Gump" Original Soundtrack. Various artists. "Turn! Turn! Turn!" performed by The Byrds. Simultaneously issued on 1-7/8 ips audio cassette and compact disc, Sony 66329, 1994.

The Best of Folk Rock. Various artists. "Turn! Turn! Turn!" performed by The Byrds. Simultaneously issued on 1-7/8 ips audio cassette and compact disc, K-Tel 3438, 1995.

Folk Hits. Various artists. "Turn! Turn! Turn!" performed by Judy Collins. Compact disc. Vanguard 79510, 1998.

Where Have All the Flowers Gone: The Songs of Pete Seeger. Various artists. "Turn! Turn! Turn!" performed by Bruce Cockburn. Two compact discs. Appleseed 1024, 1998.

Greatest Hits of the '60s, Vol. 2. Various artists. "Turn! Turn! Turn!" performed by The Byrds. Compact disc. Platinum Disc 56981, 1999.

Pop Music: The Golden Era 1951-1975. Various artists. "Turn! Turn! Turn!" performed by The Byrds. Multiple compact discs. Sony 65791, 1999.

"Universal Soldier, The" (Buffy Sainte-Marie)

It's My Way! Buffy Sainte-Marie. 33-1/3 rpm phonodisc. Vanguard VRS-9142, 1964.

Glen Campbell. 45 rpm phonodisc. Capitol 5504, 1965.

Donovan. 45 rpm phonodisc. Hickory 1338, 1965.

"Positively 4th Street" and Other Message Folk Songs. The Living Voices; Anita Kerr, arranger. 33-1/3 rpm phonodisc. RCA Camden CAL-947, 1966.

The Ballad of Two Brothers. Autry Inman. 33-1/3 rpm phonodisc. Epic 26428, 1968.

Death, Glory and Retribution. Various artists. "The Universal Soldier" performed by Glen Campbell. 33-1/3 rpm phonodisc. EMI 17187, 1985.

Songs of Protest. Various artists. "The Universal Soldier" performed by Donovan. Simultaneously issued on 1-7/8 ips audio cassette and compact disc, Rhino 70734, 1991.

Folk Hits. Various artists. "The Universal Soldier" performed by Buffy Sainte-Marie. Compact disc. Vanguard 79510, 1998.

Generations of Folk, Vol. 2: Protest & Politics. Various artists. "The Universal Soldier" performed by Buffy Sainte-Marie. Compact disc. Vanguard 78001, 1998.

"Unknown Soldier, The" (The Doors)

> The Doors. 45 rpm phonodisc. Elektra 45628, 1968.

> *Waiting for the Sun.* The Doors. 33-1/3 rpm phonodisc. Elektra EKS-74024, 1968. Reissued on compact disc.

"Viet Nam" (Mark Charron)

> *The Very Best of B .J. Thomas.* B. J. Thomas. 33-1/3 rpm phonodisc. Hickory Records LPS-133, 1966.

"Vietcong Blues" (Junior Wells)

> *The Best of the Chicago Blues.* Various artists. "Vietcong Blues" performed by the Junior Wells Chicago Blues Band. Two 33-1/3 rpm phonodiscs. Vanguard VSD-1/2, 1970.

> *Chicago Blues Today, Vol. 1.* Various artists. "Vietcong Blues" performed by the Junior Wells Chicago Blues Bland. 33-1/3 rpm phonodisc. Vanguard VSD-79216, 1972. Reissued on compact disc, Vanguard 79215.

> *Defiance Blues.* Various artists. "Vietcong Blues" performed by the Junior Wells Chicago Blues Band. Compact disc. A&M 161340, 1998.

"Vietnam" (Jimmy Cliff)

> *Jimmy Cliff.* Jimmy Cliff. 33-1/3 rpm phonodisc. Trojan 16, 1969. Reissued on compact disc, Tristar 35278, 1995.

> *Wonderful World, Beautiful People.* Jimmy Cliff. 33-1/3 rpm phonodisc. A&M 4251, 1970. Reissued on 1-7/8 ips audio cassette, A&M 75021-3189-4 and compact disc, A&M 75021-3189-2.

> Jimmy Cliff. B-side of "Come into My Life." 45 rpm phonodisc. A&M 1167, 1970.

> *The Best of Jimmy Cliff.* Jimmy Cliff. 33-1/3 rpm phonodisc. Island 6, 1975. Reissued on compact disc, 1988.

"Vietnam" (Bob Thiele)

> *Every Day I Have the Blues.* T-Bone Walker. 33-1/3 rpm phonodisc. Flying Dutchman BluesTime BTS-9004, 1969.

"Vietnam Blues" (Kris Kristofferson)

> Dave Dudley. 45 rpm phonodisc. Mercury 72550, 1966.

> *There's a Star-Spangled Banner Waving Somewhere.* Dave Dudley. 33-1/3 rpm phonodisc. Mercury MG-21057/SR-61057, 1966.

The Ballad of Two Brothers. Autry Inman. 33-1/3 rpm phonodisc. Epic 26428, 1968.

Country Shots: God Bless America. Various artists. "Vietnam Blues" performed by Dave Dudley. Simultaneously issued on 1-7/8 ips audio cassette and compact disc, Rhino 71645, 1994.

"Vietnam Blues" (J. B. Lenoir)

J. B. Lenoir. J. B. Lenoir. 33-1/3 rpm phonodisc. Crusade/Polydor 24-4011, 1970.

"Vietnam Blues" (Robert Pete Williams)

Robert Pete Williams. Robert Pete Williams. 33-1/3 rpm phonodisc. Ahura Mazda AMS 2002, 1971.

"Volunteers" (Paul Kantner, Marty Balin)

Jefferson Airplane. 45 rpm phonodisc. RCA Victor 0245, 1969.

Volunteers. Jefferson Airplane. 33-1/3 rpm phonodisc. RCA Victor 4238, 1969. Reissued on compact disc, RCA Victor 4238-2-R.

"Waist Deep in the Big Muddy" (Pete Seeger)

"Waist Deep in the Big Muddy" and Other Love Songs. Pete Seeger. 33-1/3 rpm phonodisc. Columbia CL 2705/CS 9505, 1967. Reissued on 1-7/8 ips audio cassette and compact disc, Sony 57311, 1994.

Where Have All the Flowers Gone: The Songs of Pete Seeger. Various artists. "Waist Deep in the Big Muddy" performed by Dick Gaughan. Two compact discs. Appleseed 1024, 1998.

"War" (Norman Whitfield, Barrett Strong)

Psychedelic Shack. The Temptations. 33-1/3 rpm phonodisc. Gordy 947, 1970. Reissued on 1-7/8 ips audio cassette and compact disc, Motown 5164.

Edwin Starr. 45 rpm phonodisc. Gordy 7101, 1970.

Involved. Edwin Starr. 33-1/3 rpm phonodisc. Gordy GS 956, 1971.

Rhythm & Blues: 1970. Various artists. "War" performed by Edwin Starr. Compact disc. Time-Life RHD-18, 1989.

Sounds of the Seventies: 1970. Various artists. "War" performed by Edwin Starr. Compact disc. Time-Life SOD-01, 1989.

"Billboard" Top Rock & Roll Hits: 1970. Various artists. "War" performed by Edwin Starr. Simultaneously issued on 33-1/3 rpm phonodisc, Rhino

70631; 1-7/8 ips audio cassette, Rhino R4-70631; and compact disc, Rhino R2-70631, 1990. (Note: The compact disc version of this release was included in the five-disc set *"Billboard" Top Rock & Roll Hits: 1968-1972*, Rhino 72005.)

Songs of Protest. Various artists. "War" performed by Edwin Starr. Simultaneously issued on 1-7/8 ips audio cassette and compact disc, Rhino 70734, 1991.

Best of the '60s and '70s: Protest Rock. Various artists. "War" performed by Edwin Starr. Simultaneously issued on 1-7/8 ips audio cassette and compact disc. Priority 53701, 1992.

Hitsville USA: The Motown Singles Collection, 1959-1971. Various artists. "War" performed by Edwin Starr. Simultaneously issued on 1-7/8 ips audio cassette and compact disc, Motown 6312, 1992.

Music from "The Wonder Years," Vol. 3. Various artists. "War" performed by Edwin Starr. Issued on 1-7/8 ips audio cassette, Delta 72313 and compact disc, Laserlight 72313, 1994.

Motown Year by Year: The Sound of Young America, 1970. Various artists. "War" performed by Edwin Starr. Simultaneously issued on 1-7/8 ips audio cassette and compact disc, Motown 530528, 1995.

"The Walking Dead" Original Soundtrack. Various artists. "War" performed by Edwin Starr. Simultaneously issued on 1-7/8 ips audio cassette, Motown 314530478-2; and compact disc, Motown 530478, 1995.

Rock On 1970. Various artists. "War" performed by Edwin Starr. Compact disc. Madacy 1970, 1996.

"Small Soldiers" Original Soundtrack. Various artists. "War" performed by Edwin Starr. Simultaneously issued on 1-7/8 ips audio cassette and compact disc, DreamWorks 50051, 1998. (Note: This album (and the film) also contains a recording of "War" by Bone Thugs-N-Harmony.)

Summer of Peace, Vol. 2. Various artists. "War" performed by Edwin Starr. Compact disc. Platinum Disc 18077, 1999.

"War Drags on, The" (Mike Softley)

The Real Donovan. Donovan. 33-1/3 rpm phonodisc. Hickory 135, 1966.

Like It Is, Was And Evermore Shall Be. Donovan. 33-1/3 rpm phonodisc. Hickory 143, 1968.

Donovan P. Leitch. Donovan. Two 33-1/3 rpm phonodiscs. Janus JL2S-3022, 1970.

"War Games" (David Jones, Steve Pitts)

> *Missing Links*. The Monkees. Issued on 33-1/3 rpm phonodisc, Rhino RNLP 70150; 1-7/8 ips audio cassette, Rhino R4 70150; and compact disc, Rhino R2 70150, 1987.

"War Is Over, The" (Phil Ochs)

> *Tape from California*. Phil Ochs. 33-1/3 rpm phonodisc. A&M SP-4148, 1968.

> *Farewells & Fantasies*. Phil Ochs. Three compact discs. Elektra R2-73518, 1997.

"War Pigs" (Tony Ioomi, Ozzy Osbourne, Terry Butler, William Ward)

> *Paranoid*. Black Sabbath. 33-1/3 rpm phonodisc. Warner Brothers WS1887, 1970.

"We Got to Have Peace" (Curtis Mayfield)

> Curtis Mayfield. 45 rpm phonodisc. Curtom 1968, 1972.

> *Roots*. Curtis Mayfield. 33-1/3 rpm phonodisc. Curtom Records CRS 8009, 1972. Reissued on compact disc, Rhino 75569, 1999.

"We Seek No Wider War" (Phil Ochs)

> *Farewells & Fantasies*. Phil Ochs. Three compact discs. Elektra R2-73518, 1997.

> *The Best of "Broadside," 1962-1988*. Various artists. "We Seek No Wider War" performed by Phil Ochs. Five compact discs. Smithsonian/Folkways 40130, 2000.

"What Did You Learn in School Today?" (Tom Paxton)

> *Broadside Ballads, Vol. 2*. Various artists. "What Did You Learn in School Today?" performed by Pete Seeger. 33-1/3 rpm phonodisc. Folkways BR-302, 1963.

> *The Best of "Broadside," 1962-1988*. Various artists. "What Did You Learn in School Today?" performed by Tom Paxton. Five compact discs. Smithsonian/Folkways 40130, 2000.

"What We're Fighting For" (Tom T. Hall)

> Dave Dudley. 45 rpm phonodisc. Mercury 72500, 1965.

> *There's a Star-Spangled Banner Waving Somewhere*. Dave Dudley. 33-1/3 rpm phonodisc. Mercury MG-21057/SR-61057, 1966.

"Where Have All the Flowers Gone?" (Pete Seeger)

The Bitter and the Sweet. Pete Seeger. 33-1/3 rpm phonodisc. Columbia CL-1916, 1962.

College Concert. The Kingston Trio. 33-1/3 rpm phonodisc. Capitol T-1658, 1962.

The Kingston Trio. 45 rpm phonodisc. Capitol 4671, 1962.

Who's News! Various artists. "Where Have All the Flowers Gone?" performed by The Kingston Trio. 33-1/3 rpm phonodisc. Capitol NP-1, 1962.

Peter, Paul, and Mary. Peter, Paul & Mary. 33-1/3 rpm phonodisc. Warner Brothers WS-1449, 1962. Reissued as Warner Brothers 1449, 1990. Reissued on 1-7/8 ips audio cassette, Warner Brothers M5-1449 and compact disc, Warner Brothers 2-1449, 1988.

Meet The Searchers. The Searchers. 33-1/3 rpm phonodisc. Pye 18086, 1963. Reissued on compact disc, Castle 165.

The Folk Era. The Kingston Trio. Three 33-1/3 rpm phonodiscs. Capitol STCL-2180, 1964.

Johnny Rivers. 45 rpm phonodisc. Imperial 66144, 1965.

Johnny Rivers Rocks the Folk. Johnny Rivers. 33-1/3 rpm phonodisc. Imperial LP-12293, 1965. Reissued on compact disc, BGO 299, 1996.

"Positively 4th Street" and Other Message Folk Songs. The Living Voices; Anita Kerr, arranger. 33-1/3 rpm phonodisc. RCA Camden CAL-947, 1966.

What's New Harmonicats? The Harmonicats. 33-1/3 rpm phonodisc. Columbia CS-9225, 1966. (Note: This album contains an arrangement of the song orchestrated for harmonica trio with instrumental ensemble.)

The Best of The Kingston Trio. The Kingston Trio. 33-1/3 rpm phonodisc. Capitol SM-1705, 1971. Reissued on compact disc.

Last Days and Time. Earth, Wind & Fire. 33-1/3 rpm phonodisc. Columbia 31702, 1972. Reissued on compact disc.

The World of Pete Seeger. Pete Seeger. 33-1/3 rpm phonodisc. Columbia 31949, 1973.

Very Early Joan Baez. Joan Baez. 33-1/3 rpm phonodisc. Vanguard 79436, 1983. Reissued on compact disc, Vanguard VCD-79446.

Anthology, 1964-1977. Johnny Rivers. Simultaneously issued on 1-7/8 ips audio cassette, Rhino R4-70793 and compact disc, Rhino R2-70793, 1991.

Songs of Protest. Various artists. "Where Have All the Flowers Gone?" performed by The Kingston Trio. Simultaneously issued on 1-7/8 ips audio cassette and compact disc, Rhino 70734, 1991.

Folk Hits. Various artists. "Where Have All the Flowers Gone?" performed by Pete Seeger. Compact disc. Vanguard 79510, 1998.

Where Have All the Flowers Gone? A Vietnam Veterans Memorial Album. George Grove and The Kingston Trio. Compact disc. Timber Grove Records, 1998. (Note: The song is broken up into several sections and interpolated with additional songs about the experience of Vietnam veterans sung by George Grove and poetry by Steve Mason. Note that this is a new performance by the 1998 incarnation of The Kingston Trio.)

Where Have All the Flowers Gone: The Songs of Pete Seeger. Various artists. "Where Have All the Flowers Gone?" performed by Tommy Sands and Dolores Keane. Two compact discs. Appleseed 1024, 1998.

Your Hit Parade: The Early '60s. Various artists. "Where Have All the Flowers Gone?" performed by The Kingston Trio. Compact disc. Time-Life HPD-33, n.d.

"Where Have All Our Heroes Gone?" (Bill Anderson, Bob Talbert)

Bill Anderson. 45 rpm phonodisc. Decca 32744, 1970.

Where Have All Our Heroes Gone? Bill Anderson. 33-1/3 rpm phonodisc. Decca DL75254, 1970.

Country Shots: God Bless America. Various artists. "Where Have All Our Heroes Gone?" performed by Bill Anderson. Simultaneously Issued on 1-7/8 ips audio cassette and compact disc, Rhino 71645, 1994.

"White Boots Marchin' in a Yellow Land" (Phil Ochs)

Tape from California. Phil Ochs. 33-1/3 rpm phonodisc. A&M SP-4148, 1968.

Farewells & Fantasies. Phil Ochs. Three compact discs. Elektra R2-73518, 1997.

"Who'll Stop the Rain?" (John C. Fogerty)

Creedence Clearwater Revival. 45 rpm phonodisc. Fantasy 637, 1970.

Cosmo's Factory. Creedence Clearwater Revival. 33-1/3 rpm phonodisc. Fantasy 8402, 1970. Reissued on compact disc, Fantasy 8402, 2000.

All the Way Home. Gary & Randy Scruggs. 33-1/3 rpm phonodisc. Vanguard 6538, 1970. Reissued on 1-7/8 ips audio cassette and compact disk, Vanguard 6538, 1994.

Chronicle. Creedence Clearwater Revival. Fantasy CCR2, 1976. Reissued on compact disc, Fantasy FCD-623-CCR2, 1990.

"Willing Conscript, The" (Tom Paxton)

Broadside Ballads, Vol. 2. Various artists. "The Willing Conscript" performed by Pete Seeger. 33-1/3 rpm phonodisc. Folkways BR-302, 1963.

Newport Broadside. Various artists. "The Willing Conscript" performed by Tom Paxton. 33-1/3 rpm phonodisc. Vanguard VSD-79144, 1964.

Note: The present recording was made at the 1963 Newport Folk Festival.

Ain't That News! Tom Paxton. 33-1/3 rpm phonodisc. Elektra EKL-298/EKS-7298, 1965.

I Can't Help Wonder Where I'm Bound: The Elektra Years. Tom Paxton. Compact disc. Rhino 73515, 1999.

The Best of "Broadside," 1962-1988. Various artists. "The Willing Conscript" performed by Pete Seeger. Five compact discs. Smithsonian/Folkways 40130, 2000.

The Best of the Vanguard Years. Tom Paxton. Compact disc. Vanguard 79561, 2000.

"Wish You Were Here, Buddy" (Pat Boone)

Pat Boone. 45 rpm phonodisc. Dot 16933, 1966.

Wish You Were Here, Buddy. Pat Boone. 33-1/3 rpm phonodisc. Dot DLP-3764, 1966.

"With God on Our Side" (Bob Dylan)

In Concert, Part Two. Joan Baez. 33-1/3 rpm phonodisc. Vanguard 9113, 1963.

The Times They Are A'Changin'. Bob Dylan. 33-1/3 rpm phonodisc. Columbia CL 2105, 1964.

Newport Broadside. Various artists. "With God on Our Side" performed by Bob Dylan. 33-1/3 rpm phonodisc. Vanguard VSD-79144, 1964. (Note: The present recording was made at the 1963 Newport Folk Festival.)

Manfred Mann. 45 rpm phonodisc. 1965.

Songs of Protest. Various artists. "With God on Our Side" performed by Manfred Mann. Compact disc. R2 70734, 1991.

"You're Over There (And I'm Over Here)" (Harlan Howard)

>*Country Music Special.* Johnny Wright. 33-1/3 rpm phonodisc. Decca DL-4770, 1966.

"Zor and Zam" (Bill Chadwick, John Chadwick)

>*The Birds, The Bees & The Monkees.* The Monkees. 33-1/3 rpm phonodisc. Colgems COS-109/COM-109, 1968. Reissued on 1-7/8 ips audio cassette and compact disc, Rhino 71794, 1994.

>*Missing Links, Vol. 3.* The Monkees. Compact disc. Rhino R2 72153, 1996.

BIBLIOGRAPHY

Aarons, Leroy F. 1965. FBI Checks Folk Songs—Then Mum's the Word. *The Washington Post*, November 6, 6.

Aarons, Leroy F. 1969. Sgt. Pepper Makes a Pitch for Peace. *Los Angeles Times*, June 15, 14 (Calendar).

Agnew, Spiro T. 1972. Talking Brainwashing Blues. Reprinted in *Sounds of Social Change*, ed. R. Serge Denisoff and Richard Peterson, 307-10. Chicago: Rand McNally.

Albert, George and Frank Hoffman. 1984. *The "Cash Box" Country Singles Charts, 1958-1982*. Metuchen, New Jersey: Scarecrow Press.

Allen, Gary. 1969. That Music: There's More to It Than Meets the Ear. *American Opinion* 12 (February): 49-62. (See also: Allen 1972.)

Allen, Gary. 1972. More Subversive Than Meets the Ear. In *Sounds of Social Change*, ed. R. Serge Denisoff and Richard Peterson, 151-66. Chicago: Rand McNally. (Note: The present article is a reprint of Allen 1969.)

The American Folk Scene: Dimensions of the Folksong Revival, ed. D. A. DeTurk and A. Poulin, Jr. 1967. New York: Dell Publishing, Laurel Editions.

Anderson, Omer. 1966. Army Drops Bomb on "Protests." *Billboard* (15 January): 3.

Ankeny, Jason. 2000. Review of *The Great American Eagle Tragedy* by Earth Opera. *All Music Guide* [World Wide Web Resource]. http://www.allmusic.com. Accessed October 11.

Armstrong, Dan. 1963. "Commercial" Folksongs—Product of "Instant Culture." *Sing Out!* 13 (February-March): 20-22. (Note: The present is a response to Fiott 1962-63.)

Arnold, Ben. 1993. *Music and War: A Research and Information Guide*. New York: Garland Publishing.

Arnold, James R. 1991. *The First Domino: Eisenhower, the Military, and America's Intervention in Vietnam*. New York: William Morrow and Company.

Artists Support U.S. Servicemen in Vietnam. 1966. *Billboard* (January 8): 35.

Baez, Joan. 1969. *Daybreak*. New York: Avon Books.

Banners, Buttons, and Songs. 1968. *Variety* (September 11): 88.

Battle Hymn Sales Soaring. 1971. *Music City News* 8 (March): 37.

Battle of Ideologies Set to Music Meets Deejay Resistance Movement. 1965. *Variety* (October 13): 63.

Begler, Lewis. 1970. *Rock Theology: Interpreting the Music of the Youth Culture*. New York: Bengizio Press.

Belz, Carl. 1967. Popular Music and the Folk Tradition. *Journal of American Folklore* 80 (April-June): 130-42.

Belz, Carl. 1972. *The Story of Rock*, 2nd ed. New York: Oxford University Press.

"Berets" Keep Mopping up on Sales Front. 1966. *Billboard* (March 5): 8.

Bewley, John M. 2000. Personal library reference e-mail to the author, August 29.

Bindas, Kenneth J. and Craig Houston. 1989. "Takin' Care of Business": Rock Music, Vietnam and the Protest Myth. *Historian* 52 (November): 1-23.

Birchall, Ian. 1969. The Decline and Fall of British Rhythm and Blues. In *The Age of Rock*, vol. 1, ed. Jonathan Eisen, 94-102. New York: Vintage Books, Random House.

Botkin, B. A. 1967. The Folksong Revival: Cult or Culture? In *The American Folk Scene: Dimensions of the Folksong Revival*, ed. D. A. DeTurk and A. Poulin, Jr., 95-102. New York: Dell Publishing, Laurel Editions.

Boy, 10, Leads Viets to Father's Hideout. 1964. Associated Press Wire Report (December 18).

Calley Disk Stirs Market: Supply Runs Behind Demand. 1971. *Billboard* 83 (April 24): 3.

Cap Nixes Disk: Seeks Not to "Glorify" Calley. 1971. *Billboard* 83 (April 24): 3.

Cash, Johnny. 1964. A Letter from Johnny Cash. *Broadside* n41 (March 10): 10.

Chilcoat, George W. 1992. Popular Music Goes to War: Songs about Vietnam. *International Journal of Instructional Media* 19 (Number 2): 171-82.

Chomsky, Noam. 1967. The Responsibility of Intellectuals. *New York Review of Books* (February 23): 16.

Clark, Charlie. 1986. The Tracks of Our Tears—When Rock Went to War: Looking Back on Vietnam and Its Music. *Veteran* (February): 10-23.

Cohn, Nik. 1969. *Rock from the Beginning*. New York: Pocket Books.

Coker, Wilson. 1971. *Music and Meaning*. New York: Free Press.

Col.'s Wyles also "Beret." 1967. *Billboard* (January 7): 42.

Cooper, B. Lee and Wayne S. Haney. 1997. *Rock Music in American Popular Culture II: More Rock 'n' Roll Resources*. New York and London: Harrington Park Press.

Corliss, R. 1967. Pop Music: What's Been Happening. *National Review* 19 (April 4): 371-4.

Cunningham, Sis and Gordon Friesen. 1965. An Interview with Phil Ochs. *Broadside* n63 (October 15).

Cuscuna, Michael. 1969. A New Music of Political Protest. *Saturday Review* 52 (December 13): 55-56.

Dachs, David. 1964. *Anything Goes: The World of Popular Music*. Indianapolis: Bobbs-Merrill.

Dachs, David. 1969. *American Pop*. New York: Scholastic Book Services.

Dane, Barbara. 1969-70. If This Be Treason. *Sing Out* 19 (Winter): 2-7.

Dane, Barbara and Irwin Silber. 1969. *The Vietnam Songbook*. New York: The Guardian.

Darlington, Sandy. 1969. Country Joe and The Fish: 1965-68. In *Rock and Roll Will Stand*, ed. Greil Marcus, 150-69. Boston: Beacon Press.

Dawbarn, B. 1968. Don't Laugh, But the Next Step Could Be Pop as a Political Power. *Melody Maker* 43 (October 6): 13.

Dean, Maury. 1966. *The Rock Revolution*. Detroit: Edmore Books.

DeBenedetti, Charles with Charles Chatfield, assisting author. 1990. *An American Ordeal: The Antiwar Movement of the Vietnam Era*. Syracuse, New York: Syracuse University Press.

Denisoff, R. Serge. 1969. Folk Rock: Folk Music, Protest, or Commercialism? *Journal of Popular Culture* 3 (Fall): 214-30.

Denisoff, R. Serge. 1970a. Kent State, Muskogee and the White House. *Broadside* 108 (July-August): 2-3.

Denisoff, R. Serge. 1970b. Protest Songs: Those on the Top Forty and Those on the Street. *American Quarterly* 22 (Winter 1970): 807-23.

Denisoff, R. Serge. 1971. *Great Day Coming: Folk Music and the American Left*. Urbana: University of Illinois Press.

Denisoff, R. Serge. 1972a. The Evolution of the American Protest Song. In *Sounds of Social Change*, ed. R. Serge Denisoff and Richard Peterson, 15-25. Chicago: Rand McNally.

Denisoff, R. Serge. 1972b. Folk Music and the American Left. In *Sounds of Social Change*, ed. R. Serge Denisoff and Richard Peterson, 105-20. Chicago: Rand McNally.

Denisoff, R. Serge. 1972c. *Sing a Song of Social Significance*. Bowling Green, Ohio: Bowling Green State University Popular Press.

Denisoff, R. Serge. 1973. *Songs of Protest, War & Peace*. Santa Barbara, California: American Bibliographical Center—Clio Press, Inc. (Note: There are a number of factual errors in the various discographies in the present volume. Due to the date of the publication, use of the discographies is dependent upon access to the original issues of the listed recordings on vinyl.)

Denisoff, R. Serge. 1990. Fighting Prophecy with Napalm: "The Ballad of the Green Berets." *Journal of American Culture* 13 (Spring): 81-94.

Denisoff, R. Serge and Mark H. Levine. 1971. The Popular Protest Song: The Case of the "Eve of Destruction." *Public Opinion Quarterly* 35 (Spring): 119-24. (See also: Denisoff and Levine 1972.)

Denisoff, R. Serge and Mark H. Levine. 1972. Brainwashing or Background Noise: The Popular Protest Song. In *Sounds of Social Change*, ed. R. Serge Denisoff and Richard Peterson, 213-21. Chicago: Rand McNally. (Note: The present is an expanded version of Denisoff and Levine 1971.)

DiMaggio, Paul; Richard A. Peterson; Jack Esco, Jr. 1972. Country Music: Ballad of the Silent Majority. In *Sounds of Social Change*, ed. R. Serge Denisoff and Richard Peterson, 38-56. Chicago: Rand McNally.

Downey, Pat, George Albert, and Frank Hoffman. 1994. *"Cash Box" Pop Singles Charts, 1950-1993*. Englewood, Colorado: Libraries Unlimited.

Dunson, Josh. 1965. *Freedom in the Air*. New York: International Publishers.

Dunson, Josh. 1966. Thunder without Rain. *Sing Out* 15 (January): 12-17.

E. D. 1964. Letters. *Broadside* n47 (June 30).

Eddy, Chuck. 1998. *Stairway to Hell: The 500 Best Heavy Metal Albums in the Universe*. New York: Da Capo Press.

Edmonds, Ben. 1997. Track by Track. In liner notes for *Farewells & Fantasies* (Phil Ochs): 63-89. Three compact discs. Elektra R2-73518.

Edwards, Emily and Michael Singletary. 1984. Mass Media Images. *Popular Music and Society* 9 (no. 4): 17-26.

Eliot, Marc. 1979. *Death of a Rebel: A Biography of Phil Ochs.* New York: Anchor Books.

Erlewine, Stephen Thomas. 2000. Review of *The Best of Bo Donaldson and The Heywoods* by Bo Donaldson and The Heywoods. *All Music Guide* [World Wide Web Resource]. http://www.allmusic.com. Accessed September 26.

Escot, Colin. 1988. Liner notes to *Hi Records: The Blues Sessions.* Two 33-1/3 rpm phonodiscs. Hi Records D-HIUKLP 427.

Etzkorn, K. Peter. 1977. Popular Music: The Sounds of the Many. In *Music in American Society 1776-1976*, ed. George McCue, 119-32. New Brunswick, New Jersey: Transaction Books.

Evans, Paul. 1992. *Rolling Stone Album Guide*, 3rd ed. Edited by Anthony DeCurtis, James Henke, and Holly George-Warren. *s.v.* "Creedence Clearwater Revival." New York: Random House.

Falleder, Arnold. 1966. Liner notes for *Ballads of the Green Berets* (SSgt. Barry Sadler). 33-1/3 rpm phonodisc. RCA Victor LPM-3547. Reissued on compact disc. Collector's Choice Music CCM037-2, 1997.

Fariña, Richard. 1969. Baez and Dylan: A Generation Singing Out. In *The Age of Rock*, vol. 1, ed. Jonathan Eisen, 200-207. New York: Vintage Books, Random House.

Fiott, Stephen. 1962-63. In Defense of Commercial Folksingers. *Sing Out!* 12 (December-January): 43-45. (See also: Armstrong 1963.)

Folk Music in Vietnam. 1968. *New York Times* February 13. Reprinted in *Sing Out!* 18 (June-July): 1.

Folk Songs and the Top 40—A Symposium. 1966. *Sing Out!* 16 (March): 12-21.

Forbes, C. A. 1971. New Folk Musical: Do the Answers Ring True? New Vibrations. *Christian Century* 15 (March 26): 38.

The Fort Hood Three: The Case of the Three G.I.'s Who Said "No" to the War in Vietnam. 1966. New York: Fort Hood Three Defense Committee.

Foster, Alice. 1970. Merle Haggard: "I Take a Lot of Pride in What I Am." *Sing Out!* 19 (March-April).

Friesen, Agnes. 1962. Singing on the Peace Walk. *Sing Out!* 12 (Summer): 35+.

Frith, Simon. 1981. *Sound Effects: Youth, Leisure, and the Politics of Rock 'N' Roll.* New York: Pantheon Books.

Gabree, John. 1969. Rock: Art, Revolution or Sell-Out? *High Fidelity* 19 (August): 10-11.

Garlock, Frank. 1971. *The Big Beat: A Rock Blast.* Greenville, South Carolina: Bob Jones University Press.

Geltman, M. 1966. Hot Hundred: A Surprise! Patriotic Songs. *National Review* 18 (September): 894-96.

Ginsberg, Allen. 1966. Liner notes to *The Fugs* (The Fugs). 33-1/3 rpm phonodisc. ESP-Disk 1028.

Gitlin, Todd. 1987. *The Sixties: Years of Hope, Days of Rage.* New York: Bantam Books.

Gleason, Ralph J. 1965a. Surrounded by "Subversive" Music. *San Francisco Chronicle* November 14, 23.

Gleason, Ralph J. 1965b. "The Times They Are a Changin": The Changing Message of America's Young Folksingers. *Ramparts* (April): 36-48.

Gleason, Ralph J. 1966. Liner notes for *Parsley, Sage, Rosemary and Thyme* (Simon and Garfunkel). 33-1/3 rpm phonodisc. Columbia 9363. Reissued on compact disc, Columbia CK-9363.

Gleason, Ralph J. 1972. A Cultural Revolution. In *Sounds of Social Change*, ed. R. Serge Denisoff and Richard Peterson, 137-46. Chicago: Rand McNally.

Goldstein, Richard. 1968. The New Rock: Wiggy Words that Feed Your Mind. *Life* (June 28): 67+.

Gottschalk, Earl, Jr. 1970. Love It or Leave It: New Patriotic Music Wins Fans, Enemies. *Wall Street Journal* 16 August 16, 1+.

Greenway, John. 1970. Country Music: No Talk That God Is Dead. *National Review* 22 (August 11): 853.

Grissim, John. 1970. *Country Music: White Man's Blues*. New York: Paperback Library.

Hall, Mildred. 1968. Congress Faces R 'n' R Revolution and Rights. *Billboard* (December 28).

Hammond, William Michael. 1988. The U.S. Commitment Becomes Irrevocable. In *The Vietnam War*, ed. Ray Bonds, 80-87. New York: Military Press.

Helander, Brock. 1996. *The Rock Who's Who*. Second edition. New York: Schirmer Books.

Hemphill, Paul. 1970. *The Nashville Sound, Bright Lights and Country Music*. New York: Simon & Schuster.

Hentoff, Nat. 1967. The Future of the Folk Renascence. *Sing Out!* 17 (February-March): 10-13.

Hero-Hitting Tune Stirring Rhubarb. 1970. *Billboard* 82 (October 10): 72.

Herr, Michael. 1978. *Dispatches*. New York: Avon.

Hey Brother! Let the People Sing. 1970. *Broadside* n110 (November-December): 3.

Hirsch, Paul. 1969. *The Structure of the Popular Music Industry: The Filtering Process by Which Records are Preselected for Public Consumption*. Ann Arbor: Survey Research Center, Institute for Social Research, The University of Michigan.

Hirsch, Paul. 1971. *A Progress Report on an Exploratory Study of Youth Culture and the Popular Music Industry*. Ann Arbor: Survey Research Center, Institute for Social Research, The University of Michigan.

Hodenfield, Chris. 1970. *Rock '70*. New York: Pyramid Books.

Hoffman, Abbie. 1969. *Woodstock Nation*. New York: Vintage Books, Random House.

Hoffman, Frank. 1983. *The Cash Box Singles Charts, 1950-1981*. Metuchen, New Jersey, and London: The Scarecrow Press.

Hoffman, Frank and George Albert. 1994. *The Cash Box Charts for the Post Modern Age, 1978-1988*. Metuchen, New Jersey and London: The Scarecrow Press.

Holdship, Bill. 1991. Liner notes to *Songs of Protest*. Compact disc. Rhino 70734.

Hopkins, Jerry. 1970. *The Rock Story*. New York: New American Library.

Hunt, Richard A. 1988. A Battle for the People's Hearts and Minds. In *The Vietnam War*, ed. Ray Bonds, 106-13. New York: Military Press.

Interview with Phil Ochs, Part 1. 1968. *Broadside* n89 (February-March): 11-14.

Jasper, Tony. 1972. *Understanding Pop*. London: SCM Press.

Kemp, Mark. 1997. Song of a Soldier: The Life and Times of Phil Ochs. In liner notes for *Farewells & Fantasies* (Phil Ochs): 13-62. Three compact discs. Elektra R2-73518.

Kingman, Daniel. 1998. *American Music: A Panorama*, concise ed. New York: Schirmer Books.

Korall, Burt. 1968. The Music of Protest. *Saturday Review* (November 16): 36+.

Laing, David. 1970. *The Sounds of Our Time.* Chicago: Quadrangle Books.

Landau, Jon. 1969. John Wesley Harding. In *The Age of Rock*, vol. 1, ed. Jonathan Eisen, 214-29. New York: Vintage Books, Random House.

Landau, Jon. 1972. *It's Too Late to Stop Now.* San Francisco: Straight Arrow Books.

Larkin, Rochelle. 1970. *Soul Music.* New York: Lander Books.

Law Grooves Patriotic Disk. 1966. *Billboard* 78 (March 12): 50.

Lees, Gene. 1970. Rock, Violence, and Spiro T. Agnew. *High Fidelity* 20 (February): 108.

Leitch, Donavan. 1999. Liner notes to *Donovan's Greatest Hits* (Donovan). Compact disc, Epic EK-65730.

Lembcke, Jerry. 1998. *The Spitting Image: Myth, Memory, and the Legacy of Vietnam.* New York: New York University.

Liner notes to *Distant Drums* (Jim Reeves). 1966. 33-1/3 rpm phonodisc. RCA Victor LPM-3542/LSP-3542.

Liner notes to *J. B. Lenoir* (J. B. Lenoir). 1970. 33-1/3 rpm phonodisc. Crusade/Polydor 24-4011.

Lloyd, A. L. 1962. Who Owns What in Folk Song? *Sing Out!* 12 (February-March): 41+.

Lorber, Alan. 1996. Boston Sound 1968—The Music & The Time. Liner notes to *Bosstown Sound—1968: The Music and the Time.* Two compact discs, Big Beat Records CDWIK2 167.

Lt. Calley Recordings and FCC Lyric Decision. 1971. *Cashbox* 32 (April 24): 3.

Lund, Jens. 1972a. Country Music Goes to War: Songs for the Red-Blooded American. *Popular Music and Society* 1 (Summer): 210230.

Lund, Jens. 1972b. Fundamentalism, Racism, and Political Reaction in Country Music. In *Sounds of Social Change*, ed. R. Serge Denisoff and Richard Peterson, 79-91. Chicago: Rand McNally.

Lund, Jens and Denisoff, R. Serge. 1971. The Folk Music Revival and the Counter Culture: Contributions and Contradictions. *Journal of American Folklore* 84 (October-December): 394-405.

McCombs, Larry. 1967. Broadside of Boston. *Sing Out!* 17 (April-May): 49.

MacDonald, Charles B. 1988. Communist Thrust—the Tet Offensive of 1968. In *The Vietnam War*, ed. Ray Bonds, 148-55. New York: Military Press.

McLuhan, Marshall and Quentin Fiore. 1967. *The Medium Is the Massage.* New York: Touchstone.

McLuhan, Marshall and Quentin Fiore. 1968. *War and Peace in the Global Village.* New York: Bantam.

McNamara, Robert S. with Brian VanDeMark. 1995. *In Retrospect.* New York: Times Books.

Marcus, Greil. 1969. A Singer and a Rock and Roll Band. In *Rock and Roll Will Stand*, ed. Greil Marcus, 90-105. Boston: Beacon Press. (See also: Marcus 1972.)

Marcus, Greil. 1972. A New Awakening. In *Sounds of Social Change*, ed. R. Serge Denisoff and Richard Peterson, 127-36. Chicago: Rand McNally. (Note: The present is basically a reprint of Marcus 1969.)

Marcus, Greil. 1984. In Your Heart You Know He's Right. *Artforum* (November): 95.

Martin, Harris. 1966. *Music City News* Goes to Vietnam. *Music City News* (January): 11.

Mellers, Wildrid. 1969. New Music in a New World. In *The Age of Rock*, vol. 1, ed. Jonathan Eisen, 180-88. New York: Vintage Books, Random House.

Miles, Barry. 1997. *Paul McCartney: Many Years from Now*. New York: Henry Holt and Company.

Miller, Lloyd. 1967. The Sound of Protest. *Case Western Reserve Journal of Sociology* 1 (June): 41-52.

Minstrel with a Mission. 1964. *Life* (October 9): 61-68.

Murray the K. 1967. The New Music—Telling It Like It Is. *Wall Street Journal* July 5, 12.

Music. 1965. *Time* 86 (September 17): 102.

Near, Holly. 1974. What Are My Songs? *Sing Out!* 22 (no. 6): 14+.

Neufeld, Jacob. Disengagement Abroad—Disenchantment at Home. In *The Vietnam War*, ed. Ray Bonds, 210-17. New York: Military Press, 1988.

Newsom, Jim. 2000. Review of *Mixed Bag* (Richie Havens). *All Music Guide* [World Wide Web Resource]. http://www.allmusic.com. Accessed September 26.

Newsweek. 1965. (September 20): 90.

Noebel, David A. 1966. *Rhythm, Riots, and Revolution*. Tulsa, Oklahoma: Christian Crusade Publications.

Ochs, Phil. 1963. The Need for Topical Music. *Broadside* n22 (March): 6-7.

Ochs, Phil. 1967. Have You Heard? The War Is Over! *Village Voice* (November 23): 16+.

O. S. 1965. Letter to *Broadside*. *Broadside* n55 (February 12): 12.

Orth, Michael. 1966. The Crack in the Consensus: Political Propaganda in American Popular Music. *New Mexico Quarterly* 36 (Spring): 62-79.

Paige, Earl. 1971. Jukebox Programmers Putting "Calley" on Request-Only Basis. *Billboard* (April 2): 1+.

Paul's Dream. 1966. *National Guardian* (February 19).

The Pentagon Papers: The Defense Department History of United States Decision-making on Vietnam, ed. Senator Mike Gravel. 1972. Boston: Beacon Books.

Pielke, Robert G. 1986. *You Say You Want a Revolution: Rock Music in American Culture*. Chicago: Nelson-Hall.

Pratt, Ray. 1994. *Rhythm and Resistance: Political Uses of American Popular Music*, 2nd ed. Washington: Smithsonian Institution Press.

Pratt, Ray. 1998. "There Must Be Some Way Outta Here!": The Vietnam War in American Popular Music. In *The Vietnam War: Its History, Literature and Music*, ed. Kenton J. Clymer, 168-89. El Paso: Texas Western Press.

Protest Disker Hits Draft Vandals. 1965. *Variety* (October 27): 60.

Protest Songs with a Rock Beat. 1965. *Life* 59 (November 5): 44.

Puterbaugh, Parke. 1993. Liner notes to *The Very Best of Tommy James and The Shondells* (Tommy James and The Shondells). Compact disc. Rhino R2-71214.

Pyes, Craig. 1970. *Rolling Stone* Gathers No Politix. *Sundance* 2 (October): 34-35.

Rabbi Chides Folkniks on "Destruction" Fears. 1965. *Variety* (October 13): 63.

Randal, Jonathan. 1967. Rock 'n' Roll Song Becoming Vietnam's "Tipperary." *New York Times* June 14.

RCA Dressing up "Berets." 1966. *Billboard* (January 30): 4.

Reynolds, Malvina. 1968. Letters to *Broadside*. *Broadside* n90 (April): 9.

Ribakove, Sy and Barbara Ribakove. 1966. *The Bob Dylan Story.* New York: Dell Publishing Company.

Rinzler, Alan. 1971. A Conversation with Charles Reich: Blowing in the Wind. *Rolling Stone* n75 (February 4): 30-34.

Robinson, John P. and Hirsch, Paul M. 1972. Teenage Responses to Rock and Roll Protest Songs. In *The Sounds of Social Change: Studies in Popular Culture,* ed. R. Serge Denisoff and Richard A. Peterson, 222-32. Chicago: Rand McNally.

Rock and Roll Will Stand, ed. Greil Marcus. 1970. Boston: Beacon Books.

Rodnitzky, Jerome L. 1971a. The Decline of Contemporary Protest Music. *Popular Music and Society* 1 (Fall): 44-50.

Rodnitzky, Jerome L. 1971b. The New Revivalism: American Protest Songs, 1945-1968. *The South Atlantic Quarterly* 70 (Winter): 13-21.

Rosenstone, Robert A. 1969. "The Times They Are A-Changin'": The Music of Protest. *Annals of the American Academy of Political and Social Science* 382 (March): 131-44.

Rowe, Arthur. 2000. Review of *Wish You Were Here, Buddy* (Pat Boone). *All Music Guide* [World Wide Web Resource]. http://www.allmusic.com. Accessed October 11.

Ruhlmann, William. 2000a. Holly Near. *All Music Guide* [World Wide Web Resource]. http://www.allmusic.com. Accessed October 11.

Ruhlmann, William. 2000b. Review of *Hang in There* (Holly Near). *All Music Guide* [World Wide Web Resource]. http://www.allmusic.com. Accessed October 11.

Scaduto, Anthony. 1971. *Dylan: An Intimate Biography.* New York: Grosset and Dunlap.

Schieber, Curtis. 2000a. New Boxed Set Salutes Incubator of Modern Folk. *The Columbus Dispatch* October 1, F1.

Schieber, Curtis. 2000b. Ochs's Brilliance Helped Define Protest Genre. *The Columbus Dispatch* October 1, F1+.

Schoenfeld, Herm. 1965. Fresh Talent Lifts Disk. B.O. *Variety* (October 13): 63.

Seeger, Pete. 1963-64. The Copyright Hassle. *Sing Out!* 13 (December-January): 41+.

Shaw, Arnold. 1971. *The Rock Revolution.* New York: Macmillan.

Sheehan, Neil. 1988. *A Bright Shining Lie: John Paul Vann and America in Vietnam.* New York: Random House.

Shelton, Robert. 1963. New Folk Singers. *New York Times* June 13.

Shuster, Alvin. 1971. U.S. Command in Vietnam Bars "Battle Hymn of Calley" from Radio Network Citing Pending Appeal. *New York Times* May 3, 4.

Silber, Irwin. 1967a. Fan the Flames. *Sing Out!* 17 (April-May): 33+.

Silber, Irwin. 1967b. Songs to Fight a War By: A Study in Illusion and Reality. *Sing Out!* 17 (August-September): 20-25.

Silber, Irwin. 1967c. A Study in Illusion and Reality. *Sing Out!* 17 (August-September): 20-25.

Silber, Irwin. 1968. Country Joe Unstrung. *Sing Out!* 18 (June-July): 19+.

Sinclair, John. 1970. Liberation Music. *Creem* 2 (November): 18-22.

Sinclair, John and Robert Levin. 1971. *Music and Politics.* New York: World Publishing.

Sing Out! New York: Sing Out, Inc.

Sixties in America, The, ed. Carl Singleton. 1999. Pasadena, California: Salem Press, Inc.

Skolnick, Jerome H. 1969. *The Politics of Protest.* New York: Ballantine Books.

Smucker, Tom. 1970. The Politics of Rock: Movement vs. Groovement. In *Age of Rock*, vol. 2, ed. Jonathan Eisen, 83-91. New York: Vintage Books, Random House.

Solomon, Maynard. 1964. Liner notes for *It's My Way!* (Buffy Sainte-Marie). 33-1/3 rpm phonodisc. Vanguard VRS-9142.

Songs and Vietnamese Clientele Are Sad at Nightclub in Saigon. 1969. *New York Times* December 14, 7.

Songs of Peace, Freedom, and Protest. 1970. Collected and Edited by Tom Glazer. New York: David McKay Company.

The Sounds of Social Change: Studies in Popular Culture, ed. R. Serge Denisoff and Richard A. Peterson. 1972. Chicago: Rand McNally.

Sternfield, Aaron. 1965. *Billboard* (August 21): 12.

Sternfield, Aaron. 1966. The Vietnam Conflict Spawning Heavy Barrage of Disk Tunes. *Billboard* (June 4): 1+.

Stuessy, Joe. 1990. *Rock and Roll: Its History and Stylistic Development*. Englewood Cliffs, New Jersey: Prentice-Hall.

Szatmary, David. 1996. *A Time to Rock: A Social History of Rock 'N' Roll*. New York: Schirmer Books.

Tin Soldiers and Nixon's Coming. 1970. *Rolling Stone* n61 (June 25): 9.

Traum, Artie. 1968. Richie Havens. *Sing Out!* 18 (September-October): 3+.

Universal Song. 1966. *Broadside* n71 (June): 13.

Unterberger, Richie. 2000. Review of *Death, Glory and Retribution*. *All Music Guide* [World Wide Web Resource]. http://www.allmusic.com. Accessed October 4.

The Vietnam War, ed. Ray Bonds. 1988. New York: Military Press.

The Vietnam War: Its History, Literature, and Music, ed. Kenton J. Clymer. 1998. El Paso: Texas Western Press.

Village Voice. 1968. Quoted in *Broadside* n94 (September-October).

Van Ronk, Dave. 1966. Quoted in *Sing Out!* 16 (February-March): 21.

Warmbrand, Ted. 1971. Singing Against the War in Washington. *Broadside* n113 (May-June): 2.

Weberman, Alan. 1968. Interpretations of John Lennon's "Fool on the Hill" and Jim Morrison's "Love Street." *Broadside* n95 (November-December): 1+.

Weinraub, Bernard. 1969. A Vietnamese Guitarist Sings of Sadness of War. *Broadside* n99 (June): 4.

Westergaard, Sean. 2000. Review of *Band of Gypsys* (Jimi Hendrix). *All Music Guide* [World Wide Web Resource]. http://www.allmusic.com. Accessed November 15.

Whitburn, Joel. 1989. *Top Country Singles 1944-1988*. Menomonee Falls, Wisconsin: Record Research Inc.

Whitburn, Joel. 1993. *Top Adult Contemporary Singles 1961-1993*. Menomonee Falls, Wisconsin: Record Research Inc.

Whitburn, Joel. 1997. *Top Pop Singles 1955-1996*, 8th ed. Menomonee Falls, Wisconsin: Record Research Inc.

Williams, Roger Neville. 1971. *The New Exiles: American War Resisters in Canada*. New York: Liveright Publishers.

Wolfe, Paul. 1964. Report on the Newport Folk Festival of 1964. *Broadside* n53 (December 20): 11.

Wolfe, Paul. 1972. Dylan's Sellout of the Left. In *Sounds of Social Change*, ed. R. Serge Denisoff and Richard Peterson, 147-50. Chicago: Rand McNally.

Woody's Boy. 1966. *Newsweek* (May 23): 110.
Wright Clicks on Viet Tune. 1965. *Billboard* (July 24): 37.
Young, Israel G. 1967. Frets and Frails. *Sing Out!* 17 (April-May): 35.

SONG TITLE INDEX

"'2+2=?'" (Bob Seger), **54**, 109.

"19" (Paul Hardcastle), **73**, 107, 109.

"'A' Team, The" (Leonard Whitcup, Phyllis Fairbanks, Barry Sadler), **85**, 109.

"Alice's Restaurant Massacree" (Arlo Guthrie), 16, 29, **46-47**, 109.

"America, Communicate with Me" (Ray Stevens), 10, **99-100**, 109-110.

"American Eagle Tragedy" (Peter Rowan), 54, 110.

"American Woman" (Randall Bachman, Burton Cummings, Michael James Kale, Garry Peterson), **62**, 100.

"Americans (A Canadian's Opinion), The" (Gordon Sinclair), **104-105**, 110.

"Are You Bombing with Me, Jesus?" (Shurli Grant), **58**.

"Ball of Confusion (That's What the World Is Today)" (Norman Whitfield, Barrett Strong), **63**, 111.

"Ballad of the Fort Hood Three, The" (Pete Seeger), **46**, 111.

"Ballad of the Green Berets, The" (SSgt. Barry Sadler, Robin Moore), 10, 34, 46, **82-85**, 111-112.

"Ballad of L.B.J., The" (Mortimer Frankel), **36**.

"Ballad of Song My" (Mike Millius), **61**.

"Ballad of Two Brothers, The" (Bob Braddock, Curly Putnam, Bill Killen), 33, **96-97**, 101, 112.

"Battle Hymn of Lt. Calley, The" (Julian Wilson, James M. Smith), 5, 8, 10, 17, **101-102**, 112-113.

"Battle Hymn of the Republic" (traditional), 71-72, **94-95**, 97, 101-102, 113.

"Beware: Here Come Friends" (Richard Kohler), **43**.

"Big Draft Medley, The" (various), **20**, 29, 113.

"Billy and Sue" (Mark Charron), **74-75**, 113.

"Billy, Don't Be a Hero" (Mitch Murray, Peter Callander), **70**, 113.

"Blowin' in the Wind" (Bob Dylan), 13, 16, **21-25**, 34, 43, 49, 83, 113-114.

"Born in the U.S.A." (Bruce Springsteen), 73, 104, **106-107**, 114.

"Born on the Fourth of July" (Tom Paxton), 73, **105**, 114.

"Bring the Boys Home" (Gregory Perry, Angelo Bond, General Johnson), **65-66**, 115.

"Bring Them Home" (Pete Seeger), 10, **43-44**, 115.

"Buy a Gun for Your Son" (Tom Paxton), **29**, 115.

INDEX

About the Author

JAMES PERONE is an Associate Professor of Music at Mount Union College and the author of many books on music, including *Paul Simon: A Bio-Bibliography* (Greenwood, 2000), *Carole King: A Bio-Bibliography* (Greenwood, 1999), and *Orchestration Theory: A Bio-Bibliography* (Greenwood, 1996).